What Is To Be Done?

Proposals for the Soviet Transition to the Market

What Is To Be Done?

Proposals for the Soviet Transition to the Market

Merton J. Peck and Thomas J. Richardson
Editors

With Contributions by

Wil Albeda
Petr O. Aven
Richard N. Cooper
Alfred E. Kahn
William D. Nordhaus
Kimio Uno

Foreword by Stanislav S. Shatalin

An IIASA Study

Yale University Press
New Haven and London

Set in Baskerville type by The Composing Room of Michigan, Inc., Grand Rapids, Michigan.
Printed in the United States of America by Vail-Ballou Press, Binghamton, New York.

Library of Congress Cataloging-in-Publication Data

What is to be done? : proposals for the Soviet transition to the market / Merton J. Peck and Thomas J. Richardson, editors ; foreword by Stanislav S. Shatalin.
p.   cm.
"An IIASA study."
Includes bibliographical references and index.
ISBN 0-300-05466-1 (cloth). — ISBN 0-300-05468-8 (paper)
1. Soviet Union—Economic policy—1986–   2. Economic stabilization—Soviet Union.   3. Privatization—Soviet Union.
I. Peck, Merton J.   II. Richardson, Thomas J., 1958–   .
III. International Institute for Applied Systems Analysis.
HC336.26.W43   1992
338.947—dc20   91-30064 CIP

The paper in this book meets the guidelines for permanence and durability of the Committee on Production Guidelines for Book Longevity of the Council on Library Resources.

10 9 8 7 6 5 4 3 2 1

Contents

Tables

Foreword

I am pleased to add a brief foreword to this book, for it represents the culmination of a project that I initiated in the fall of 1989. My view was, and continues to be, that Western economists could contribute to formulating plans for the very difficult transition of the Soviet economy to a market system. I further thought that the International Institute for Applied Systems Analysis would be the best forum for providing such assistance.

The record of the last eighteen months has vindicated my views. This Institute was able to attract distinguished Western economists to study and to write about the problems of the transition. During several conferences, they engaged in a true dialogue with my Soviet colleagues that we found very helpful. In their preliminary reports presented in the summer of 1990, these Western economists provided valuable materials for the report of the Working Group formed by the joint decision of M. S. Gorbachev and B. N. Yeltsin. I was the head of the task force that wrote the report, also known as the Five-Hundred-Day Plan.

This book is the final report of the Western economists who were enlisted in this project by the Institute. It offers the best analysis by Western economists of the problems of economic reform in the Soviet Union, and it presents proposals that would create an effective market system for our economy.

This book, written in a lively style, is a major contribution to the scholarly literature concerning the transition of centrally planned economies to a market system. Economists, policy makers, journalists, and all those who are concerned with how the largest European nation can share in and contribute to world prosperity should read it. I highly recommend it.

Stanislav S. Shatalin

Acknowledgments

This book is a product of the Economic Reform and Integration Project at the International Institute for Applied Systems Analysis (IIASA) rather than the work of a single scholar. A large number of individuals contributed to the project. We are pleased to recognize them here.

As the introduction explains, the project owes its inception to the vision of Academician Stanislav Shatalin, who saw the need for an analysis of Soviet economic reform by Western economists. He launched the project and has been its steadfast supporter throughout. Professor Evgenii Yasin, department chief of the USSR State Commission on Economic Reform, has worked closely with us in planning our work. He attended all of our conferences.

Petr Aven served as project coordinator with the responsibility for organizing the work of Soviet experts for the project and undertaking the coordination with the USSR State Commission. To both the authors and editors he made available his great knowledge of the economic institutions of the Soviet Union and of the previous reform efforts. His contributions enabled us to make our work more realistic and to reflect better the current situation in the Soviet Union.

IIASA directors Robert Pry and Peter de Jánosi fully supported this unique project and provided valued advice. Professor Friedrich Schmidt-Bleek, leader of IIASA's Technology, Economy, and Society Program, of which this project was initially a part, taught us the mysteries of planning international conferences and gave us counsel on the substance of the project. Considerable help was given to us by IIASA staff members János Gács, Shari Jandl, Gabrielle Schibich, Christoph Schneider, and Sabine Malek. Eryl Mädel and Robert Duis of the IIASA Publications Department helped prepare the final manuscript.

Much of the editing was done in New Haven, Connecticut. Roberta Dulong typed successive drafts of many of the chapters with dispatch. Yale students Tyrone Agar and Carolyn Kalhorn were able research assistants. Martha Ullberg typed the drafts of chapter 3.

As the introduction indicates, the main outlines of the ideas in this volume were developed at a conference in Sopron, Hungary, in July and August of 1990. About fifty economists from East and West were willing to interrupt their busy schedules and family vacations to contribute their knowledge to our discussions of economic reform. They are identified in Appendix B.

We pay particular tribute to the five study group chairmen: Wil Albeda, Richard N. Cooper, Alfred E. Kahn, William D. Nordhaus, and Kimio Uno, who wrote the various memoranda that form the chapters of this book. This was truly a labor of love and one that made this book possible.

Financial support for the project was provided by the USSR State Commission on Economic Reform, the Ford Foundation, the Pew Charitable Trusts, the Japan Foundation, the Sasakawa Foundation, and IIASA. Of course, these organizations and the individuals who have helped us are not responsible for the views expressed here, which are solely those of the authors.

The editors thank all those who have made our work possible.

Merton J. Peck and Thomas J. Richardson

Contributors

Wil Albeda is the Belle van Zuylen Professor of Social Economic Policy at Utrecht University (Utrecht, Netherlands) and a part-time professor of economics at the University of Limburg, Maastricht. He studied economics at the University of Rotterdam. Professor Albeda has written on economics, social policy, and labor relations; his most recent book was *Neocorporatism*. He also participated in a study on tripartism sponsored by the International Labour Organisation, for which he wrote the section on the Netherlands. Professor Albeda was minister of labor for the Netherlands from 1977 to 1981, and chairman of the Scientific Council for Government Policy from 1985 to 1990. He is currently chairman of the Public Service Advisory and Arbitration Committee in the Netherlands.

Petr O. Aven is a research scholar at the International Institute for Applied Systems Analysis (Laxenburg, Austria). He received his M.S. and his Ph.D. from Moscow State University. Dr. Aven has taken part in several research projects concerning Soviet economic reform, and his major research interests are the methodology of socioeconomic comparisons, comparative economics, and economic reforms in centrally planned economies. He is the author of the book *Functional Scaling*. Dr. Aven was an economist at the Institute of Systems Studies of the USSR Academy of Sciences in Moscow from 1981 to 1989.

Richard N. Cooper is the Maurits C. Boas Professor of International Economics at Harvard University (Cambridge, Massachusetts). He received his B.A. from Oberlin College and his Ph.D. from Harvard University. He has written extensively on questions of international economic policy, including most recently *The International Monetary System* and *Debt and Stabilization in Developing Countries*. Professor Cooper has served the U.S. government on several occasions, including as under secretary of state for economic affairs from 1977 to 1981. He is currently chairman of the Federal Reserve Bank of Boston.

Alfred E. Kahn is the Robert Julius Thorne Professor of Political Economy Emeritus at Cornell University (Ithaca, New York). He received his B.A. degree from New York University and his Ph.D. degree from Yale University. His main areas of research are government regulation, antitrust policies, and the organization and performance of industries. Professor Kahn's latest publication is a new printing of his two-volume *Economics of Regulation*. He has served as chairman of the New York State Public Service Commission (regulating public utilities), the U.S. Civil Aeronautics Board, and as adviser to President Carter on Inflation.

William D. Nordhaus is the A. Whitney Griswold Professor of Economics at Yale University and is on the staff of the Cowles Foundation for Research in Economics, Yale University (New Haven, Connecticut). He received his B.A. from Yale University and his Ph.D. from the Massachusetts Institute of Technology. He has specialized in macroeconomic and energy economics and his recent publications include *The Efficient Use of Energy Resources* and *Reforming Federal Regulation*. He is also the coauthor with Paul Samuelson of *Economics,* the classic introductory textbook. Professor Nordhaus was a member of the U.S. government's Council of Economic Advisers from 1977 to 1979; he served as the provost of Yale University from 1986 to 1988.

Merton J. Peck is the Thomas Dewitt Cuyler Professor of Economics at Yale University. He is also the leader of the Economic Reform and Integration Project at the International Institute for Applied Systems Analysis. He received his B.A. from Oberlin College and his Ph.D. from Harvard University. Professor Peck has written on the economics of competition, government regulation, and technical change, and his most recent publication is *The World Aluminum Industry in a Changing Energy Era*. He served as a member of the U.S. government's Council of Economic Advisers from 1968 to 1969.

Thomas J. Richardson is assistant professor of economics at Yale University. He received his B.A. from the Evergreen State College and his Ph.D. from Columbia University. He is a specialist on the Soviet economy, and his research has focused on the microeconomic theory of economic planning. Professor Richardson's dissertation centered on strategic models of the dynamic principal-agent planning problem, with application to the Soviet economy.

Kimio Uno is professor of economic policy at Keio University (Fujisawa City, Japan). He received his B.A. from Keio University and his Ph.D. from the University of Illinois. Professor Uno has specialized in the analysis of industrial structure, industrial policy, technological change, and international economic relations. His recent publications include *Japanese Industrial Performance, Measurement of Services in an Input-Output Framework,* and *Technology, Investment, and Trade.* Professor Uno was a staff member of the Technology, Economy, and Society Program at the International Institute for Applied Systems Analysis from 1989 to 1990. He is currently associated with the National Institute of Science and Technology Policy and is a member of the Statistical Council of the Japanese government.

The International Institute for Applied Systems Analysis

is a nongovernmental research institution, bringing together scientists from around the world to work on problems of common concern. Situated in Laxenburg, Austria, IIASA was founded in October 1972 by the academies of science and equivalent organizations of twelve countries. Its founders gave IIASA a unique position outside national, disciplinary, and institutional boundaries so that it might take the broadest possible view in pursuing its objectives:

To promote international cooperation in solving problems arising from social, economic, technological, and environmental change

To create a network of institutions in the national member organization countries and elsewhere for joint scientific research

To develop and formalize systems analysis and the sciences contributing to it, and promote the use of analytical techniques needed to evaluate and address complex problems

To inform policy advisors and decision makers about the potential application of the Institute's work to such problems

The Institute now has national member organizations in the following countries:

Austria
The Austrian Academy of Sciences

Bulgaria
The National Committee for Applied Systems Analysis and Management

Canada
The Canadian Committee for IIASA

Czech and Slovak Federal Republic
The Committee for IIASA of the Czech and Slovak Federal Republic

Finland
The Finnish Committee for IIASA

France
The French Association for the Development of Systems Analysis

Germany
Association for the Advancement of IIASA

Hungary
The Hungarian Committee for Applied Systems Analysis

Italy
The National Research Council (CNR) and the National
Commission for Nuclear and Alternative Energy Sources (ENEA)

Japan
The Japan Committee for IIASA

Netherlands
The Netherlands Organization for Scientific Research (NWO)

Poland
The Polish Academy of Sciences

Sweden
The Swedish Council for Planning and Coordination of Research
(FRN)

Union of Soviet Socialist Republics
The Academy of Sciences of the Union of Soviet Socialist
Republics

United States of America
The American Academy of Arts and Sciences

Chapter One

Introduction

Merton J. Peck

The Soviet economy is engulfed in a crisis. One of its manifestations is the breakdown of retail distribution. Television viewers in the West have repeatedly been shown the empty shelves in the state stores and the long lines. One product after another is no longer freely available—first, meat and sugar, then cigarettes, soap, toilet paper and, most recently, watches. The grim saying in Moscow is that only socialism can create a shortage of almost everything. What depresses Soviet citizens is not just the shortages but also their unpredictability; goods here today are gone tomorrow. Essentially, the ruble has not been freely convertible into foreign currencies since the outbreak of World War I. Now the ruble cannot easily buy even those consumer goods and services produced in the Soviet Union, and this internal inconvertibility is increasing daily.

The breakdown of the state's wholesale distribution network—supplies from one enterprise to another—is a less visible but equally critical manifestation. Factories are idle because they lack materials, and this shortage leads to a slowdown in production. For the first time since World War II, Soviet industrial production declined in 1990. Again the breakdown in distribution reflects a flight from the ruble. Allocation through the state supply system (*Gossnab*) is no longer effective, and enterprises are reluctant to sell directly to one another because the rubles they receive cannot assure them of materials. In the traditional Soviet system, materials are supposed to flow from one enterprise to another according to government plans or, more recently, state orders (*goszakazy*). Yet planning directives are often ignored and state orders unfulfilled. Thus the Soviet economy is said to have neither plan nor market.

BARTER TRADE AND HOARDING

With the decline in the internal convertibility of the ruble for consumer goods, barter trade is increasing. Consumers survive by exchanging goods and services with one another. John LeCarré's novel, *Russia House,* gives some sense of how complex and time consuming such barter trade can be:

> As soon as she got to the office . . . [Katya] would collect the two tickets for the Philharmonic which the editor Barzin had promised her as amends for his drunken advances at the May Day party. . . . At lunchtime after shopping she would trade the tickets with the porter Morozov who had pledged her twenty-four bars of imported soap wrapped in decorative paper. With the fancy soap she would buy the bolt of green check cloth of pure wool that the manager of the clothing shop was keeping locked in his storeroom for her. . . . This afternoon after the Hungarian reception she would hand the cloth to Olga Stanislavsky who, in return for favours to be negotiated, would make two cowboy shirts, . . . one for each twin in time for their birthday. . . .[1]

A fictional account to be sure, but it captures well the complexities of barter trade that Soviet consumers face daily.

Barter trade is also common among enterprises. Many have specialists (*tolkachi*) who engage in many-sided trade with other enterprises, offering their output either for materials to keep the enterprise running or for consumer goods to distribute to their workers. Enterprises often have a twice weekly distribution of food products to their employees, and some have set up small canteens to sell otherwise hard-to-get products. Many consumer durables—noticeably automobiles—are distributed through enterprises rather than freely sold in the market. Special stores with a restricted clientele have long been a feature of Soviet society. Formerly these were limited to a small elite clientele; now many enterprises engage in distribution of goods for most of their employees.

Barter trade extends beyond enterprises and consumers to in-

---

1. John LeCarré, *Russia House* (New York: Knopf, 1989), 113–14.

clude republics and local governments. With the breakdown of distribution, heads of governments have acted aggressively to protect their residents and local enterprises. They have taken control of local production and then concluded agreements with other localities to exchange that production for materials and consumer goods. Thus the mayor of Leningrad trades textiles for milk with the head of the Estonian Republic.

With barter trade has come hoarding. The uncertainties of the state supply system have always forced firms to maintain large inventories. But in recent months, the increasing reliance on barter trade has led both households and enterprises to hold still greater stocks of goods rather than rubles. Even more significant is hoarding in anticipation of both further reductions in availability and increases in prices. Holding goods is also a protection against such actions as the recent confiscation of 50 and 100 ruble notes and the freezing of large bank accounts. Saving now takes the form of stockpiling goods rather than rubles.

Money, the textbooks say, serves as a medium of exchange and a store of value. Its evolution dates back to the Middle Ages when money was found to be much more efficient than the cumbersome use of goods for trade. Since then bartering as a basis for trade has survived only in primitive economies or in times of economic crisis. The rise of bartering is the most obvious and pervasive indicator of an economic crisis.

THE CRISIS AND SYSTEMIC PROBLEMS

The current manifestations of the recent deterioration of Soviet economic performance are striking. Yet as the appendix by Petr Aven makes clear, Soviet economic growth rates have been steadily declining since the early seventies and by the mid-seventies were well below those of the industrialized market economies. Per capita gross national product (GNP) comparisons place the Soviet Union in the upper-middle income range in terms of the categories established by the World Bank Development Report—that is, with such countries as Greece, Portugal, Brazil, or Malaysia.[2] In 1990 Soviet per capita

2. Calculations by the author and data from the *World Development Report, 1987* (Oxford: Oxford University Press, 1987), 202–3.

GNP was 5,060 in U.S. dollars compared with 21,000 for the United States.[3]

Industrialization came late to the Soviet Union. Some other nations that were late to industrialize have caught up with the early industrializing countries in the years since World War II, the striking example being Japan. The Soviet Union ceased catching up in the early seventies, and since then it has fallen further behind the industrialized market economies.

International comparisons of per capita GNP overstate the welfare of Soviet citizens in several important respects. First, these comparisons make no allowance for the low quality of most Soviet goods relative to those available in market economies. Second, they make no allowance for the unavailability of goods, the time spent in shopping queues, as well as the general hassle and frustration involved in obtaining goods and services. Finally, they make no allowance for the low percentage of GNP that goes to household final consumption. In 1987 that figure was 54 percent for the Soviet Union compared to 66 percent for the United States, 62 percent for the United Kingdom, 61 percent for France, and 58 percent for Japan. Soviet citizens live significantly poorer than their per capita GNP indicates.[4]

Averages do not, of course, identify the extent of poverty. Using official Soviet definitions, between 43 million and 80 million persons are below the poverty line, depending on where it is drawn. Here poor means poor, for using roughly comparable definitions, around 30 to 40 percent of the population in developing countries are below the poverty line used in the Soviet Union.[5]

Such data indicate that several longer-run systemic problems have damaged Soviet economic performance. First, when compared to a market system, the economic planning system has proven a cumbersome and markedly inefficient way to coordinate a complex modern industrial economy. A modern economy involves many

3. *PlanEcon Report,* vol. 6, no. 52, December 28, 1990, 17. Since many goods were unavailable at official prices, purchasing power parity calculations overstate Soviet per capita GNP.

4. *SSSR i Zarubezhnie strany, v 1988* (The USSR and foreign countries in 1988) (Moscow: Finansy i statistika, 1989).

5. *A Study of the Soviet Economy* (Paris: International Monetary Fund, World Bank, Organization for Economic Cooperation and Development, and European Bank for Reconstruction and Development, 1991), 2:154–55.

firms selling to one another, thus pròviding inputs for the output of final goods. The inputs must match up with the outputs. In the Soviet economy this was achieved by mandatory planning. By contrast, in a market system coordination is achieved by the price system, which balances demand with supply. A market system allows decentralization of decision making to enterprises and individuals and has proved to be a vastly superior way of coordinating the needs of customers and suppliers. The incentives provided by self-interest have proved to be more effective than directives issued by the planners. Furthermore, a market system allows for choice by both enterprises and households among competing suppliers. As we emphasize repeatedly in this book, the spur of competition has no substitute in promoting economic efficiency in all its dimensions.

Second, the planning system has failed badly with respect to innovation. Postwar economic growth in the West has primarily resulted from the technological development of new products and processes. Innovation is inherently unpredictable and requires flexibility. That is something that the planning system cannot easily provide, but the decentralized market system is well equipped to handle. The flexibility to adapt to changing demands cannot be routinized or planned. Lack of flexibility was less of a drawback when growth in the Soviet economy depended on adding more steel mills. It is a critical failing when growth requires introducing new microchips.

Third, the planned economy does not allow for easy integration into the world economy where the market economies are the major players. Rather the planners act as gatekeepers carefully controlling access from abroad to the domestic economy. This control precludes the decentralized import and export characteristic of the market economies, as well as the spur of competition of imports and the impact of technological change occurring elsewhere. In the postwar economic growth of market economies, the increasing role of international trade has been considered a major factor. Trade increases competition, permits economies of scale to be realized, and allows nations to specialize in what they do best. Adherence to the planning system has kept the Soviet Union isolated from one of the major sources of economic growth for other industrialized nations.

Fourth, the planning system serves the preferences of the planners rather than of the consumers, who are considered sovereign in a market economy. Of course, in theory planners are thought to

represent the long-run interests of society, but in reality they respond to political pressures, bureaucratic interests, passing fashions,
and the desires of the top leadership. More fundamentally, in the
absence of markets, planners lack accurate information concerning
consumer preferences. Governments in market economies find
themselves politically overloaded by the more modest tasks of maintaining macroeconomic stability, taking care of various nonmarket
institutions such as education and providing a social safety net for
individuals inadequately provided for by the market economy. This
political overload is increased by several orders of magnitude when
the state tries to run the economy and almost everything else. Of
course, the practice of central planning has never been quite as fully
directed by central commands as the concept suggests. In reality, it
has involved major elements of bargaining—enterprises with their
ministries, ministries with one another and with the central planning
agency, and even enterprises with one another. Within the Soviet
governmental structure, localities bargain with the republics and the
republics with the center. The Communist Party has had a pervasive
role as mediator and arbitrator, for its members have been influen-
tial throughout the bureaucracy. The Party was indeed the glue that
held the Soviet economy together.

In the absence of complete information, Soviet planners had to
rely on their subordinates for planning data, thus giving those subordinates bargaining power in the planning process. This bargaining power weakened the central planning mechanism, imposing
costs and efficiency losses that are, to a greater extent, ameliorated
in a decentralized market system.

Finally, the Soviet economy has suffered from a progressively
worsening macroeconomic disequilibrium. This imbalance is the
most striking feature of the current crisis and the one on which our
opening paragraphs have focused. Some would say that the critical
macroeconomic situation is not a systemic fault. Although repressed
inflation in which aggregate demand exceeds supply is a long-
standing characteristic of the Soviet economy, it has become severe
only in the last few years. The problem could be attributed to a series
of bad macroeconomic decisions of the kind that have occurred in
market economies.

We are inclined to an alternative view—that macroeconomic disequilibrium is systemic rather than the consequence of particular

policy errors. In the Soviet system, the banking system serves as a passive instrument to finance the government deficit and the economic plan. The structure provides no clear and immediate signals warning of a macroeconomic disequilibrium nor does it make its adverse consequences immediately apparent. In market economies, macroeconomic disequilibrium becomes apparent in the open inflation of rising prices and the depreciation of the exchange rate. These signals lead to a political backlash that forces policymakers to take note.

The systemic character of the macroeconomic disequilibrium is confirmed by the fact that this imbalance occurs in almost all centrally planned economies from Yugoslavia to China. However, its prevalence still does not explain why macroeconomic disequilibrium became worse in the seventies and eighties. The answer may lie in the fact that by that time slack resources could no longer be mobilized by the planning system and that political changes of those decades created pressures for rising monetary income in excess of productivity gains.

The following chapters and the policy proposals they make are directed in the first instance to resolving the current crisis. Yet the proposals—all part of a transition to a market economy—are also solutions to the long-run systemic problem. We have taken as a starting point the current crisis only because it is so visible and pressing.

This statement in the *Shatalin Report* may be a bit strong, but we agree with it:

> Mankind has not created anything more efficient than the market system. It gives strong incentives to materialize man's abilities, to activate labor and business and to expedite greatly the progress of science and technology. Its own self-adjustment and self-regulation gears take care of the best possible coordination of activities of all economic subjects [and the] rational use of labor, material and financial resources [to] balance the national economy.[6]

6. *Transition to the Market: A Report of a Working Group Formed by M. S. Gorbachev and B. N. Yeltsin,* Part 1: *The Concept and Program* (Moscow: Cultural Initiative Foundation, 1990), 7. This report is also known as the *Five-Hundred-Day Plan* or the *Shatalin Report* after the Chairman of the Task Force, Academician Stanislav Shatalin, and is henceforth cited as the *Shatalin Report.*

FROM CRISIS TO COLLAPSE

Although President Gorbachev originally introduced *perestroika* as a way to deal with the precrisis situation inherited from the Brezhnev era, the last six years have culminated in what can only be called a crisis. This crisis could now become a collapse. The remaining ruble trade could disappear so that transactions would be largely by barter. Industrial production could decline precipitously as materials become harder to obtain. Food supplies for urban areas could become a problem as farmers withhold their output, which they might do if consumer goods from the cities become less available. Republics and regions could become increasingly autarkic. The political consequences of a collapse could be dramatic. Some observers see such a collapse occurring in as little as twelve to twenty-four months.

It is more likely that the Soviet economy will lumber along in its present state of crisis. Forces of inertia are strong in any industrialized economy. Emergency decrees may cope with the worst of the problems. Partial reform measures such as the administrative reform to raise prices and the just-completed abortive currency reform will be repeated. Such measures, for reasons to be discussed, will not eliminate the crisis, but they may keep the economy afloat. Yet even if the crisis does not become a collapse, the present condition of the Soviet economy is so perilous that it seems unlikely to continue indefinitely.

The least likely outcome is for the old planned economy to be restored. Its restoration would require that thousands of enterprises cooperate with directives from the center. Until recently, enterprises did more or less fulfill their assigned roles. Central planning did allow the Soviet economy to function, albeit inefficiently. A planned economy, however, requires obedience, or as Soviet conservatives say, discipline. That is now in short supply, particularly as the various republics assert their sovereignty and annul directives from Moscow. The centrally planned economy can be restored only with the kind of repression that would reverse the political changes of the last six years.

MEASURES FOR ECONOMIC REFORM

In the next chapter, we propose five measures to resolve the crisis.

1. Liberalize prices.
2. Corporatize enterprises.
3. Stabilize government spending and restrict credit.
4. Moderate the social costs of unemployment.
5. Open the economy to competition, both internally and internationally.

These measures are presented as a comprehensive program. We consider these five steps the minimal conditions necessary for creating an effective market economy. The success of each depends on the others. If adopted singly or over time, they are likely to fail; if adopted promptly and introduced simultaneously on what we call D-day (D for deregulation), they promise a resolution of the present crisis.

The measures we propose are similar to those described in two other proposed programs of reform: the Five-Hundred-Day, or Shatalin, Plan, and the plan developed by international agencies in response to the Houston Summit.[7] Our program differs from the other two by being bolder and by reflecting a greater sense of urgency. Our proposals are more integrated and consistent with one another and, of course, they differ from the other plans in details. We make the case for simultaneous action in greater detail than do previous authors. Yet our suggestions share with the other two reform proposals the ultimate goal of creating a market economy.

THE HISTORY OF THE PROJECT ON ECONOMIC REFORM

The proposals set forth here are the result of an eighteen-month collaboration involving many economists. The story is complicated enough that it is best told chronologically.

7. The Shatalin plan is outlined in the *Shatalin Report*. The plan from the Houston summit is contained in *The Economy of the USSR: Summary and Recommendations*, a study undertaken in response to a request by the Houston Summit (Washington, D.C.: International Monetary Fund, International Bank for Reconstruction and Development, Organization for Economic Cooperation and Development, and European Bank for Reconstruction and Development, 1990).

In the fall of 1989, Academician Stanislav Shatalin, then a senior economic adviser to President Gorbachev, approached the International Institute for Applied Systems Analysis (IIASA) in Laxenburg, Austria, with a request for recommendations on Soviet economic reform. IIASA is a unique international organization that applies systems analysis to policy problems. It has fifteen national member organizations including those from four formerly centrally planned countries as well as the Soviet Union, the United States, Japan, Canada, and seven Western European countries.

In asking for IIASA's involvement, Academician Shatalin noted:

> The experience of Western specialists is invaluable both in our efforts to achieve structural adjustment in socialist economies and in ensuring other countries are fully informed about and can adjust to the changes being made. IIASA is ideally placed to establish a neutral and objective dialogue between economic experts in the East and West to translate *perestroika* into tangible economic results.[8]

Several points require underscoring and elaboration. We would stress the word *dialogue,* for the project was conducted on the basis of free and frank interchange among Soviet economists and economists from other nations. The intent was to create a forum for joint problem solving, not for presentations in which one group would lecture the other. IIASA was instrumental in providing a setting in which economists from a wide range of countries felt comfortable and where tradition encouraged a problem-solving orientation. It was also an environment that allowed economists to let their imaginations run freely. (Contrary to popular belief, economists do have imaginations!) IIASA was, then, the setting that this work required.

Once the formal proposal was made by the USSR State Commission on Economic Reform and approved by IIASA officials, events moved quickly. Professor Schmidt-Bleek of IIASA convened the first planning meeting in December 1989 and another in March 1990. At the March meeting, Merton J. Peck of Yale University was appointed project leader and five study groups were established. The groups and their chairmen were as follows:

8. Quoted in an IIASA News Release, May 17, 1990.

1. Prices and Competition: Alfred E. Kahn, Cornell University (USA)

2. Economic Stabilization: William D. Nordhaus, Yale University (USA)

3. Opening of the Economy: Richard N. Cooper, Harvard University (USA)

4. Labor Markets and Employment: Wil Albeda, Universities of Utrecht and Limberg (Netherlands)

5. Capital Markets and Privatization: Kimio Uno, Keio University at Shomaw Fujisawa (Japan)

The March conference was still an exploratory one, but it initiated substantive discussions of the problems of economic reform. Soviet experts presented papers that served as starting points for the discussions at this conference.

The planning began immediately for the next conference, to be held in Sopron, Hungary, in July and August 1990. This conference was to be organized by study groups, each consisting of about nine members, from the United States, Japan, Western Europe, and Eastern Europe. Particular mention should be given to the contributions made by economists from Poland, Czechoslovakia, Hungary, and Bulgaria. Economists in these countries have been forced to think long and hard about economic reform. The successes and failures of previous reforms in these four countries were particularly relevant to the problems facing the Soviet Union.

Two to four Soviet experts joined each study group, having prepared papers as a background for the study group discussions.[9] Appendix B lists the participants at the Sopron meetings.

During the Sopron meetings, word arrived from Moscow concerning a significant change. A joint decision reached by Mikhail Gorbachev, Soviet president, and Boris Yeltsin, chairman of the Russian Parliament, led to the formation of a new joint task force to be headed by Academician Shatalin, with a staff of experts to be drawn in large part from the economists who had been associated with the USSR State Commission on Economic Reform. (Three of the eleven

9. Five of these papers are to be published in a volume edited by Petr O. Aven and Thomas J. Richardson, *Essays in the Soviet Transition to the Market* (Laxenburg, Austria: IIASA, forthcoming). The reader is urged to consult this forthcoming book for further details of the transition as well as for insights into how Soviet experts approach the problems of transition.

members of the Shatalin task force were at Sopron, and two others had attended the March conference.)

We were asked to prepare preliminary reports as soon as possible for use by the Shatalin task force. The diligence of the chairmen resulted in preliminary reports that were completed by mid-August and were discussed by the Shatalin group in the process of preparing their report.

We had decided that the reports would be the work of the chairmen who wrote them. There was surprising agreement within the study groups on the major points—thus contradicting the old saying that economists never agree. Still, it would have been pushing our luck to produce an agreed report and the schedule precluded it. The chairmen were asked to write their reports on the basis of the group discussions, but the report was to express their personal view.

The study group chairmen met again in New Haven, Connecticut, in November 1990. (They were joined by myself and fellow editor Thomas Richardson; Petr Aven; Barry Bosworth, of the Brookings Institution; and Professor Evgenyi Yasin, department chief of the USSR State Commission on Economic Reform.) The original purpose of the meeting was to make plans to revise the preliminary reports. Professor Yasin, however, asked that the Western experts instead prepare a policy memorandum of fewer than twenty pages that would set forth our views on the essential economic reforms to deal with the current economic crisis in the Soviet Union.

We did this, although given our geographical dispersion doing so required considerable use of fax technology. The memorandum was sent to Moscow and translated into Russian, and in December, the Russian translation was given to President Gorbachev. This policy memorandum has since been published as an IIASA report[10] and has been the subject of articles in several publications in the Soviet Union and in the West. The policy memorandum is chapter 2 of this book, and it is followed by the five final reports of the study group chairmen, which elaborate the reform proposals in the policy memorandum. In varying degrees these later chapters also add further proposals that are consistent with the principal ones described in the policy memorandum.

10. *The Soviet Economic Crisis: Steps to Avert Collapse,* Executive Report 19 (Laxenburg, Austria: IIASA, February 1991).

The five chapters presented here differ from the preliminary reports of August 1990. In part these changes reflect modifications made when the chairmen reconsidered their preliminary reports and incorporated the discussions of the November meeting. These five chapters also contain data drawn from *Economy of the USSR* and the *Shatalin Report*, all published after the preliminary reports were finished.[11] We have not systematically drawn on the extensive literature on the Soviet economy, preferring timeliness over comprehensiveness. We have responded to those that urged the value of early publication, and particularly to those in the Soviet Union to whom we promised publication at this time.

Despite the changes, the remaining chapters contain the imprint of the discussions at Sopron and could not have been written without that conference. Chapters 3 to 7 were written in February and March 1991, and chapter 2, the policy memorandum, was written in November 1990. Obviously much will have happened in the Soviet Union by the time the book is published, but it was not feasible to make revisions to reflect the latest events. We think, however, that little will have happened that would change the general character of our proposals.

The proposals in chapters 3 to 7 are consistent with one another in their main outlines with one exception: chapter 6 assigns considerable importance to incomes policies whereas chapter 4 is skeptical about their value. This difference reflects the division of views among Western economists and, indeed, experience in market economies concerning the use of incomes policies. The degree of consistency elsewhere is striking, although the careful reader may also find some differences in details among the chapters. We take comfort in the saying, "Consistency is the hobgoblin of little minds."

The chapters generally reflect the views expressed in the discussions of the study groups at the Sopron Conference. Nonetheless, the chairmen in writing their chapters have not considered themselves bound by these discussions and in a few cases they have departed widely from what was expressed there.[12]

11. After the manuscript for this book was substantially completed, we received the three-volume work *A Study of the Soviet Economy*. This work contains a wealth of detail on the Soviet economy that we were able to incorporate in the present work only to a very limited extent. Readers who wish more details are urged to consult these three volumes.

12. The reader should note that the term *price liberalization* is used in the policy

THE OUTLOOK FOR ECONOMIC REFORM

When this project began in December 1989, there was a high probability of significant economic reform in the Soviet Union. The economists involved from both East and West had a great sense of excitement and enthusiasm. Many of the Soviet economists working with us had been assigned major responsibility for working out plans for economic reform. The top leadership of the Soviet Union appeared to be committed to economic reform. The conflict between the union and the republics was not so marked or at least not so apparent at that time.

A little more than a year later, the political situation has changed dramatically. The Shatalin plan was devised and then rejected by President Gorbachev, and another reform plan was approved by the Supreme Soviet.[13] A new prime minister, Valentin Pavlov, took office in January 1991. He has followed quite different policies than the ones we have set forth; he is apparently committed to the gradual introduction of a regulated market economy whatever that may mean. In his first month in office he announced a version of the plan set forth by his predecessor, Nikolai Ryzhkov, in May 1990 and rejected at that time by the Supreme Soviet. Its main feature is an administrative increase in retail prices, with controls on retail prices still retained. The price increase is to be compensated for by increasing everyone's income by a significant fraction of the losses due to the price increases. The reader need not go beyond our policy memorandum to see why we think this measure is bad economics. His other major initiative is a monetary reform that invalidated 50 and 100 ruble notes and limited withdrawals from bank accounts. Chapter 4 shows why that measure was again bad economics.

The outlook for economic reform is uncertain. Yet we believe that uncertainty does not diminish the value of this book. First, economic

---

memorandum in chapter 2, whereas in the subsequent chapters the term is *price deregulation*. Deregulation is the more accurate term, since what is involved is removing the state control of prices. Nonetheless we have retained the term *liberalization* in the policy memorandum because we wish to keep that memorandum in the form in which it was presented to President Gorbachev in December 1989.

13. From time to time throughout the book we refer simply to the Soviet parliament when the distinction between the Supreme Soviet and the larger Congress of People's Deputies is not important.

events in the Soviet Union affect the welfare of almost 300 million people. They also have an impact on the welfare of the rest of us, particularly those people who live in the formerly centrally planned economies of Eastern Europe for whom the USSR is a major trading partner. We hope this book will provide a better understanding of the complexities of the transition from a centrally planned economy to a market system as well as some insight into the specific problems facing the Soviet Union. Second, we feel an obligation to those Soviet colleagues who worked with us. Most have left their government posts and returned to their research institutes and universities. They continue, however, to work on problems of economic reform. They expect us to do likewise and finish the tasks we set for ourselves.

The final reason we think this book is of interest is due to our conviction that in the long run economic reform will come to the Soviet Union. Politics cannot keep Soviet citizens forever from the gains of a market economy or the advantages of integration into the international economy. One might say that it has done so since 1917 but that ignores two factors; the last six years have changed the political landscape in an irreversible fashion and one would have to return to 1920, the era of war communism, to find the economy in such disarray. The worse the economy, the greater the pressure for reform.

The authors are economists, and we have tried to avoid political questions and speculation, beyond the occasional asides and the few preceding paragraphs. Much of economic policy is ultimately political, with the decisions to be made by the Soviet government and people. Still, a market economy has a certain logic and obeys certain rules whether the economy is located in Latin America, Asia, or Eastern Europe. Culture and politics matter, but so do economics.

We recognize that almost any economic policy measure creates winners and losers, some of whom are powerful interest groups. The task of policymakers is to persuade, conciliate, outmaneuver, and provide concessions to opponents sufficient to neutralize their opposition. The transition to a market economy surely threatens the many who thrive under the present system: It is a classic case of measures for the general good invoking the opposition of specific losers.

It is said that the losers in economic reform go well beyond those thriving in the present system to include almost everyone. The problem of reform is considered one of enduring widespread short-run losses from declining production, falling real income, unemployment, and industrial unrest to achieve the long-run gains of greater efficiency and improved economic growth. Such a view is based on Latin America's experience with economic reform, as well as the experience of market economies with the elimination of budget deficits and shifts from easy to tight monetary policy. Such policy shifts often result in a short-run decline in output, real income, and employment. Yet, this conventional view may be inaccurate for the present Soviet situation.[14]

The reason is that the Soviet Union is already in an economic crisis, as the opening pages indicate. Hence, doing nothing is the right measure of the short-run cost of the proposals contained here. The current crisis is already producing the usual consequences of a sharp shift in economic policy. Soviet net material product (the closest Soviet measure to GNP) is down 10 percent in the first quarter of 1991 compared to the first quarter of 1990, and the decline for all of 1991 is estimated to be 15 to 20 percent.[15] Economic reform is also said to result in rising unemployment and strikes, but the present course of the Soviet economy is creating both.[16] Indeed, the Soviet estimates of economic decline are comparable to those for

14. Some distinguished Western economists have voiced that view. Hence, they believe the proposals made here for reducing the budget deficit and tightening monetary policy will reduce real output. That is the usual outcome in market economies, where real output is typically limited by aggregate demand and thus its reduction by macroeconomic policies leads to falling output. The situation in the Soviet Union—extreme inflationary pressures coupled with sharply falling real output—is uncharacteristic of market systems. Output in the Soviet case is falling because consumer goods and industrial inputs are no longer reliably available for rubles; individuals and enterprises are instead hoarding commodities and resorting to barter trade, a form of trading that reduces the efficiency of exchange.

The measures proposed here aim quickly to restore the internal convertibility of the ruble for domestic goods and services and thus to permit real output to return to its 1989 level. In a market economic *every* good cannot simultaneously be in short supply, but the USSR has a special kind of shortage economy.

15. The net decline in net material product for the first quarter of 1991 is reported in *Izvestiia*, April 10, 1991, and in *Pravda*, April 23, 1991. Estimates of 15 to 20 percent for all of 1991 are based on discussions with Soviet economists. See also Dirk W. Damaru, John C. Reed, John F. H. Purcell, and Joyce Chang, *The Soviet Union: Approaching Crisis* (New York: Salomon Brothers, 1991), 4–5, which estimates a decline of 15 percent.

16. See *Study of the Soviet Economy*, 1:44–45.

Poland in the early months of its dramatic economic reforms.[17] Polish policy is termed shock therapy; present Soviet policy is then a shock without the therapy.

The measures proposed here are intended to reverse the present decline of the Soviet economy. To the extent they do so, they may represent a short-run gain, instead of a short-run cost. The chapters that follow set forth the analysis that demonstrates why the proposed measures are likely to stem the economic decline in the short term and provide the basis for economic growth in the long term.

The existence of specific losers from the proposed measures, however, means that exceptional leadership and political skill will be required for their adoption. Fortunately, a market economy is robust enough to tolerate a fair number of concessions to particular interest groups. Nevertheless, overuse of concessions can eliminate most of the gains of economic reform.

We do not spell out the political tactics for achieving reform, for that is not where our expertise lies. We do caution, however, against too quick a judgment that the measures proposed here are politically infeasible, since events of the past decades have shown that what is called infeasible today often happens easily tomorrow.

That brings us to our second caveat. There is little experience with the massive task of converting a large centrally planned economy into a market one. Economic reform in Latin America and in postwar Europe and Japan faced somewhat similar issues of stabilization, but not the task of creating a market system *ab initio*. The guidance from economic analysis can only be the most general.

Finally, economic reform takes time, particularly when the reforms involve creating new institutions. We do not mean to paint a picture in rosy hues of instant bliss or to suggest that the shift to a market economy will solve all economic problems. Indeed, a market economy provides its own continuing problems of maintaining macroeconomic stability and creating a rising standard of living. The

17. Comparisons between Poland and the Soviet Union are necessarily impressionistic, given the lack of comparable data. The Polish Ministry of Finance reports industrial output fell 20 percent in the ten months following the reform, a rate of decline per quarter comparable to that in the Soviet Union in the first quarter of 1991 and to estimates for 1991. Polish data reported in David Lipton and Jeffery Sachs, "Creating a Market Economy in Eastern Europe: The Case of Poland," *Brookings Papers on Economy Activity*, no. 1 (Washington, D.C.: Brookings Institution, 1990), 124.

transition to a market economy should be considered a new beginning rather than the end of economic problems and controversies.

We offer, then, our proposals with some inner qualms that are not quite captured by our rhetoric. Yet we believe economic history and theory supports the proposition that an effective market economy gives the best chance for the Soviet people, educated and resourceful as they are, to realize their potential and to move toward the living standards of the other industrialized countries.

Postscript

As this volume was about to go to the printer, dramatic events unfolded in Moscow. On August 19, 1991, a group of eight hard-liners formed a State Committee on the Extraordinary Situation, arrested President Gorbachev, and declared a State of Emergency. They did not, however, arrest Boris Yeltsin, president of the Russian Federation, and two days later the coup collapsed.

For fifty-six hours the prospects looked bleak for a radical economic reform any time soon; now they seem quite promising. The failure of the coup may eliminate much of the high-level opposition to a reform of the sort outlined in this book, since these were the people and the forces that have blocked radical reform for almost a year. Although the situation in Moscow is still fluid, it seems possible that the democratic, pro-reform forces may prevail, and this would make the need for Western economic advice more pressing than ever. We thus reiterate our hope that the suggestions contained in this volume will prove useful to our Soviet colleagues as they begin what now may be a real transition to the market.

Chapter Two

The Soviet Economic Crisis
Steps to Avert Collapse

The Soviet economy faces a worsening economic crisis that makes it essential to take steps immediately to complete market reforms, stabilize the budget and credit, and open the economy. This memorandum lays out the reforms that must be taken in the next few months if the Soviet economy is to arrest and reverse the economic collapse that is underway.

I. INTRODUCTION

The Current Situation

The symptoms of repressed inflation become more acute every day. The state shops have empty shelves, citizens and enterprises are hoarding goods and materials, trade within the Soviet Union deteriorates toward barter, and the ruble buys little. The real gross national product has fallen sharply in 1990.

Creating a Market Economy

The question is, what is to be done? Reform measures have been frequent in the last five years but the result has been neither to create a market nor to improve the planning system. Any economic system needs a mechanism to coordinate and discipline its enterprise. No effective system now exists. Enterprises have been partially freed, but the incentives and competition necessary for an effective market

Note: This memorandum was prepared by the study group chairmen, Barry Bosworth, Merton J. Peck, and Thomas J. Richardson, in November 1990 and in cooperation with Evgenii G. Yasin and Petr O. Aven. It was submitted to President Gorbachev in Russian translation in early December 1990. The original text has not been changed since we wish to preserve it in the original form in which it was submitted to the USSR State Commission and the form in which it was translated into Russian. The memorandum was given to senior officials, including President Gorbachev, in December 1990. In subsequent chapters it is cited as chapter 2.

have not been introduced. The banking system accommodates the demands of enterprises in a way that allows ballooning credit and no constraints on enterprise spending.

Prices at the procurement and wholesale level have been raised, but retail prices are still frozen. Such partial liberalization means that state subsidies have increased substantially. The increase in subsidies from freeing wholesale prices is likely to add 100 billion rubles or more to a government deficit that is already over ten percent of the gross national product.

The solution lies in abandoning the search for halfway houses, in abandoning the dream of a regulated market economy. It is crucial to move quickly to an effective market system. The need for a market system is widely recognized in all the reform plans considered in the last year. What has not been recognized is that it takes a few bold but simple steps to make it effective. Otherwise a market system cannot deliver the benefits that the economic texts promise and the Western economies have achieved.

The Soviet Union now has a large market with a common currency and almost 300 million people in its boundaries. Thus it already has the unified market that has been so successful in America and has taken Western Europe decades to achieve. The forces of separatism, now so pervasive, threaten to destroy it. Trade barriers would be particularly costly for the Soviet Union because its plants and facilities have been built on the basis of geographic specialization and exchange across the unified market. All of the republics have a large fraction of their economic activity dedicated to inter-republic trade.

Proposals for Economic Reform

Economic reforms must be adopted quickly if the current economic crisis is to end. The policies must be simple and effective; they must provide at least the minimum essentials for an effective market system.

One of the characteristics of a market economy is its interdependence. What happens in one sector feeds back to other sectors. The failure to recognize this interdependence doomed earlier partial reforms.

The minimum measures are five:

1. Liberalize prices.
2. Corporatize enterprises.
3. Stabilize government spending and restrict credit.
4. Moderate the social costs of unemployment.
5. Open the economy to competition, both internally and internationally.

The five measures must be taken simultaneously and, in view of the present crisis, as soon as possible, that is, early in 1991. The time for careful sequencing of reform plans is past. Furthermore, as discussed below, each of the five measures reinforces the others. If adopted together, the five can be successful; if adopted only singly or over time, they are doomed to failure.

II. LIBERALIZE PRICES

Definitions

To "liberalize" means freeing prices so that sellers can set whatever prices they choose. Sellers will then set prices at "market-clearing" levels—that is, prices will equate the demand of buyers with the supply of sellers. Thus freeing prices means goods in the shops, albeit at higher prices. It also means sellers will set prices that will cover their costs, so that they will no longer require state subsidies to operate.

The Soviet Union has already freed many prices. As of November 15, 1990, retail prices are now free of central control on such items as television sets, higher quality furniture, and such luxury items as jewelry. On January 1, 1991, all wholesale prices are to be freed of central control, along with prices at which enterprises sell to one another.

Retail prices, however, remain controlled for more than 80% of total retail sales. With retail prices fixed below market-clearing levels, the government must provide subsidies for the difference between wholesale and retail prices. In 1991, such subsidies will greatly add to the already excessive government deficit. The deficit is financed with new money, so the consequence of freeing wholesale prices without freeing retail prices is that even more rubles will be chasing the goods in the shops.

The Failures of Administrative Reform

To equate supply and demand without ever increasing government deficits, retail prices must be increased in the near future. But
that change can occur effectively only if prices are set free, rather
than by administrative decree.

This is true for several reasons. First, administrative reforms typically fail to raise prices to market-clearing levels. As a result, consumers are not compensated for increased prices by goods becoming plentiful on the shelves.

Second, it is simply impossible to calculate the correct set of relative prices for several thousand commodities; economic conditions
simply change too often, and in unpredictable ways, for a correct
administrative reform to be possible.

Third, administrative reform results in a succession of price
jumps; before each jump, which will be much discussed in parliament and the media, consumers will anticipate the price increases by
hoarding. The result will be periodic shortages that will further
strain the public's patience. In contrast, freeing market prices will
result in thousands of frequent and small price adjustments that
consumers and producers will not anticipate with extensive hoarding.

The Impact of Price Liberalization

The freeing of all retail and wholesale prices will lead to immediate price increases for most goods, threatening to trigger inflation,
and possibly lowering the real income of many households.

1. There are a number of ways to estimate the size of the increase
in prices. One technique examines the increase in household money
balances, and produces an estimate that prices are likely to rise by
about 50 percent after they are freed. Some estimates suggest a rise
of 150 percent, while other estimates are based on prices in free
markets, which in mid-1990 were around three times the official
prices. Much depends on the amount by which wages are allowed to
rise in step with prices. If they increase fully as much as do prices, an
explosion is possible. While there is no way of choosing definitively
among these estimates, there is no doubt that liberalization will result in a price increase of serious proportions.

It is important to recognize, however, that these are estimates of
the increase in official prices. By contrast, grey- or black-market

prices are already at market-clearing levels, and they are likely to fall with liberalization while official retail prices increase sharply. Hence for consumers the price increase will be on only a portion of their purchases. Consumers who currently buy only in the state shops will, of course, experience the entire burden of the rise in official prices.

It is true that rationing by price means that consumers will face a reduction in their real wages. But they will also benefit from reduced time spent in lines, as the current system of rationing by queues requires. The ruble will buy less but it will buy *something*.

2. The serious threat to the Soviet economy is not the one-time price jump but the possibility that this jump would set off a wage-price spiral in which price increases lead to wage increases that in turn lead to further price increases. A price-wage spiral can turn into hyperinflation, as prices and wages chase one another at an accelerating rate. Only with tough macroeconomic stabilization measures can the government keep the one-time price jump following upon price liberalization from turning into hyperinflation.

3. The price increase will lower the incomes and reduce the real value of the savings of some households. There are two measures that could moderate the social costs of price changes. First, some basic necessities can be guaranteed to low-income households and pensioners at prices they can afford to pay. This can be accomplished through the distribution of coupons for specific minimum quantities of selected items, or by controlling the prices of a few items such as bread, milk and cheap meat. It is important, however, to keep the fraction of items subject to price controls few; otherwise the required subsidies will vastly increase the budget deficit and cause inflation to soar. In view of the geographic diversity of the Soviet Union, such controls might be best administered by the Republics or localities.

The Benefits of Liberalization

First and foremost, by freeing prices to equate supply and demand, liberalization means that people's rubles will be able to buy things. Currently that is not so. Goods are disappearing from shelves, and Republics and localities are driven to ration basic goods like soap, meat, bread, and cigarettes. The ruble is less and less

convertible *internally* by Soviet residents into Soviet goods and services. Free prices will make the ruble once again convertible into
domestic goods.

One advantage of the Soviet economy was that it had a common
currency used in all the fifteen Republics. But that advantage becomes a liability when the common currency is no longer acceptable
because prices are severely distorted. With the ruble not freely convertible into goods internally, trade between enterprises and localities has shifted to a complex and inefficient barter system.

By bringing goods back on to the shelves of the shops, the decontrol of prices eliminates the long lines waiting to make purchases.
It brings goods from the back of the shop, where they are sold
illegally for high prices to a select few, to the front, available to all
willing to pay the now higher prices. Under the pressure of low
official prices that do not equate demand and supply, alternative
distribution channels have developed. A recent study found that
only 40 percent of the food is currently distributed in state stores,
with the balance distributed in enterprise stores, farm markets and
special stores serving veterans, invalids and pensioners. Such a
breakdown of the normal distribution channels is a clear sign of
repressed inflation and unrealistic official prices.

Second, liberalization makes an important contribution to stabilization. Stabilization requires reducing the growth of money incomes. That requires first reducing the government deficit that is
financed by printing more rubles. Price liberalization eliminates or
reduces the need for subsidies for enterprises which now make up a
large part of government expenditures.

Finally, price liberalization sets the stage for greater economic
efficiency, by giving enterprises the incentive to serve the consumers, on whom they will now be totally dependent. They will no
longer need to obey the Ministries who provide their subsidies, and
who pay for whatever they produce, however poor the quality.

Competition among enterprises will begin to develop, leading to
improved productivity. Though the process will take time, it will be a
major benefit of moving to a market economy, and the only possible
basis for improving the standard of living of the people of the Soviet
Union.

III. CORPORATIZE STATE ENTERPRISES

To be most effective, liberalization of prices requires that enterprises be converted into independent, self-financing, and profit-maximizing organizations. The most important step, which we call *corporatization*, immediately establishes enterprises as independent and financially autonomous entities; once corporatized, enterprises must no longer be under the direction of the Ministries or dependent on the government budget for subsidies and investment funds. This step is distinct from privatization, which will require more time.

The two key elements of corporatization are independence and self-financing for all the enterprises. *Independence* means the directors of an enterprise must have the authority to set prices, output, and wages, as well as determine inputs and financing. Corporatization would ensure the legal and actual separation of the enterprise from the state.

Self-financing, or financial autonomy, means the enterprise can obtain money to pay its workers, build plants, buy equipment, and to pay its suppliers from only three sources: sales of its products, borrowing from banks at realistic rates of interest, or by the sale of its assets. The objective of self-finance is to impose hard budget constraints on all enterprises. An enterprise operating under a hard budget constraint must accept the fact that it cannot turn to the Union, the Republics, localities, or banks for subsidies or unlimited credit. The enterprise must know that unprofitability ultimately means bankruptcy for the firm and economic ruin for the managers. The possibility of bankruptcy provides a market system with the stick that makes enterprises efficient.

A market system also needs a carrot; enterprises must retain a portion of their profits for bonuses to managers and to expand and to improve their facilities. While a tax on corporate profits is consistent with a market system, the rate must be uniform across enterprises, non-negotiable with the tax authorities, and must be set at levels that still leave a significant reward for success.

Preconditions for Corporatization

Corporatization requires the government to create certain additional conditions:

1. The government must enact and enforce laws of property. There must be clear rules for ownership transfer and a system of contract enforcement to encourage longer term agreements and the development of capital markets. Creditors must have the right to seize quickly the assets of debtors who are unwilling or unable to meet their obligations.

2. Banks must refuse to issue credit to enterprises that have poor economic prospects. [This issue is discussed further in chapter 4.]

3. There must be rules of bankruptcy and liquidation to govern what happens when the claims on an enterprise exceed its liquidation value.

The Steps in Corporatization of Large State Enterprises

The joint-stock company is the best organizational form for making large state enterprises independent and self-financing. The existing management could serve as the initial directors.

As the initial owners of the capital stock, governments should create Property Management Agencies (PMA) of the Union, Republics, and localities. The appropriate governmental level would depend in part on the type of company and in part on a political decision as to the distribution of ownership among the present levels of government.

The PMA will hold all the stock and collect the dividends. It should have an interest in seeing that its corporations maximize profits. The PMA will have important duties, which basically are to behave as a traditional stockholder. It must select directors on the basis of their competence; it must provide as much protection as possible against abuses of managerial discretion while avoiding interference with day-to-day operations; it must resist political interference with the firm; it must not seek subsidies for its failing corporations. This asks much of governmental property agencies, but fulfilling these responsibilities is essential to a market economy, and will help produce the benefits it alone is capable of providing.

An enterprise so transformed into a joint-stock company, with its stock initially assigned to the PMA, will have the ability to decide on prices, production, product mix; on the inputs of labor, materials, and capital, as well as the prices it will offer for these inputs; and on the level and financing of investment. It will have the right to enter freely into contracts with the government, other enterprises, and foreign entities. It will have the right to hire and fire workers. All these rights will, of course, be subject to the laws of the land, but those laws must not preclude the kinds of discretion and behavior generally provided businesses in market economies.

At the outset, enterprises would be government-owned corporations. While corporatization is an imperfect substitute for private ownership, it is a crucial and useful first step. Corporatization can be done quickly—in a month if necessary—once the division of ownership between various levels of government has been resolved and the property to be assigned to each enterprise has been established. Privatization should be the ultimate goal, but privatization takes time. To wait for privatization would delay the reforms which are so urgent. In the short run, corporatization is a necessary compromise that will bring a measure of independence and self-financing.

The Monopoly Problem

Many of the state enterprises are monopolies. By freeing them from government restraint, the combination of corporatization and price decontrol will create the possibility of monopolistic behavior and monopoly profits. Yet reform should not be postponed until effective competition is established. Nor should most monopolies be subject to special price controls at the time of liberalization.

In a market system, high profits attract the entry of new rivals, and thereby sow the seeds of destruction of the monopoly power that made them possible. The retention of price controls for these enterprises would interfere with that healthy competitive process, and preserve all the distortions created by the present ubiquitous administrative price controls. The best remedy, therefore, is encouragement of competition itself.

The most crucial element of such a policy is to ensure legally free entry of enterprises into whatever markets they wish to enter. Opening the economy to the competition of imports will further effectively limit monopoly power, and it will do so promptly. In addition, laws can be enacted, like the American antitrust laws, prohibiting enterprises from combining or agreeing among themselves to limit competition.

The one exception to this general principle would be the natural monopolies, such as the railroads, some communications services, or the local distribution of electricity, water, or gas. In these cases, either the technological advantages of large scale or the existence of monopoly bottlenecks give a single firm a cost advantage over all possible rivals. For such natural monopolies, and for them only, the kinds of price regulation practiced in most market economies would continue to be necessary in the Soviet Union as well.

The Soviet economy is unlikely to become consistently and pervasively competitive overnight. A successful demonopolization effort will take time. That is one of the most important reasons why we emphasize the necessity for opening the economy to international trade at the earliest possible moment. It is also one possible reason to delay ultimate privatization, since private owners may successfully resist demonopolization. Still, we think that thorough conversion of the Soviet economy into a competitive one cannot be considered an essential precondition for the reforms recommended here. They cannot be delayed.

Small Business and Agriculture

Corporatization applies largely to large state enterprises. A different approach can apply to small businesses. Retailing, services, and small-scale manufacturing are activities that can be quickly privatized by sale or leasing. This denationalization can probably best be done by local governments. Improving retailing and services by introducing competition is a step that can improve consumer welfare quickly at little cost in resources.

Entry of new enterprises is likely in these activities. All requirements to enter new markets or activities should be abolished except the minimum necessary to protect public health and safety (e.g., sanitary standards for restaurants and food stores).

Agriculture is a special case in which a mix of corporatization and small-scale individual ownership may prove most appropriate. Individual farmers should have the opportunity to own or lease land to engage in small-scale farming—mainly in fruit, vegetables, meat and dairy production. Large-scale agricultural organizations are likely to be most efficient in grain production, and such units should be converted to joint-stock companies along the lines discussed above.

IV. STABILIZE GOVERNMENT SPENDING AND RESTRICT CREDIT

The Problem Today

In addition to the microeconomic issues of pricing, the Soviet Union today faces a huge and growing government budget deficit, money incomes that are rising much more rapidly than output, worsening open and repressed inflation, and a flight from the ruble.

In a free market, rising incomes and stagnant production would result in a rise in prices—inflation—sufficient to ration out the increased demand. Since most retail prices are fixed in the Soviet Union, the increased demand manifests itself in barer and barer shelves in state stores and lines that get longer and longer. The few goods left in the state stores are rusty tins and rotten cabbages. Free-market or black-market prices rise sharply, and the street price of hard currency diverges even more from the official rate.

Once shortages appear, the dynamics of hoarding take over as people begin to worry about the value of their rubles and begin to use goods as a store of value. Republics are driven to ration basic goods like soap, meat, cigarettes, and sugar. Overvalued rubles drive out undervalued goods. In other words, the ruble is less and less convertible *internally* by Soviet residents into Soviet goods and services.

Diagnosis

All of these are the familiar symptoms of *severe repressed inflation*. It is a syndrome that has been seen in many countries over the twentieth century. In understanding the issue, we separate the causes into three categories:

• Ruble overhang. The "ruble overhang" signifies that households have excess spending power in currency and savings accounts. This is the result of past budget deficits.

• Budget deficit. The current budget deficit adds continuously to the ruble overhang. The official budget deficit (expenditures less receipts) is on the order of 10 percent of GNP. This deficit will explode in 1991 if retail prices are not raised when wholesale prices are liberalized. Because of the structure of the Soviet finan-

cial system, budget deficits are effectively monetized immediately; they are turned automatically into cash or savings
accounts.

• Hoarding. As people come to expect price increases, there occurs an outbreak of hoarding and attempts to flee the ruble.
Particularly after the announcement of future price increases in
May 1990, the shelves in state stores were cleaned out of goods.
The black-market exchange rate of the ruble has fallen in 1990,
another indication of price disequilibrium and widespread
hoarding. More recently, there has been considerable "dollarization," or use of foreign currencies inside the Soviet Union—a
further indication of a deteriorating confidence in the ruble and
of a repressed inflation.

Stabilization Policies in the Short Run

As late as last summer, it might have been possible to stabilize the
economy—bringing total demand in line with total supply by monetary and fiscal measures—prior to taking some of the other steps.
This is no longer possible; the crisis is too severe, and stabilization
now requires the support of the other measures.

The immediate threat is that the deterioration of economic activity and the disruption of the distribution system will get worse:
fewer goods in state stores, more dollarization, greater divergence
between official and black-market prices, and spiraling inflation. In
response to the breakdown of the price system, Republics and localities will turn increasingly to rationing, coupons, substitute currencies, border controls, and restrictions on movement of goods.
The major goal of stabilization policy should be to restrain the
growth of money incomes. The primary tools for accomplishing this
are through reducing the budget deficit, tightening credit, and liberalizing prices.

Given the existing budget policies and the "ruble overhang," it
will be difficult to avoid a major increase in the average price level in
the period ahead. If liberalization of prices is postponed, the flight
from the ruble will intensify, inflation will accelerate, and hyperinflation will become a real possibility. The best hope for avoiding
this kind of total breakdown is price liberalization and a tough curb
on budget and credit policies. The sooner prices are liberalized, the

smaller will be the price jump and the less will be the risk of hyperinflation.

The following steps will help stabilize the economy and prevent runaway inflation:

1. The first priority is to reduce the budget deficit. A balanced budget would effectively control the growth of incomes. If the budget is not controlled, incomes will continue to rise, and an uncontrolled price-wage-price spiral may begin.

The priorities for reducing the budget deficit are, in every country, subject to controversy and political debate, but we have a few concrete recommendations. The most important action in the short run would be to liberalize prices and remove subsidies; without such a measure, the budget deficit will rise by at least 100 billion rubles. Liberalization today is an essential step toward stabilization.

More generally, we recommend focusing on spending reductions rather than tax increases. There is clear room for reduction of subsidies to unprofitable industries; this is in any event essential to establish market discipline. Central investments are thought to be highly inefficient and can be cut. The allocation of hard currency might be immediately reformed, say by hard-currency auctions; this would reduce the budget deficit substantially.

2. We believe that a substantial tightening of credit is essential to subject enterprises to hard budget constraints. It is neither possible nor necessary in the short run to privatize the banking system in order to have tough credit policies. In the longer run, however, creating a private banking system will help ensure that result.

In the near term, Gosbank must make enterprises financially independent by extending credit only to firms that can repay it; this implies curbing credits to unprofitable enterprises. In addition, the banking system must place overall credit limits on the enterprise sector, much as western central banks do today. We envision that banks will charge high interest rates to enterprises under a regime of tight credit. In the period surrounding liberalization, real interest rates (equal to money interest rates less the rate of inflation) must be positive; this implies that money interest rates must be well above today's level. After inflation has stabilized, interest rates can be reduced to levels prevailing in market economies.

3. We believe that the current structure of taxes is on the whole viable for the immediate future. However, one major point is vitally

important: all "specific" turnover or other taxes (i.e., taxes denominated in ruble terms per unit) must be replaced with percentage or "ad valorem" taxes (i.e., taxes set as a percent of the product price). This step will prevent the erosion of real taxes as prices rise. We understand this proposal is under consideration and endorse it strongly. More generally, government expenditures should be budgeted in rubles rather than in real terms so as to prevent the development of an inflationary psychology and to slow any inflationary spiral.

Some economists advocate a monetary reform to solve the stabilization problem. For example, existing rubles might be exchanged for new rubles at, say, 2-to-1 or 3-to-1; other suggestions are "parallel rubles" or "gold rubles." We believe these approaches should be avoided unless budget and monetary stability are *absolutely* guaranteed. If a monetary reform fails, as it surely will in the absence of strict fiscal and monetary discipline, the government will lose most of its remaining credibility. On the other hand, if monetary stability is achieved, then monetary reform is likely to be unnecessary.

A major question is whether it is desirable, by indexing, to compensate various groups for price increases. We recommend minimizing the amount of automatic indexation. There is no way to index the entire economy. Indexation cannot produce goods; it simply redistributes real resources from one group to another. The more the system is indexed, the greater is the threat of hyperinflation. Many countries have indexed their economies and have lived to regret it; indeed, in the country with the greatest price stability, the Federal Republic of Germany, wage indexation is illegal.

The only exception we would recommend is for transfer payments to low-income households, like pensioners, who must be protected against the hardships of a severe inflation. Indexation of wages should be altogether avoided if at all possible.

What about the possibility of "incomes policies," designed to control wages and prices directly? We believe that tight fiscal and credit policies are the crucial ingredient for the containment of inflation. The only certain way to check inflation is the threat of unemployment and bankruptcy that prevents firms from raising prices; for this, tight budget and credit policies are essential. Incomes policies may help, but they must not be used as a substitute for fiscal and monetary discipline.

V. MODERATE THE SOCIAL COSTS OF UNEMPLOYMENT

Perhaps the most serious adverse consequence of the essential reforms we identify here will be a sharp increase in open unemployment. The weaning of State enterprises from governmental subsidies and easy credit, the authority and incentives managers will and must have to reduce costs and increase efficiency, the introduction of competition both domestic and foreign and the elimination of inflation, will all inevitably mean the displacement of large numbers of workers from their current employments.

In a dynamic economy, the resources released in this way will be absorbed in the expansion of output, the springing into existence of new enterprises, the opening up of opportunities for exports, and in the increase in effective consumer demand and real income that improvements in productivity make possible. And that kind of economic progress is impossible if every worker is instead given a one hundred percent guarantee of retaining his or her job in its present location.

Unemployment compensation is the only possible way of reconciling this requirement of reversing the present disintegration and stagnation of the Soviet economy with the prevention of severe hardships for workers in the transition. Such a system will provide workers who are laid off with temporary support. However, that support must be substantially below the wages of those who continue to work and should decrease with the length of unemployment, in order to preserve incentives for workers to relocate, retrain, and accept alternative employment.

Given the geographic diversity in the Soviet Union in terms of wage levels and the cost of living, it would be desirable to have the unemployment compensation system administered by the Republics and localities. Of course, these levels of government must have the tax revenues necessary to meet the costs of an unemployment compensation system.

VI. OPEN THE ECONOMY INTERNATIONALLY

In a sense, the several steps we have recommended to this point are all steps to create an open, competitive market economy *within* the Soviet Union. These also require avoiding the imposition of trade barriers among the several republics.

In addition, as the Soviet Union liberalizes and stabilizes its economy, opening the economy internationally can play a critical role. We recommend moving to a convertible currency and removing import and export restrictions very quickly. Opening the economy will provide consumer goods, will speed the introduction of foreign technology, will ensure that prices reflect competitive world market prices, and will restrain monopolistic forces inside the Soviet Union.

We recommend that the ruble be made freely convertible for all imports and exports, with limitations only on "capital-account" transactions. In addition, we recommend that all quantitative restrictions be replaced by low and uniform tariffs, in the neighborhood of 10 percent.[1]

Reasons for Opening the Economy

There are several reasons for opening the economy very quickly. The principal reason is that it would expose the Soviet Union to the competitive world marketplace. The Soviet economy must make the transition to new lines of production and more efficient productive techniques. History shows that the quickest way to achieve an efficient pattern of production is to allow the price signals of the market to get transmitted to domestic enterprises. By removing quantitative restrictions on imports and allowing ruble convertibility, Soviet enterprises will have a price and quality standard that they must match in order to sell at home or abroad.

Second, currency convertibility will ensure that Soviet prices will move to market-clearing levels. Foreign firms are adept at finding the combination of prices, quantity, and quality appropriate to each

1. The reader should also note that chapter 5 recommends additional transitional tariffs for industries that are not initially internationally competitive but have the potential to become so. We do not intend so rapid a dismantling of protection as this sentence, standing alone, might imply. The original text has not been changed because, as noted earlier, we wish to retain the form in which it was submitted to the USSR State Commission. (Footnote added by the editors.)

country; they will force the newly corporatized Soviet firms to align internal prices with the world prices of tradable goods, adjusted for quality differences. The sooner convertibility is introduced, the quicker will be this alignment.

Third, opening the economy will provide goods to Soviet workers whose incentive to produce is at present severely undermined by shortages and the unavailability of domestic and foreign goods and services. Opening the economy will offer a wide array of new goods, albeit at high prices; ironically, however, these prices are likely to be lower than the ones prevailing in today's black markets.

Finally, as noted earlier, corporatization and price liberalization will allow some Soviet enterprises to charge high prices. Introduction of foreign competition will be the most effective and immediately available method of restraining the exercise of monopoly power for tradable goods. Easy entry by foreign firms into the Soviet market will provide some check on nontradable sectors as well.

These are compelling reasons to place opening the economy near the top of any serious move to a market economy. We propose taking these steps as soon as possible, either simultaneously with or very quickly after most prices are liberalized.

Concrete Steps

1. The ruble should become freely convertible into other currencies for all "current" transactions. Current account convertibility means that Soviet enterprises and individuals have free access to foreign exchange for the purchase of foreign goods and services, and that foreigners have free access to sell in the Soviet market. All Soviet and foreign enterprises will be allowed to buy and sell rubles and foreign currencies for the purposes of export and import of goods and services. Foreign firms should be allowed to hold ruble accounts and to repatriate their profits. We propose an initial limitation on "capital" transactions, however. Soviet residents would not be permitted to hold foreign securities or large quantities of foreign currencies.

2. In the long run, it would be desirable to have a fixed exchange rate for Western currencies. In the near term, this will not be feasible, because of the prospect of severe inflation. It is therefore recommended that the ruble be allowed to float, although the government

will probably want to intervene to prevent excessive short-term exchange-rate fluctuations.[2]

A freely floating ruble will initially move to a level between the official rate and the black-market rate. Thus, depreciation upon floating is both inevitable and desirable. A lower exchange rate will balance supply and demand for foreign exchange, will ensure that enterprises can buy foreign goods when that is most efficient, and will provide a wider variety of goods and services to consumers.

We warn against an overvalued exchange rate. It would be better to have the ruble priced too low than too high. An undervalued ruble ensures that doing business in the Soviet Union would become a bargain, and foreign firms and technology would be attracted to set up production there.

3. We recommend replacement of all quantitative restrictions on imports with a uniform tariff on all imports in the neighborhood of 10 percent. Tariffs are more evenhanded than quotas as a way of protecting domestic industry, and they avoid the administrative system that currently dominates and distorts Soviet foreign trade. In addition, tariffs can provide a source of valuable government revenues. It may be desirable to subsidize importation as well as domestic production of some food products, such as bread and vegetable oils, which are exceptionally important to households. Energy exports, particularly oil and gas, may need to have a temporary export tax to cushion domestic consumers from large price increases, although permitting domestic energy prices eventually to increase to world levels—which we strongly recommend—will free up resources for exports and generate an important source of export earnings.

Economic Union

One of the critical issues facing Soviet policymakers concerns the economic relationships between the Union and the Republics. From an economic point of view, maintaining free trade among the different regions would contribute to an efficient division of labor and use of resources. In many ways, the existence of the United States as a continental free trade zone has contributed to the success of the

2. The reader should note that in chapter 5 we recommend adopting a fixed exchange rate. As explained there, a floating exchange rate is presented here as a second-best proposal because the macroeconomic stability that a fixed exchange rate requires is unlikely to be achieved in the near future. (Footnote added by the editors.)

American economy, and the European Community is moving to-ward a free-trade region.

The centrifugal forces leading Republics and localities to seize control and demand autonomy arise from the breakdown of the current administrative system. When administrative prices deviate so far from realistic prices, nobody wants to sell and everybody wants to keep goods at home. It is futile to try to negotiate agreements between the Union and the Republics in a world where the terms of trade—the prices—are so distorted, where trade is involuntary, and where everyone feels exploited.

There are powerful gains from maintaining a free-trade zone when the price mechanism is functioning effectively. However, only when prices are freed and reflect genuine scarcities and costs, and the ruble regains value and stability, will the economic conditions be propitious for forging a political consensus about the shape of the new Soviet Union.

VII. CONCLUSION

To succeed, these measures must be explained to the parliament, to the media, and to the people. Successful adoption will require a firm, wholehearted, and consistent commitment by Soviet leaders and the reaching of an accord with the leaders of the Republics.

We recognize that the proposals will be painful and controversial. They impose major social costs in the short run as the Soviet society makes the transition from a centralized administrative approach to the decentralized direction of individuals through markets. More-over, it is not possible to provide an ironclad guarantee that these measures will cure the nation's ailments. But we can say with confidence that history shows again and again that allowing markets to direct an economy offers the best hope for resuscitating the sick economy and for raising living standards toward those in Western Europe and the United States.

Chapter Three

Price Deregulation, Corporatization, and Competition

Alfred E. Kahn and Merton J. Peck

This chapter is an elaboration of two of the key proposals summarized in the policy memorandum (chapter 2)—the deregulation of prices[1] and the corporatization of large state enterprises, along with their logical complement, the promotion of competition.

DEREGULATE PRICES

The intent of our recommendation is that sellers throughout the economy, with a limited number of exceptions, be allowed to set their prices wherever they choose—or wherever the market will permit—free of direct state control. Along with our corporatization proposal—that is, simultaneously converting the present state enterprises into financially and managerially independent organizations—we would expect the liberated enterprises to be guided, in setting prices, by the profits they would be expected to produce: ideally, their goal should be to maximize profits.

Note: Although our report is based in part on the discussions of the study group that met at Sopron, Hungary in July 1990 and the study group chairmen's meeting held in New Haven, Connecticut, in November 1990, and on the papers prepared by Soviet colleagues for the Sopron Conference, we alone are responsible for the present version. We wish to thank Dr. V. Shironin of the All-Union Institute of System Studies in Moscow for his provision of statistics previously unavailable, as well as his suggestions on an earlier draft.

1. In the policy memorandum, we characterized our recommendation in terms of price "liberalization." That characterization could be misleading, because it could be taken to mean only the *relaxation* of governmental controls, whereas the intention of our recommendations is that prices be totally liberated from such controls.

The Benefits of Deregulation

The essence of an effectively functioning market system is that the prices of all products are determined by the interaction of competitive supply and demand. Prices set in this way equate the quantities sellers offer for sale and the quantities buyers demand: at those prices there are no unsatisfied would-be buyers or sellers. Buyers are free to choose among all products and services, guided only by their own evaluations of them and by the necessity of having to pay prices that reflect the costs to society of meeting their demands. This encourages buyers to economize in the use of their limited incomes, and producers, under pressure of competition and the need to attract buyers, to strive for efficiency. The overall consequence is that—income distributional considerations aside[2]—society extracts the maximum level of satisfaction from its limited total resources.

We are aware, of course, that the transition from a tightly controlled to a market economy can involve severe disruptions and hardships. Indeed, as of April 1991, the union government evidently thinks that because of the present economic crisis, genuine and comprehensive decontrol of prices is out of the question. We draw exactly the opposite conclusion: the current crisis in the Soviet Union is primarily the result of the halting and incomplete nature of the reforms to date. Greater autonomy for the state enterprises has led to an explosion of wages, but because corporatization is incomplete and prices still state-controlled, the result has been a corresponding explosion of state subsidies and soft credits. Similarly, substantial decontrol of wholesale prices and channels of distribution has further multiplied the need for state subsidies to hold retail prices down and has led to large-scale diversion of products from normal channels, recourse to barter, breakdown of interrepublic trade and a firestorm of hoarding.

2. It is possible to believe that the market does what it does with extremely great efficiency, as we do, while also recognizing that the distribution of income and social benefits that it yields is inconsistent with widely held conceptions of fairness. Most Western economists, therefore, would qualify this endorsement of a market economy by recognizing the desirability of governmental interventions in the interest of greater fairness—whether by direct redistributions of income, or by protecting individuals from the vicissitudes of the market, or by providing to all citizens some minimum standard of living and, at the very least, to ensure a greater degree of equality of opportunity.

The present crisis has many aspects and causes, but its most visible and painful manifestation is the breakdown of retail and wholesale distribution.[3] Official prices are so far below market-clearing levels that everyone is loath to sell and everyone wants to buy. The result is hoarding and widespread recourse to inefficient barter. Supplies are diverted from the established channels into more profitable black markets. The shelves in the state retail stores are empty and the queues long, and production is down as factories find materials difficult to obtain. The present economic disintegration provides the clearest possible evidence that an economy partly liberalized but in major part still centrally controlled does not work.

In these circumstances, there are only two real alternatives—to return to thoroughgoing central control or to proceed with immediate and comprehensive price deregulation. We have already made clear our conviction that the latter is far preferable to the former.

Price deregulation would make sellers eager once again to sell for rubles. To achieve this end it must be *comprehensive*: individual sellers will want to accept rubles only if they can in turn use them to buy both consumer products and the raw and intermediate materials they need to continue producing and distributing products. This means that prices throughout the economy must be market-clearing: people and enterprises that have rubles must be able to purchase what they want, as long as they are prepared to pay prices fully reflecting the costs of supplying them.

The way in which prices are determined in an economy is intimately connected with all the other ways in which its economic activities are coordinated. Comprehensive price decontrol is therefore a necessary condition of all the other reforms that we advocate in the policy memorandum (chapter 2); and these reforms, in turn, are necessary to make price deregulation effective.

For example, corporatization, as we have already pointed out, cannot work as long as prices are rigidly controlled: the liberated enterprises can be neither independent nor self-financing if the government determines the prices they can charge. Corporatization, in turn, is necessary if enterprises are to respond to profit opportunities and price signals, and thus make a free market econ-

3. Wholesale distribution is used here, as in the USSR, to include sales of all intermediate inputs between enterprises rather than, as in the West, only sales by manufacturers and distributors to retailers.

omy work. Similarly for macroeconomic stabilization: price decontrol will eliminate the justification for subsidies to enterprises, which have in turn been a major source of inflation. There are estimates that the enterprise subsidies accounted for as much as 10 percent of gross national product (GNP) in 1990 and may double in 1991.[4] Under corporatization, the former state enterprises will have to cover their costs through the revenues they can generate in an uncontrolled market or go out of business. Elimination of the subsidies—which will be possible only if prices are comprehensively deregulated—would therefore make a major contribution toward fulfilling the most important component of any macroeconomic stabilization program—the reduction of government spending, as is emphasized in chapter 4.

Control of inflationary pressures will be essential, in turn, if the one-shot general upward surge in prices that is likely to follow decontrol is not to be converted into a runaway inflation—which would discredit price reform and prevent a market economy from functioning efficiently.

Once again, opening the economy of the Soviet Union to world trade would be both pointless and ineffective if it were not accompanied by a freeing of its price-making mechanisms. Only then will both businesses and buyers receive the signals that will result in the country specializing in areas in which it has inherent competitive advantages and having recourse to imports of goods and services in the supply of which it is at a competitive disadvantage. On the other hand, opening the economy to imports is an essential part of the program to subject domestic enterprises to the constraints of competition, thereby mitigating the danger that corporatization and price decontrol will merely result in monopolistic exploitation of consumers.

Similarly, both privatization and the establishment of capital markets, the subject of chapter 7, obviously require the liberation of prices from government control; private investment is simply not going to be forthcoming if the state continues to fix prices. And, once again, the causal connection runs in the opposite direction as

4. *The Economy of the USSR: Summary and Recommendations,* a study undertaken in response to a request by the Houston Summit (Washington, D.C.: International Monetary Fund, International Bank for Reconstruction and Development, Organization for Economic Cooperation and Development, and European Bank for Reconstruction and Development, 1990), 17.

well: private enterprise and well-organized capital markets are necessary if the economy is to respond efficiently to the signals provided by free market prices.

Finally, although the decontrol of prices is not a necessary condition for enacting our various proposals for alleviating unemployment, it is inconceivable that prices could be freed, state subsidies to enterprises eliminated, and the economy opened to competition were these reforms not accompanied by some system of transitional social support for the people who are likely to be thrown out of work as a result of them.

In short, in any society or economy, everything depends on everything else; and this is certainly the case with respect to a market economy. For this reason, our several reform proposals are inextricably interdependent.

The Costs of Liberalization

If the deregulation of prices were painless, it would have been accomplished a long time ago, in view of the enormous long-term benefits it promises. Unfortunately, it will also inevitably involve severe costs, especially in the short-term. Because of the severe suppressed inflation now afflicting the Soviet economy, reasonable estimates of the probable average increase in official prices upon decontrol range between 50 and 300 percent: it is impossible to estimate more precisely, since the size of the increase will depend on how consumers and enterprises respond. The more they respond by rushing to spend their accumulated monetary holdings, the more prices will rise.

It is necessary immediately to qualify these frightening estimates in two very important ways. The first is that these estimates concern the expected increase in *official* prices. If the ceilings on those prices are lifted, prices in the farmers' and black markets are very likely to fall.[5] The *free* market price of chickens in Moscow in December 1990

5. It is worth pointing out that there are a whole range of markets in the USSR, only some of which are legal. The state stores sell goods at heavily regulated prices and are, of course, perfectly legal. Prices on the illegal black market are unregulated, as are the prices on the legal collective farm market. In addition, as the official distribution system has grown less effective, the last few years have witnessed increasing reliance on distribution and sale of hard-to-get goods through individual places of employment.

was ten times the official price in the state stores—where chicken was seldom available. Once the state stores are free to pay the free market price, farmers and distributors will no longer have an incentive to divert their sales to the free or black market, or to hold them on the farm for use in bartering transactions; and buyers who today can satisfy their wants only outside official channels—and can afford it—will no longer find it necessary to do so, and in so doing to drive up those prices. As a result, although decontrol could mean a threefold increase in the price in the state stores, it is highly likely to mean a decrease for consumers who today patronize the free or black markets.

The same is true of the prices that enterprises are likely to have to pay for their raw materials or semifinished inputs. The ones that are able today to obtain those supplies at the official prices will undoubtedly experience a substantial price increase; those who now have to do so through complicated barter arrangements are likely to experience decreases.

Moreover, the present dual distribution system, on top of a great deal of simple barter, is extraordinarily inefficient. The return to an effectively functioning money economy, in which goods are freely bought and sold for rubles, will have a powerful salutary influence in holding down price increases generally.

The second consideration is that an increase—even a substantial increase—in the prices of goods and services that consumers will then find readily available in the shops, as compared with the official prices of those same goods that were previously simply unavailable, is in a very real sense no price increase at all.[6] This beneficial aspect of deregulation—increased availability of goods in the shops—is likely to be very large. As of the summer of 1990, 42 percent of the meat and meat products, 55 percent of the vegetables, 20 percent of the milk, 75 percent of the potatoes, and 44 percent of the eggs were sold outside the state retail distribution system.[7] At the very least,

6. One is reminded of the story during World War II of the customer who, upon being quoted a price of a dollar a pound for coffee by a shopkeeper, complained that the price in the shop across the street was only half that; when the shopkeeper asked him, then, why he didn't buy his coffee across the street, the customer responded, "But they don't have any coffee."

7. *Transition to the Market: A Report of a Working Group Formed by M. S. Gorbachev and B. N. Yeltsin*, Part 1: *The Concept and Program* (Moscow: Cultural Initiative Foundation,

against the negative effect on consumer welfare of the increase in official prices, consequent on the freeing of markets, must surely be weighed the complexities, uncertainties, and arbitrariness of the present system; the anger that it understandably generates; the vexations of having to wait in long queues for long periods of time and finding the shelves bare; the stark choices Soviet consumers find themselves forced to make between shoddy merchandise and no merchandise at all; and the time and energy expended in bartering goods and services that could thenceforth simply be bought with rubles.

All these things must be said, without any intention to minimize the distress that the price increases in the state stores will inflict on low-income consumers to whom the vexations of long lines, empty shelves, and wasted time are of less moment than the higher prices they would have to pay in the future.

The one-time jump in official prices, then, is a necessary and inescapable cost of moving to a market economy. The critical necessity will be to keep that one-time inflationary jump from turning into hyperinflation, in which prices and wages chase one another at an increasing rate. That would be a disaster; and that is why the freeing of prices must be accompanied by the kinds of macroeconomic measures to control inflation that are discussed in chapter 4.

Exceptions and Measures to Ease the Transition

Although the case for freeing prices from controls applies to all goods and services except ones supplied under conditions where effective competition is impossible, we conceive the probable necessity of a more gradual transition in a few very limited cases, along with other measures to mitigate the severe distress that total decontrol could inflict on low-income families.

Decontrol would necessarily result in wide variations among goods and services in the extent to which their prices increase above their present official levels. One important reason for this is that the present state subsidies are not spread evenly across all products, and, since in a free market prices must cover costs, this obviously means

---

1990), 67. The task force was headed by Academician S. Shatalin, and it is henceforth cited as the *Shatalin Report*. The document is also known as the Report on the Five-Hundred-Day Plan.

Table 3.1
Ratio of Input Costs to Producers' Price for Selected Consumer Goods, 1989

Subsidized Items	Input Costs/Price
Housing and utilities	6.02
Communication	2.67
Meat	1.86
Milk	1.81
Transportation	1.62
Fruits and vegetables	1.22
Unsubsidized Items That Are Profitable or Taxed	
Confectionery	0.76
Clothes	0.74
Durables	0.54
Wine	0.43
Vodka	0.10

Source: V. Shironin, "Product Prices in the USSR" (Paper presented at the IIASA Conference on Economic Reform and Integration in Sopron, Hungary, July–August 1990).

that highly subsidized products will experience greater increases than unsubsidized ones.

Table 3.1, which compares the input costs of various products with their regulated producer prices, provides a rough indication of the kinds of variations that are likely to be experienced. The table was calculated by adjusting prices of inputs by the tax or subsidy applied to them, including the taxes and subsidies on the inputs used to produce the inputs. Producer prices are the equivalent of what are called elsewhere wholesale prices, that is, the prices to retail establishments.

A ratio of input costs to price of more than one indicates a subsidy, less than one, taxes or profits: the 6.02 for housing and utilities suggests costs are an astounding six times the official price; at the other extreme, the 0.10 ratio for vodka clearly reflects prices far in excess of costs.

Housing is obviously very heavily subsidized; this is not surprising, considering that Soviet families on average pay only 3 percent of their income for rent; the roughly comparable ratio in market economies is on the order of 30 percent. Meat, milk, fruit, and vegetables are also heavily subsidized.[8] When a consumer buys milk at a state store, the price covers only 55 percent of its cost.

These facts strongly suggest the advisability of gradualism in decontrolling the prices of goods and services that are of importance, either symbolic or real, to low-income groups. These families live under desperately difficult conditions and must have some protection from sudden and extreme price increases, such as seem likely to occur in housing, meat, milk, and public transportation, particularly since they are the most dependent upon the official sources of supply. Decontrol of rents, similarly, must clearly be permitted to take place only over a number of years.

Confinement of state subsidies to this very important but relatively small bundle of goods and services will still permit very sharp reductions in their total, and therefore not be inconsistent with macroeconomic stabilization.

On the other hand, price controls are a very inefficient way of helping poor people. Many in the lowest income group are pensioners; the most straightforward way of protecting them would be to raise their pensions—a possibility discussed in chapter 6. Another option would be for local governments to provide people with low incomes ration coupons carrying the right to purchase a fixed quantity of selected items at a low price, although the International Monetary Fund report suggests that such a means-tested program might be too complicated to administer.[9] A less efficient and more costly alternative would be to give everyone such ration coupons, with purchases above the quantities covered by the coupons having to be made at market prices.

Another way of making the transition to higher market prices more acceptable to consumers would be to ensure adequate inventories at the time of deregulation. The pain of higher prices would then be offset to some extent by the greater availability of goods in the shops. The inventory build-up might be accomplished by increased imports, using foreign exchange reserves; such imports

8. The best-known subsidized price was that of bread, which, until its recent trebling, had remained unchanged since 1962, at 20 kopecks. The subsidy for bread would not have been reflected in the calculations reproduced in table 3.1 because it is provided at the retail level; table 3.1 captures only subsidies at the wholesale level—that is, before the products or services reach the retailer.

9. *Economy of the USSR*, 5.

would also be excellent candidates for temporary foreign aid. Providing ample stocks in retail stores at the time of deregulation should moderate panic buying. We emphasize that such a recourse to borrowing or foreign aid for this purpose should be a one-time measure, as part of an effort to build confidence in the economic reforms.

Low-income families can also be helped by other kinds of direct subsidy, without the distortions of price control. We assume, for example, that medical care and education will continue to be provided by the state at nominal or no charges.

Although they are not directly reflected in table 3.1, except insofar as they are included in the category "housing and utilities," energy prices in the Soviet Union are far below market-clearing levels. It might appear that these prices, too, provide a case for retaining price controls, considering the importance of energy prices in the economy at large: the USSR hardly needs an oil shock such as afflicted most countries of the world in 1973–74 and 1979–81.

On the other hand, precisely because oil is so very important in the economy and conservation in its use so necessary—partly because of the importance of oil exports as a source of precious foreign exchange—we would be inclined to resist the retention of price controls—which encourage wasteful consumption, breed shortages and queues, and are extremely inefficient. The way to help poor families with their utility bills, for example, would be to have special means-tested lifeline rates, such as many electric and gas utilities offer in the United States. Similarly, the way to cushion low-income families from soaring rents and prices of essential foods is, as in Western countries, to provide means-tested rent subsidies, food stamps and the like.

Chapter 5 proposes an attractive transitional compromise, in consideration of its estimate that the present prices of oil and gas in the Soviet Union are at only about 20 percent of the world levels, and simple deregulation and an immediate opening of the Soviet economy would impart a very painful shock to all energy-consuming enterprises. Its proposed solution is a large export tax on oil, sufficient at the outset to maintain the present relationship between domestic and world prices, but scheduled to be reduced regularly over a five- to seven-year period—conceivably, if the supply is believed to be sufficiently elastic, to zero.

We reemphasize the importance of keeping the exceptions to price decontrol few. Market economies can function reasonably well if a few items are singled out for controls; but the controls that are defensible are, typically, of commodities supplied under conditions of natural monopoly, whose purpose is to prevent monopolistic exploitation rather than to hold prices below cost. And so while it may be necessary to phase out controls on the prices of housing, milk, and meat, it is far better to help poor people through the transition in ways that do not prevent prices from fulfilling their essential role of eliciting supply—for example, by specific subsidies to the low-income groups, or by free or subsidized provision of food, rental accommodations, and modest quantities of utility services.

Partial, Gradual, and Administered Liberalization

It is widely recognized in the Soviet Union that the present structure of prices is grossly distorted—that is to say, that the prices of its millions of individual goods and services are in widely varying degrees out of line with their respective costs, and therefore with one another. It is widely recognized also that official prices at both the retail and producer level are too low. The official response has been partial deregulations and gradual correction by administrative decree, rather than the immediate, close to universal decontrol that we propose.

This emphasis on gradualism and the reluctance to dismantle the entire framework of governmental price controls that it reflects is, of course, understandable. As we have already recognized, the price increases following total removal of governmental restraints are likely to be very large, particularly at the retail level. And while the historic regime of stable, artificially suppressed official prices has had as its inevitable accompaniment long lines at the shops, shoddy quality, and empty shelves, that is the tradeoff to which the Soviet public has been accustomed; violent departures from it, however large the offsetting advantages and promise of long-term benefits, are likely to generate a severe political reaction.

The fact remains—and we cannot emphasize it too strongly—that any attempts to move only partially or gradually, under continued governmental management, are almost certainly going to create new distortions, shortages, and hardships—as, we submit, the experience of the last five years has clearly demonstrated—while at the same time at best delaying and at worst putting off indefinite achievement of the ultimate free market system that holds the key to genuine improvement in living standards.

There are several fundamental reasons why governmentally administered price reform, within a framework of continued comprehensive price controls, can only make matters worse rather than better—indeed, has demonstrably already done so.

The first reason is that administrative price reform or correction will inevitably be extended over a considerable period of time. An effective market economy requires that the price of *every* good and service be set at levels that equate its demand and supply. The sheer size of the administrative problem of achieving such a result by governmental correction is staggering. Ed Hewett reports that *Goskomtsen,* the price control agency, reviews annually about 200,000 proposals for price changes—700 each working day. An estimated 300,000 more are handled by the economic ministries or other authorities.[10]

Moreover, the continued responsibility of the government for prices, under such a process, means that the decisions will continue to be subject to political considerations and pressures. In circumstances in which commodities and services are almost all in short supply, these pressures will inevitably constrain administrative corrections to relatively modest levels;[11] as a result, the price reforms, as long as the will to continue them persists—and that itself is subject to doubt—will inevitably consist of a series of successive increases, each one too little and too late. As long as the government is responsible for setting prices, it will inevitably introduce unpopular changes only grudgingly, so that when adjustments finally become inevitable, they are likely to come in big and painful jumps. Moreover, as long as prices are not free to equate supply and demand, administratively enacted increases cannot reliably be offset by full availability of

10. Ed A. Hewett, *Reforming the Soviet Economy: Equality versus Efficiency* (Washington, D.C.: Brookings Institution, 1988), 192.

11. This statement, which was written before the price reforms that went into effect during the first week of April 1991, would seem to be belied by the extremity of some of those corrections: as we have already observed, for example, the price of bread is reported to have been tripled. The fact remains that the new levels are evidently still substantially below market-clearing levels.

goods at those prices. Only market-set prices can provide that kind of assurance.

Indeed, piecemeal, administered reform will probably aggravate shortages rather than mitigate them. This is because each of the corrections will necessarily be debated in parliament, reported in the press, and therefore be widely anticipated. The result will inevitably be refusals to sell, panic buying, and hoarding, as buyers—ultimate consumers and enterprises both—stock up in anticipation of the increase. The result will be continued obstruction of normal channels of sale, bartering, and shortages of supplies in open markets, which will further discredit the process. Moreover, such repeated price increases give rise to widespread inflationary expectations, which are hard to combat, and severely aggravate the problem of macroeconomic stability.

Apart from the political pressures, this result is inescapable because a system of economywide price controls can never get the complex and constantly changing relationships among prices even remotely close to right. The price control agency in the USSR may be reviewing a few hundred thousand proposals for changes each year, but the number of prices in a modern economy is hundreds of times as large as that. In the United States, the trucking industry alone quotes prices numbering in the millions: this should not be surprising, considering the almost limitless variety of products carried and routes served for each.

Moreover, prices in a market economy are interdependent in the most complicated ways. Some goods and services complement one another; others are substitutes; in both cases, purchasers of any one are therefore influenced not just by its price but also by the prices of its substitutes or complements. Producers are—and economic efficiency *requires* that they be—guided by the prices of their various inputs relative to the wholesale prices at which they can sell; by the price of aluminum relative to that of copper, of labor relative to that of capital (and in a market economy, capital must have a price that reflects its opportunity cost—that is, of what it can add to output in alternative uses), by the price of coal and gas relative to that of oil and by the price of each relative to the cost of transporting it; traders and arbitragers must be guided by the prices of products at one geographic location relative to the prices of those same products at other locations, along with the costs of moving them from where they are relatively cheap to where they are relatively scarce or costly; consumers must be guided by the price of television sets relative to the charges for movies, and so on in an infinite set of combinations. There is simply no way in which the administrative agency can get these interdependencies right.

Moreover, prices in free markets are constantly changing under the influence of changing balances between supply and demand. Regulated prices, which are inevitably set preponderantly on the basis of *average* costs, cannot possibly be adjusted flexibly in the same way. Efficient, market-clearing prices will at some times and places have to be far above average costs, at others far below, depending on whether supplies are short or capacity is excessive.[12] "Administrative price reform" is almost a contradiction in terms.

Of course, this kind of wholly flexible, market-driven pricing is by no means the universal rule in Western economies either: many of our prices too are set at standard or average cost and held relatively stable over time. But even in concentrated industries like automobiles and steel, the effective prices are far from totally rigid: when demand drops, the automobile companies break into low-interest rate financing promotions and rebating wars, steel companies find various ways of providing extra fabricating and other services without charge, and large customers successfully bargain for discounts.[13]

12. A striking example of the failure of administered prices to recognize these differences is provided by the intense public protests in Minsk against the sharp price increases enacted in April 1991. According to the account in the *New York Times*: "Commentators pointed out that supplies there had been relatively stable, leaving the public unprepared for the sudden doubling and trebling of prices on basic foods and commodities." The *New York Times* quotes the vice president of the Byelorussian parliament as pointing out: "Unlike Moscow or other capitals we maintain a supply of meat, flour and other essentials. These prices were an explosion." (See *New York Times*, April 11, 1991, pp. A1–9.)

The administered price increases had the fatal flaw of being *uniform* across the entire Soviet Union, evidently ignoring wide disparities in local balances between supply and demand. In an effectively functioning market economy those disparities automatically produce corresponding differences in prices, which in turn encourage both the flow of goods from where they are relatively plentiful to where they are relatively scarce and regional specialization in production.

13. Moreover, it is in precisely those areas that American industries have performed most badly in the past. The upward wage-price spiral in the American automobile and steel industries in the late 1970s and early 1980s, in the face of declining demand, epitomized the problem of stagflation, which Western economies have not entirely solved to this day. At the same time, it was the introduction of market competition,

Finally—and in a sense most fundamentally—as long as it is the government that sets prices, it will be impossible to put into effect all the other major institutional changes that are a necessary part of moving to a free market economy, and so the hardships of the transition will be unnecessarily extended and multiplied.

To take a single example, if enterprises must continue to turn to the governmental authorities for approval of their prices, they cannot enjoy the autonomy that is an essential aspect of corporatization; they will continue to be subject to the historic planning and command system. Nor, in these circumstances, can they be cut loose from subsidies; if they suffer losses, they can blame excessively rigid price controls, and the government will be unable to resist their demand and that of their employees for continued subsidization. As a result, the critical goals of corporatization—independence of each enterprise and responsibility for its own destiny—and the sharp reduction in governmental subsidies essential to the control of inflation will be unachievable. (Of course, that may be one of the reasons that administrative rather than market-driven price reform is popular among Soviet officials: it enables them to retain their control over the economy, whereas the purpose of true economic reform is to liberate the economy from these officials.)

Just as is true of gradual administrative price reform, so the decontrol of only some prices and not others, in the hope of easing the pains of the transition, is likely to create more problems than it solves. In November 1990, the prices of "luxury items"—amounting to about 20 percent of retail sales—were liberated from state control. Although the reason for retaining price controls on the remaining products—to protect citizens with modest incomes from the burden of price increases—was both understandable and laudable, this selective decontrol had the inescapable effect of exacerbating the problem of availability of the latter goods to those same people. For example, it made production of expensive furniture, the prices of which were deregulated, much more profitable than inexpensive furniture, which remained subject to price ceilings; the result, as any

---

stemming from foreign manufacturers, that both protected American consumers from suffering the full consequences of the deteriorating performance of their own industries and exerted very powerful pressures on domestic suppliers to improve both their productivity and the quality of their products—another example of the superior performance of competitive markets.

economist would have predicted, was that manufacturers shifted their production from the latter to the former.

It was the purpose of the various economic plans and state orders to prevent that outcome, but, as the experience of the last several years clearly demonstrates, they are largely ineffective because they run contrary to the incentives of producers. Moreover, they necessarily preserve the old command-and-control system, in ways flatly inconsistent with the independence of enterprises, which is in turn necessary if production is to become more efficient.[14]

Another variant of partial liberalization, as the foregoing discussion suggests, has been to permit enterprises to sell some fraction of their output in the free market, with the remainder still subject to official prices, plans, and state orders. This kind of "reform" involves problems similar to freeing the prices of luxury items: the partial decontrol gives enterprises strong incentives to divert all their output to the more profitable, decontrolled markets; as a result, ever more intensive controls and enforcement are required to prevent them from doing so. The virtue of a competitive market economy is of course that private incentives coincide with the public interest, rather than conflict with it.

Yet another method of gradual deregulation that has been proposed is to liberate one industry at a time, while continuing to control prices of the others. There is indeed a case to be made for proceeding sector-by-sector. Some industries have considerable numbers of enterprises in them and are less capital and technology intensive than others—both conditions facilitating entry and effective competition. One of the many benefits of their quick deregulation would be that it would open up opportunities for large numbers of entrepreneurs, which would help spread the idea and enhance the acceptability of private entrepreneurship. Obvious candidates for such treatment are agriculture, services, and small-scale manufacturing.

The critical flaw of the sector-by-sector approach, however, is that

14. State orders (*goszakazy*) are mandatory production assignments, obligatory on the enterprises in exactly the same way as the old planning targets were obligatory. They were created under the 1987 Law on State Enterprises, and were intended to cover only a fraction of the firms' output, the rest being available for sale on the relatively free wholesale market. In practice, the fraction was usually close to 100 percent, and the wholesale market did not develop.

it ignores the complex interdependence of all sectors of the economy. Consider the situation of a small clothing manufacturer, itself freed of controls but functioning in an otherwise controlled economy. How does it obtain all the inputs it needs—textiles, factory space, machines, electricity, trucks? And how does it sell its products in a free market, unless wholesalers and retailers are likewise decontrolled? The liberated manufacturer would have to operate outside the system of state orders, which ordinarily provides the required inputs and controlled distribution: however profitable its business, it could not legally use money to bid for items whose distribution and prices are controlled. The manufacturer might be able to barter some of the clothing it makes with suppliers, which would use them in turn to reward their workers; but barter is a very inefficient way of doing business. In the context of a generally controlled economy, evasion of controlled channels of distribution will also seem (indeed, may actually be) corrupt or illegitimate. In free markets, in contrast, the clothing manufacturer could always obtain the inputs and services it needed by offering the market price; and this would be the normal and accepted way of doing business.

One question that needs to be answered about the transition is the extent to which long-term contracts among enterprises in existence at the time of deregulation should continue to be honored and enforced. The *Shatalin Report* proposed that "the existing economic ties will be unconditionally maintained until July 1, 1991"—that is, approximately six months after the price deregulation it advocated would have gone into effect. The *Report* rightly points out that "by preserving all existing ties (for a long period) we would run the risk of hindering market development and free exchange of commodities between enterprises."[15]

Although we are in no position to say whether or not six months is the right transition period, we agree that it must be short. A long period is obviously inconsistent with immediate price decontrol. Conceivably, indeed, enforcement of existing long-term contracts should simply cease the moment general price deregulation occurs: since those contracts were entered upon in the context of a comprehensively controlled economy, comprehensive decontrol would constitute such a radical change in circumstances as to justify invalidating any such preexisting obligations, leaving it to enterprises

15. *Shatalin Report,* 26.

either to reestablish these relationships or to drop them, depending upon their conception of their own interests.

We have encountered concern over the rapid changes and confusion that release of enterprises from long-term contractual commitments may occasion, as sellers seek new customers and buyers new sources of supply. Of course, there will be some milling about and uncertainty; but in a market economy sellers tend to serve customers for long periods of time, and economic ties are abandoned only for good reason. We expect that upon liberalization most enterprises will continue to maintain their previous economic interrelationships; and where they do not, it will be because the ties established under central planning were economically irrational, for both the enterprise and the economy, and are best abandoned.

Governments at all levels will still need to purchase goods and services to fulfill their various responsibilities, as governments do in all market economies. Their "orders" will, however, have no more standing or power than those of other purchasers. This means that all such contracts will be voluntary; governments will make their acquisitions at market prices, not by commands and controls.

Liberalization at the Several Levels of Government

Until recently the Soviet Union was a vast common market of close to 300 million people, and trade across republic borders was extensive. Eight of the fifteen republics delivered over half, and six others between 30 and 50 percent of their net material product to other republics. The exception was the Russian Republic, which is so large and diverse that it can meet more of its needs within its borders.[16] The comprehensive economic planning system has assumed, historically, that the USSR was to be one unified economy; investment in production facilities reflected that principle.

The progressive failures of that system in recent years—the appearance of pervasive shortages, the increasing severity of repressed inflation and the consequent decreasing ability of the ruble to command goods and services—have given rise to powerful centrifugal forces, both political and economic. Trade among the republics is breaking down and being replaced increasingly by crude barter: just as within the republics, so among them, the ruble has been less and less relied upon as the medium of exchange.

16. *Economy of the USSR*, 51.

With prices fixed at artificially low levels and goods in scarce supply, localities and republics have tended to take control of the goods they produce, either for the use of their own citizens and enterprises or to barter with other localities and republics. Various republics have signed trade agreements with one another providing for the bilateral exchange of goods. Decontrol of prices, by making it profitable once again to sell goods and services in the open market, would reestablish the conditions for free trade: because the ruble would once again effectively command goods and services, enterprises and republics would willingly sell their own products for rubles, without regard to whether the buyers were located within the republic or outside.

In short, comprehensive price deregulation would restore to the Soviet Union the benefits of the common market—the efficiencies of specialization and the benefits of competition. The history of the United States economy and, more recently, of the European Economic Community both clearly demonstrate the advantages of a free-trading continental market in producing high and growing standards of living.

These benefits will be most fully achieved only if the extent and pace of liberalization are uniform among the fifteen republics. If some of them continue to control prices while others deregulate, there will be a tendency for goods to flow from the former to the latter, and, to prevent that occurring, the former will impose restrictions on trade—restrictions that will tend to spread, as other republics retaliate. Achievement of a common market therefore requires coordination of the pertinent economic reforms across the entire union.

Our own strong recommendation would be to adopt the model of the American Constitution, which flatly prohibits direct restraints by individual states on interstate trade. As the *Shatalin Report* puts it: "No quotas, limitations or Custom barriers shall be allowed within the Union for goods defined by inter-Republican agreement."[17]

The coordination of price deregulation among the republics would not necessarily preclude local or regional regulation of essentially local services. Regulation of public utility services in the United States at the state level has created some problems, resolvable only by interstate coordination, as the operations of the telecommunica-

17. *Shatalin Report,* 12.

tions, electric, and gas companies have increasingly extended across state lines. This coordination does not operate perfectly, but it produces acceptable results. Similarly, individual government units may, without creating serious problems, enact their own labor and public health standards—to the extent, again, that the activities in question are primarily local, and their regulation therefore does not distort or interfere with interregional and interrepublic specialization and trade.

CORPORATIZATION

The policy memorandum (chapter 2) proposes that large state enterprises be corporatized—cast loose from state ownership and control and converted into managerially and financially autonomous entities—at the earliest possible moment. We propose that this be done comprehensively and simultaneously with the enactment of the other proposed reforms, including, of course, price deregulation. Each enterprise must be required to stand on its own feet, financially, making a profit or failing to do so on the basis of its own success in satisfying market demand. This means also that credit must be made available, but only on a commercial basis, with all elements of subsidy removed—a topic discussed more fully in chapter 7.

Corporatization will require the elimination of both government subsidies and differential taxes. The former is an extremely important component of any program of overall economic stabilization. The latter is necessary if the Soviet Union is to achieve the benefits of a market economy: successful firms must be rewarded for their success and unsuccessful ones must be penalized, not insulated from the consequences of their failures. Although we cannot claim to have resolved to our satisfaction all important aspects of the corporatization process, there are a few that we discuss in more detail here than in the policy paper.

Corporatization and Privatization

Effective functioning of a market economy clearly requires private ownership of productive enterprises. Unless and until the interests of the managers and owners are made somehow to coincide—with management effectively responsible to the owners—the former will never have the incentive, essential to the functioning of a market economy, to maximize the present value of the enterprises.

It seems very clear, however, that privatization is going to take time. Despite a commitment to the concept of private ownership, perhaps stronger than in the USSR, Hungary, Poland, and the Czech and Slovak Federal Republic have made little progress in privatizing their large state enterprises.

The Soviet Union has about 46,000 industrial and about 760,000 retail and service enterprises, all owned by the state.[18] That is a staggering number for which to find private owners quickly, even if the many political issues associated with that process were resolved. But, in point of fact, there has as yet been no consensus reached about the levels of government at which the privatization should be carried out, or how the ultimate owners shall be selected and owner-ship distributed among them.

As for the first, there is as yet no consensus about which enter-prises are to be regarded as initially owned by which levels of govern-ment: the Soviet Union has no clear rules to serve as a starting point. Enterprises are assigned to union or republic ministries or to local governments for planning and supervision, but these assignments can be changed easily. Industrial and commercial property is re-garded as owned by society and its citizens, but when everybody is an owner, none of them is in effective control. To complicate the situa-tion further, there is considerable support within the Soviet Union for distributing ownership of the enterprises among their own workers; in view of their widely varying prospects for success, how-ever, that method of distribution would produce gross inequities among workers, depending upon where they happened to be working.

In view of the diversity and size of the USSR, we are inclined to favor assigning most enterprises to the republics in which they are located, giving each republic the right to reassign ownership of smaller and locally oriented enterprises to lower levels of govern-ment. We recognize the danger that those governments might sim-ply accept that favor and not move on to distribute the stock to private owners; but as long as they are not in a position to obstruct the entry of competing providers of the goods and services, it seems to us the injury to the public would be acceptable in that event.

18. Ibid., 53.

As for the question of how ownership is to be distributed, the form of corporatization that we propose—converting the state enterprises into joint-stock companies—would permit a wide range of ultimate decisions when that question is resolved. The shares might be sold to citizens or distributed to them without charge, sold to foreign investors or other Soviet enterprises and institutions, or assigned to managers and workers of the enterprises, in any combinations and proportions. Chapter 7 considers in greater detail the advantages and disadvantages of these various possible methods of distributing the stock.

The point about our present proposal, in any event, is that by setting aside for later decision the issues associated with privatization, corporatization can be accomplished quickly and simultaneously with the deregulation of prices; and for reasons that we have already set forth, we believe that both of these reforms must be undertaken synchronously and as quickly as possible. So the corporatization that we recommend is the equivalent of the *Economy of the USSR*'s proposed "commercialization," that is, "the establishment of the enterprise without necessarily implying private ownership."[19]

Several additional measures will be required if the newly created joint-stock enterprises are to play their proper role in a market economy. We list them in our policy memorandum (chapter 2) but repeat them here because they are so important, and because the interrelatedness of the several recommendations cannot be overemphasized:

1. Governments must enact and enforce laws of property and must respect property rights in their own actions. The legitimization of private ownership and rules providing for its transfer are necessary if capital markets are to develop; legal methods must be provided for the enforcement of contracts, including obligations of debtors to creditors, voluntarily entered upon.

2. Rules must be promulgated for the treatment of enterprises that go bankrupt—for the orderly settling of creditors' claims, either by restructuring those obligations to permit the firm to continue to operate, if there is reasonable prospect of its being able to do so successfully, or for the distribution of its assets, if there is no such reasonable prospect.

3. Banks must be available to provide credit, but only on commer-

19. *Economy of the USSR,* 48.

cial grounds: specifically, they must refuse to issue credit to enterprises that are not financially viable and, in their strict commercial judgment, unlikely to be able to repay.

4. Governments—at the union, republic, and local levels—must cease to subsidize the enterprises, whether with direct subsidies or soft credits, except as part of limited and targeted programs, such as we have already described, to protect low-income families and ease the transition to a market economy.

The purpose of all these measures is to place the enterprises under stringent budget constraints. As we said in the policy memorandum,

> An enterprise must know that unprofitability ultimately means bankruptcy for the firm and economic ruin for the managers. The possibility of bankruptcy provides a market system with the stick that makes enterprises efficient.
>
> A market system also needs a carrot; enterprises must retain a portion of their profits for bonuses to managers and to expand their facilities. Although a tax on corporate profits is consistent with a market system, the tax rate must be uniform across enterprises, must be nonnegotiable with tax authorities, and must be set at levels that still leave a significant reward for success.[20]

Corporatization involves, at its heart, a total surrender of authority and responsibility for enterprises and industries by the union and republic branch ministries. Since the skills, attitudes, and policies of these agencies are all inflexibly oriented to their present functions of operating a state-owned command and control economy, we see no way of their playing a productive role in a market economy. We therefore recommend their abolition.

Control of the Enterprises during the Transition to Privatization

Since under our conception corporatization, which must be enacted promptly, will almost inevitably precede the ultimate disposition of ownership of the state enterprises, we have proposed a transitional arrangement during which the stock of the newly liberated

20. Page 23 above.

companies would be held by state property management agencies (PMAs) of the union, republics, or local governments. Such a transitional arrangement, we recognize, poses the danger that the PMAs will simply operate like their predecessors, the economic ministries. The only safeguards we can conceive would have to be incorporated in the legislation setting up the PMAs, as part of the corporatization process, clearly stipulating as its primary intention the autonomy of the enterprises themselves.

We assume the heads of the PMAs and their boards would be selected by the sponsoring governments, with instructions to pursue the goal of long-run profit maximization for the enterprises entrusted to them. Their role would be limited to selecting directors, who would in turn select the full-time managers. Directors must be selected for the contributions they can make to the effective management of the corporations, not for their political connections. Some of the managers may also be directors; but American corporations have found it valuable to have outsiders as a substantial fraction of their directors, independent of the full-time managers, serving, in effect, as trustees representing the interests of the owners. One possible way of enhancing the incentives of both PMAs and outside directors to serve the goal of maximizing the value of the enterprises would be to compensate them with ownership shares.

The PMAs must evaluate the performance of their corporations just as stockholders do in a market economy. This means they should focus on profitability as the key criterion of success, bearing in mind that this means maximizing not necessarily short-term profits, but the long-term value (more specifically, the discounted present value) of the firm. In their role as trustees for the stockholders, they have a clear responsibility to hold management accountable for its performance, alert to the danger of managers using their positions to serve their own personal interests at the expense of the owners.

Just as important as these positive duties is the list of negative ones. It is *not* the obligation of the PMAs to advance such social goals as the provision of employment, where these conflict with the interests of the stockholders. Nor should they use the revenues from profitable operations to subsidize unprofitable ones—either particular operations of individual firms or unprofitable firms. Nor must they seek subsidies or preferential tax treatment for companies in financial difficulty. Nor, as stockholders, should they have the right to interfere with the day-to-day operations of the firms. Above all, they must not assume the role previously played by the economic ministries.

In view of the large number of state enterprises involved, we recommend that a number of PMAs be established at each level of government, particularly since the one plant/one enterprise rule proposed in the next pages will increase their number. In making this recommendation, we are influenced by the experience in Germany, where the shares of public corporations in the former German Democratic Republic are held by a single agency, the *Treuhandanstalt*, in trust for the German government. The use of one agency creates a large bureaucracy with tremendous power. It seems to us better to divide and decentralize this task, perhaps even to the extent that two or more PMAs might hold stock in one enterprise, acting as a check on one another—a point discussed further in chapter 7. The experience in Hungary suggests that PMAs should not have responsibility for demonopolization; that function should be assigned to a separate agency, as we will recommend below. It may also be useful to establish intermediate levels of organization, such as joint-stock holding companies, which could act as shareholders for groups of companies. This might make the tasks of selecting and overseeing management simpler, especially during the transition to the one plant/one enterprise organization that we contemplate. If such an expedient is adopted, it would be important to avoid organizing the holding companies by industries—with one such company, for example, holding the stock of all the companies in the steel industry; that would run the risk of the holding companies serving as agencies for restricting competition, or acting too much like the economic ministries that we envision them replacing.

THE PROMOTION OF COMPETITION

The Soviet economy is highly monopolistic, reflecting the historic belief of its founders and of Soviet planners generally that competition is wasteful and large-scale production units and centralized planning are the most efficient methods of economic organization.

This inherited structure of Soviet industry poses a severe obstacle to economic liberalization, since it means that price deregulation and corporatization are likely to result in monopoly prices and profits. This seems indeed to have been one of the effects of the liberalization of the Polish economy, as a group of Western economists have recently concluded: "[T]he evidence points strongly to the important role of monopoly power. . . . [P]rofits have been unexpectedly high, especially in the face of a sharp decrease in domestic demand, . . . The constraints on prices from convertibility and a fixed exchange rate do not appear to have been powerful enough to have prevented monopoly pricing in large segments of the economy, at least for the time being."[21]

We anticipate that high monopoly profits will materialize in the Soviet Union as well. We believe, however, that it would be a mistake to postpone deregulation and corporatization until monopolies have been thoroughly eliminated; on the contrary, we regard these two fundamental reforms as an important part of the process for reducing the power of monopoly. At the same time, these considerations strongly underline the importance of accompanying those reforms with specific measures aimed at accelerating the introduction of competition.

The Extent of Monopoly

There are no good measures of the extent of monopoly in the Soviet Union, or, indeed, in the West. Nor have we been in a position to undertake an authoritative survey of the available evidence. It is clear, however, that the phenomenon is very much more widespread in the Soviet Union than in Western economies.

The *Shatalin Report* states that 2,000 manufactured products are produced by a single enterprise.[22] This statement may exaggerate the prevalence of monopoly, because the *Report* may have defined products so narrowly as to exclude effective substitutes supplied by other firms. At the same time, the facts cited in the report, that 96 percent of all diesel locomotives, 100 percent of all air conditioners, 100 percent of all deep water pumps, and 66 percent of all batteries are supplied by a single enterprise clearly suggest genuine monopoly.

21. Olivier Blanchard, Rudiger Dornbusch, Paul Krugman, Richard Layard, and Lawrence Summers, "Reform in Eastern Europe," Report of the WIDER World Economy Group (Cambridge, Mass., 1990, mimeographed), I-18–19.

22. *Shatalin Report*, 54.

Table 3.2
Distribution of Soviet Manufacturing Product Groups According to the Share of
the Largest Producer in Total Output, 1988

	Share of Output			
Branches	100–75%	75–50%	50–0%	Number of Product Groups
Power machinery	64.7	14.7	20.6	34
Railroad machinery	23.0	46.2	30.8	13
Lifting and transport machinery	18.1	18.2	63.7	22
Oil and chemical machinery	12.4	18.8	68.8	16
Construction and road machinery	16.7	58.3	25.0	12
Metallurgical equipment	23.5	35.3	41.2	17
Sledge-press machinery	65.8	23.7	10.5	38
Motor cars and bearings	22.7	22.7	54.6	22
Tractors and agricultural machinery	60.5	15.8	23.7	38
Machinery for livestock farming and fodder crops	63.3	16.7	20.0	30
Electronics	4.7	14.3	81.0	21
Ferrous metallurgy	30.3	51.5	18.2	33
Chemistry and timber industry	6.5	6.5	87.0	31
Consumer goods	23.5	29.4	47.1	17
In all branches	36.6	24.1	39.2	344

Source: Calculations by V. Capelik and A. Yakovlev from 1989 Goskomstat data,
"The Monopolization Problem in the USSR," in P. Aven and T. Richardson, eds.,
Essays in the Soviet Transition to the Market (Laxenburg, Austria: IIASA,
forthcoming).

Our Soviet colleague, V. Capelik, has supplied us with the com-
pilation for table 3.2, showing the distribution of so-called manufacturing product groups according to the share of total output accounted for by a single firm. These figures are apparently roughly
comparable with the concentration ratios regularly reported by the
U.S. Census of Manufactures in its "4-digit" industries, which are
frequently used by American economists as rough indicators of the
possible presence of monopoly. ("4-digit" refers to the numerical
code used by the U.S. Census Bureau to identify industries. Soviet
manufacturing output is divided for reporting purposes into 344
product groups; U.S. manufacturing into 441 4-digit industries.)

Table 3.3 therefore presents a distribution of U.S. manufacturing
industries side by side with the summary (bottom line of table 3.3)
for the Soviet Union. In comparing the two, it is necessary to bear in

Table 3.3
Distribution of Concentration Ratios: Soviet Product Groups and U.S. 4-Digit
Manufacturing Industries

Market Share	Soviet Groups: Share of Single Largest Producer, 1988	U.S. Industries: Share of Four Largest Producers, 1982
0–50	39.2	72.6
50–75	24.1	21.3
75–100	36.6	6.1
Total	100.0	100.0

Sources: The Soviet data is taken from table 3.2; the U.S. data is calculated from
U.S. Bureau of Census, *1982 Census of Manufactures, Concentration Ratios in Manufacturing* (Washington, D.C.: U.S. Bureau of Census, April 1986).
Note: The figures show the percentage distributions of product groups and 4-
digit industries according to the shares of total output counted by the single largest
and four largest producers, respectively. The Soviet column does not add to 100
due to rounding error.

mind the one extremely important difference between the two sets
of statistics: the U.S. ratios show the distribution of industries according to the share in total output of the top *four* companies,
whereas the Soviet figures are for the single largest producer.

This quick comparison shows dramatically how much more concentrated Soviet output is than American, and how much more pervasive monopoly is therefore likely to be: in almost two-thirds of the
Soviet product groups, *a single enterprise* accounts for more than
half—between 50 and 100 percent—of total output; in less than
one-third of the U.S. 4-digit industries do the *top four* companies
account for a comparable percentage of output. Simple interpola-
tion yields a median *one-firm* concentration ratio of 61 percent for
the Soviet Union and 37 percent for the top *four* firms in the American case.

It would be preferable to show the distribution of product groups
or industries not by numbers but by the value of output falling within
each percentage range: this would have the effect of weighting the
groupings by their relative importance. These data are unavailable.
At the same time, the data in our two tables are clearly broadly
consistent with the assertion in the *Economy of the USSR* that "30 to 40
percent of total industrial output [in the USSR] is accounted by
products for which there is but a single manufacturer,"[23] an estimate

23. *Economy of the USSR*, 26.

consistent in turn with the views of Soviet experts with whom we have worked.

The figures in the foregoing tables underestimate the prevalence of monopoly power in both countries for one important reason: because they show the share of total *national* output accounted for by either a single producer (in the case of the Soviet Union) or the top four (for the United States), they tend to exaggerate the number of potentially competing sellers available to buyers in markets that are not nationwide but local or regional, because of the importance of transportation costs. The cement industry illustrates this phenomenon very clearly:[24] there are ninety such enterprises in the Soviet Union, but only about four in each of the nineteen economic regions.[25] In eleven of these regions, 80 percent or more of the cement consumed is produced within the region, and, on average, one enterprise accounts for 47 percent of the output.

Whether the tendency of the figures at the national level that we have used to compare the prevalence of monopoly in the two countries understates that prevalence more for the one country than the other cannot be determined *a priori*. On the one side, the far larger number of instances in which the national Soviet figures already show a single firm accounting for the major share of total output means that regional markets could not be significantly more highly concentrated: if there is only one supplier nationally, then there is unlikely to be fewer than one in regional markets (although we cannot exclude that possibility, in view of the widespread shortages in the Soviet Union); whereas the fact that it may take four suppliers in the United States to account for the major share of total output clearly does not exclude the possibility that individual regions may have significantly fewer competitors available to them. On the other side, however, is the fact that the transportation system in the Soviet Union is far less developed than in the United States; this would tend to make regional markets more interdependent in the United

24. Even in the United States, where the transport system is more highly developed than in the USSR, 90 percent of all cement is shipped 200 miles or less. F. M. Scherer, *Industrial Market Structure and Economic Performance* (Chicago: Rand McNally, 1980), 63.

25. A. Yakovlev, "The Monopolization Level of Some Branches and Production Markets in the USSR" (Paper presented at the IIASA Conference on Economic Reform and Integration in Sopron, Hungary, July–August 1990), 10.

States than in the Soviet Union, and regional monopoly therefore more pervasive in the latter country.

The Inevitability of Monopoly Pricing during the Transition

It seems clear that the Soviet economy is one of the most monopolized in the world, in important measure because most of the monopolies are what Soviet economists call "organizational"—that is, created by an explicit decision of planners—rather than "natural"—that is, dictated by technology.

This fact poses an undeniable dilemma for us in our advocacy of comprehensive and immediate decontrol of most prices, because of course it means that such a policy would open the door to a considerable amount of monopoly exploitation. Without in any way minimizing the severity of this dilemma, we nevertheless reaffirm our advocacy of comprehensive deregulation—except for the "natural monopolies," to which we will allude shortly. We do so for a number of reasons.

The first is our conviction that it is impossible for the Soviet Union to move promptly to the institution of a market economy while retaining comprehensive price controls. In view of the pervasiveness of monopoly, any policy of retaining controls on the prices of monopolized industries would effectively block the process of economic reform. For this reason, we also reject the retention or imposition of special taxes in an attempt to recapture monopoly profits: there is no way the government can distinguish profits generated by monopolistic exploitation from profits that are the reward for successful enterprise of precisely the kind that the Soviet Union must encourage.

Our second reason is that even monopoly prices are, as a general rule, preferable to state-regulated ones. Such prices will clear markets: they will equate demand and supply. In so doing, they will eliminate queues and incentives to resort to barter; they will therefore effectively reestablish the ruble as the medium of exchange. Moreover, although monopoly prices tend to be higher than competitive ones, the motive of profit maximization itself sets limits on them: monopolists cannot be unconcerned about exceeding the point at which higher prices so discourage purchases as to reduce their profits. Nor, in an open economy, can they ignore the danger that excessively high prices or poor quality of product or service will attract competitors. For this reason, although elements of monopoly are pervasive in all market economies, they also tend to be transitional and temporary. To a large extent, monopoly power and profits are the reward for successful innovation and are therefore also a sign and consequence of successful competition; and they tend to be eroded as competitors are attracted and attempt to duplicate or improve upon the original successes.

The fact that so much of the monopoly in the Soviet Union is the artificial construct of state policy provides additional ground for optimism that it will be subject to substantial erosion once competition becomes legally permissible and governmental protections are removed. So does the frequently expressed concern—to which we will return—that the state enterprises are generally inefficient and will be unable to survive, once deprived of state subsidies and exposed to competition.

And so, finally, does the fact that in the supply of consumer and producer durables, where concentration and the dangers of monopoly are likely to be greatest, the availability of a second-hand market typically provides customers with powerful protection against excessive monopolistic exploitation. If this protection is to be effective, repair services must be readily available, on reasonable terms; but this is the kind of service in the supply of which competition is likely to spring up promptly, once the state removes barriers to entry.

The conclusion that price deregulation should proceed promptly even in the presence of widespread monopoly has not been an easy one for us to reach. Effective competition is indispensable to the effective functioning of a market economy. It is essential also if such an economy is to have political legitimacy and acceptability. At the same time, it is also our view that, objectively, private monopoly under private ownership—with incentives such as only private ownership can provide—even if unregulated, is as much superior to the present Soviet system of organization as competition is to private monopoly; and we know of no way of breaking through to a market economy without accepting a good deal of private monopoly during the transition.

This recommendation does however lend additional urgency to

the immediate initiation of the most radical efforts possible to make that transition short, by encouraging the flowering of competition.

We see important, early opportunities for such competition even within the existing structure of state enterprises, once all governmental limitations on the range of products that each enterprise can produce are eliminated, as of course they must be, at once.

For example, the industry that produces the chemical fibers used to make textiles is made up of thirty-three enterprises; the largest, Mogiliev, accounts for only 16 percent of total output. Since transportation costs are low, the market is unionwide.[26] Such an industrial structure appears to be consistent with effective competition. Of the 375 different fibers, however, 288 are produced by a single enterprise; and this situation has remained essentially unchanged for several five-year plan periods.

Since fibers can in varying degree substitute for one another, we can provide no definitive, summary view of how much monopoly power this extreme specialization confers on the separate enterprises, but we have little doubt that it is substantial. Some fibers are in short supply; for others, output has more or less consistently exceeded demand. In a competitive economy, the prices of the former would rise, perhaps thereby generating monopoly profits; but these would in turn induce other enterprises to undertake their production, thereby eliminating any such excess returns. We see no reason why this kind of competitive process could not operate effectively here: we are skeptical that the present pattern of extreme specialization, in which one of the thirty-three enterprises now producing chemical fibers is the exclusive supplier of 288 of the 375 made in the Soviet Union, reflects technological or commercial imperatives.

Competition among those several enterprises would operate not just to hold costs and prices down but to improve quality. The chemical fibers manufactured in the Soviet Union are inferior to the ones produced in other countries,[27] for no apparent reason other than the absence of competition.

The production of passenger cars in the Soviet Union exhibits the same kind of extreme specialization and consequent repression of potential competition. There are seven enterprises in this industry—

26. Ibid., 8.
27. Ibid., 9.

a larger number than in any Western economy except Japan—yet all
but the largest one, VAZ, which accounts for 58 percent of total
production, manufacture only a single model, directed at a particular stratum of the market:[28] ZIL, for example, manufactures only
large limousines; and VAZ dominates the very profitable middle-
sized automobile market. Most Western firms, in contrast, make a
large number and variety of models, and so compete with one another across the board. We would certainly expect the other Soviet
manufacturers, once free and motivated to do so, to exploit the
potential production and marketing economies and opportunities
for profit by broadening their product lines, thereby challenging
VAZ itself.

The fear has at times been expressed that cutting-off Soviet enterprises from subsidy and exposing them to competition will force so
many of them to close down resulting in more monopoly, not less: it
is estimated that one-third of them now operate at a loss, and survive
only with state subsidies. There are at least two major responses to
that fear.

The first is that the present reliance of so many enterprises on
state subsidies is a consequence of price controls. With deregulation,
prices will rise to whatever level is necessary to elicit supply sufficient
to satisfy demand; and those higher prices will clearly make a much
larger percentage of Soviet enterprises financially viable than is the
case today. For example, the automobile manufacturer AZLK is today
in financial difficulty; but automobiles sell in the second-hand market for three times the official price. At such levels, AZLK's financial
problems would almost certainly be solved.

The second answer is that if, even after price decontrol, some
companies cannot survive in the face of competition, their disappearance would, at least in the first instance, be a manifestation of
the effectiveness of competition. And the Western experience is
that, in the great majority of industries, open competition rarely
ends up eliminating so many competitors as to give way to monopoly.
In view of the pervasiveness of monopoly in the Soviet economy
today, and the fact that so much of it is an artificial construct of state
policy, it would certainly be a perverse policy that continued to ob-

28. Ibid., 6.

struct the entry of competitors, both domestic and foreign, out of a fear that competition would prove to be only temporary.

Restructuring the Large State Enterprises

Erosion of the unbridled monopoly power that would be enjoyed by so many state enterprises upon corporatization, through the operation of competitive processes, may well be insufficient to establish workable competition within a politically acceptable period of time. This is particularly likely to be the case in capital-intensive industries, with high barriers to entry.

For this reason, we consider it likely to be necessary to restructure those enterprises themselves as close as possible to the time of their liberation from the economic ministries.

One way of accomplishing this, recommended by the *Shatalin Report,* would be for some government agency to decide, enterprise by enterprise, whether the public interest required that it be broken up. In our judgment, such a process would be intolerably slow and would be objectionable also because it would require government agencies to make an enormous number of judgments that they are probably not competent to make. We strongly prefer a more automatic and comprehensive approach, which would in the last analysis leave it to the market to determine the most efficient structure for each industry and the most efficient size and scope of its component enterprises.

Our proposal is to have each separate physical plant constituted as a separate enterprise. Although we were unable to obtain data on how many additional enterprises such a rule would create, it appears that this would be a prompt and effective way of establishing the structural prerequisites for competition.

We are encouraged to make this proposal by the assurances of Soviet experts that the present state enterprises are inefficiently large. Most studies of market economies conclude that, at least at the production level, the economies of multiplant operations are not great. We can think of no more practicable way of quickly creating the possibility of competition in what are now highly monopolistic industries.

Our recommendation is that application of the one plant/one

enterprise rule take place simultaneously with corporatization. If this proves infeasible, the rule would clearly have to be applied before privatization can take place—at least if the firms are to be *sold*—since the prospective owners will have to know under what conditions the enterprises they acquire will be operating. Purchasers of a firm with a monopoly would rightly regard themselves as defrauded if their newly purchased enterprises were broken up after they had acquired them.

We recognize, of course, that this kind of dissolution might entail some loss of nonproduction economies of multiplant operation—in marketing, procurement and other aspects of management. We recommend therefore that *re*unification of some of the newly created enterprises via mergers be permitted, subject to approval by an antitrust or antimonopoly agency. Since the newly separated enterprises would be financially independent, succeeding or failing on the basis of their own profitability, there would be a greater presumption after corporatization than exists today that any proposed reintegration was motivated by a quest for improved efficiency.

This was what we meant when we asserted that under our proposal the market itself, guided by the independent judgment of firms seeking to maximize profits, would in the last analysis decide to what extent and where, precisely, multiplant operations were conducive to efficiency.

On the other hand, of course, such reunifications or new combinations might be motivated by a desire to regain or achieve monopoly. For this reason we would make proposed mergers exceeding some minimum size subject to approval or disapproval by some sort of antitrust agency, guided by the following general rules:

- Direct horizontal unions of competitors would be presumed illegal; the applicants would have to demonstrate convincingly that the mergers would confer economies of integration sufficiently large to override their presumed anticompetitive effects;
- Vertical mergers in which one or more of the parties was a monopoly would be subject to the same presumption of illegality, with the same opportunity as in the horizontal cases for the proponents to override that presumption;
- All other mergers would be presumed legal; in these cases the antitrust authorities would have the opportunity and burden of

demonstrating that any possible benefits would be outweighed by a substantial threat to competition.

In short, the second part of our proposed program for creating competition with and among big state enterprises—after removal of all restrictions on what each is permitted to produce and in what markets it is permitted to sell—would involve simultaneously (a) breaking them up on a one plant/one enterprise basis while, (b) readily permitting nonhorizontal reintegration by merger or by contract.

We would leave two problems to be solved by the enterprises themselves, under pressure of competition and in quest of higher profit. Even individual plants in the Soviet Union may be too large for efficiency: such a possibility is suggested, for example, by the fact that the average production of their cement plants is two and one-half times as large as in the United States.[29] Any governmental attempt to try to correct such inefficiencies at the plant level would involve exactly the same intrusive, judgmental government interventions we have just rejected in opposing the Shatalin plan for governmental industry-by-industry restructuring at the enterprise level. It seems to us far preferable to leave it to competition and the market to force plant sizes to evolve to efficient scales.

The other problem is that many Soviet enterprises produce many of their own inputs today merely in order to protect themselves against the uncertainties of relying on the central plans to provide them with the supplies they need, even though much of this production would otherwise be highly inefficient. As it becomes possible to rely on the market to provide such inputs, in simple exchange for rubles, the present enterprises—particularly if they are under competitive pressure—can be expected to shed operations that can no longer be justified on efficiency grounds.

Opening the Economy to Foreign Competition

Although this particular recommendation is fully discussed in a later chapter, we must mention it here, because opening the Soviet economy to the world is an essential component of a program to promote competition. Automobiles, once again, provide a striking

29. Ibid., 12.

illustration. The USSR produces 1.3 million cars annually. Imports
are estimated to be about 4,000—not even 1 percent of the market.
In striking contrast, imports account for about 30 percent of sales in
the U.S. market and have, over the last ten to fifteen years, been the
major factor undermining the previous dominance by the three
domestic manufacturers and the primary source of competition in
price and product quality.

Perhaps superfluously, we reemphasize the importance of each of
the two major sources and forms of potential competition—open
entry domestically and internationally. Although in some ways
opening the Soviet economy to international trade offers the prospect of the most immediate source of competitive discipline, because
the competitive producers already exist outside of the Soviet Union,
it is highly likely, as the Polish experience demonstrates, that imports
will be expensive at the exchange rates likely to prevail under convertibility. But this in turn should provide an important stimulus to
competitive domestic manufacture—provided, once again, that all
restraints on competitive entry and market interpenetrations by domestic Soviet enterprises are removed.

Antimonopoly Policy and Its Enforcement

As we have already suggested, another necessary component of a
policy of fostering competition is the establishment of an antimonopoly enforcement agency. Indeed, in view of the division of
responsibility for economic policies between the union and the republics, antitrust agencies will be required at both levels of government: the United States has a federal assistant attorney general
charged with enforcing the antitrust laws, and so do most of the
individual states. Although this kind of dual authority involves con-
flicts and inconsistencies, agencies at both levels have important
roles to play, and the courts have been generally successful in defin-
ing the boundaries of their several jurisdictions to minimize such
problems.

These agencies require adequate financing and high-quality
staffs who are dedicated to preserving and promoting competition.
This means that they must be kept separate from the state PMAs and
any ministries charged with promoting industry.

The antitrust agencies would presumably be involved in implementing our proposed one plant/one enterprise rule, depending of course on when this rule is applied. And, as we have already proposed, these agencies would be involved in approving or disapproving any proposed reintegrations of separated firms.

Once the structural problems are resolved, antimonopoly agencies will have the same responsibility they have in most market economies: to be vigilant in prohibiting agreements and combinations that suppress competition and exercises of monopoly power that exclude rival enterprises from a fair opportunity to compete.

We urge that these agencies be empowered to go beyond merely preventing and dissolving suppressions of competition and be given responsibility for actively promoting it as well. One important way in which they might do so would be by exerting influence on the decision making of all other government agencies whose policies may have pro- or anticompetitive effects—for example, by the way they dispose of surplus military plants, administer tax policies, or license enterprises for health or safety reasons. Promotion of competition is the responsibility of all government agencies; the antimonopoly agencies could play an important role in encouraging all of them to fulfill that responsibility.

Small Business

There are some 700,000 state enterprises operating in the service sectors. These are typically small in scale, require relatively little capital, employ relatively simple technologies, and therefore present relatively few problems of monopoly. For these reasons they are candidates for direct privatization by public auction, sale to present managers (perhaps with deferred payment) or lease to individuals with an option of eventual purchase. In view of the large numbers involved, these privatizations can best be supervised by local governments.

Personal attention to customers is an important aspect of how well the service industries perform; it is precisely in this respect that their performance in the Soviet Union is notoriously deficient. One of the greatest benefits of competition is that it would force such firms to treat customers well; the result would be a very substantial improvement in general welfare, at very little cost in the use of society's total resources. For these several reasons, we urge prompt privatization of service establishments, as well as of small-scale manufacturing.

Privatization is likely to be comparatively easy to effect in these sectors of the economy, because they are already characterized by a significant amount of private enterprise. In the provision of repair services, for example, private activity accounted in 1984 for 45 percent of the repairs in the case of apartments, 50 percent for clothing, 30 percent for home appliances, and 40 percent for auto repairs.[30] At that time much of this activity was of doubtful legality and was conducted largely by state enterprise workers during their evenings and weekends—a record, incidentally, that refutes the stereotype of Soviet citizens as lazy and lacking in entrepreneurial spirit. Since 1988, cooperatives have been legal; as of October 1990, there were 200,000 of them, producing an output estimated at 40 billion rubles annually.[31]

Our proposal, thus, does little more than incorporate the present reality and recent trends, except that we would go further and ensure complete freedom of entry, by abolishing the present requirement of governmental permits authorizing such operations. We would positively encourage entry by making sure all enterprises have access to credit on reasonable commercial terms. That is of course the function of a commercial banking system—perhaps not limited to the provision of short-term credit, as in the United States, but permitted also to acquire long-term debt or equity in new ventures. Such banks might also play an important role by providing useful management advice.

Cooperatives do not enjoy a good reputation in the Soviet Union; they have frequently been criticized by the media and the parliament, and are unpopular with many of the people. These criticisms reflect the fact, however, that they are small islands of free enterprise in the sea of a planned economy; they are not fairly reflective of the kind of role such institutions would play in a genuinely market economy.

For example, the most vigorous criticism is that the cooperatives

30. Hewett, *Reforming the Soviet Economy*, 180.

31. *Shatalin Report*, 57.

charge prices much higher than the state stores. But that of course is because the prices of the latter are held artificially low.

For this reason, many cooperatives are highly profitable—another basis for widespread criticism. But that of course is, once again, because they provide goods that are not available through normal distribution channels and are rendered additionally scarce by the way in which the Soviet economy is now regulated. It is also because entry into competition with them is obstructed by many barriers, formal and informal; the solution is to remove all such barriers.

Cooperatives are also criticized for diverting supplies from the state-controlled distribution systems, often by bribery; but that, once again, reflects the distortions of the present system and the absence of a competitive wholesale distribution system. Some cooperatives are financed with profits from criminal activity. That can of course occur in any society; in the Soviet Union it also reflects the difficulty that private enterprises have in obtaining start-up and working capital in the absence of a private banking system and capital markets such as exist in market economies.

Legitimization of competitive private enterprise would eliminate the basis for most of these criticisms and would permit cooperatives and other private enterprises to play a productive economic role. It would also help relieve the present victimization of cooperatives by protection schemes organized by criminal gangs; the need for such protection reflects police indifference to their legitimate right to protection.

In a full-scale market system, these various problems and sources of criticism would be very substantially mitigated, just as would the many problems confronting any private enterprises that attempt to function today in an essentially planned system. Privatization and liberation of small-scale enterprise will make a major contribution to the welfare of the Soviet citizens; but it can do so only within the context of a general market economy.

Agriculture

Agriculture engages 25 percent of the total labor force in the Soviet Union. Although we have not been able to do justice to its

special problems, we see no reason to doubt the applicability to
agriculture of the general principles and recommendations we have
enunciated—corporatization of the state farms and open opportunities for private ownership and operation, where—presumably
mainly in the growing of fruits, vegetables, and possibly meat and
dairy products—small-scale farming is likely to be feasible. Similarly, our recommendations for price deregulation and the elimination of state-controlled distribution are clearly applicable to agricultural products and their inputs: as for the latter, there is obviously
no way in which the production, pricing, and marketing of farm
products could be effectively liberated so long as the production,
prices, and distribution of the necessary inputs, on the one side, and
of processed agricultural products, on the other, continued to be
tightly regulated. A free market for agriculture requires a free market in fertilizers, fuel, farm equipment, parts, repair services, transport, processing, and distribution services.

The necessity for comprehensive liberalization is made even
clearer if we consider that although the USSR is the world's largest
producer of wheat, it is nevertheless a large net importer of both
grain and food generally. As the *Economy of the USSR* explains, "the
need to import arises in large part from the inability to process
efficiently and distribute the substantial domestic production of
food and fiber. Wastage and losses are roughly equal to imports."[32]
Only elimination of the comprehensive system of state controls and
the institution of competitive markets, in our judgment, can remedy
the deplorable situation in which a very large proportion of last
year's record grain harvest failed to reach the market—whether
because of inadequate supplies of fuel and repair parts for farm
equipment or trucking, or because of the neglect under Soviet planning of efficient systems of distribution.

The Exceptions: Residual Areas of Direct Regulation and Nonmarket Sectors

There are two sectors of the economy where the possible inade-
quacy of competition and therefore continued price regulation must
be considered. The first would be the concentrated industries—

32. *Economy of the USSR*, 39.

primarily newly separated state enterprises—that continue to be characterized by substantial monopoly power. We have already discussed and explained our disinclination to recommend price controls in these situations.

The second is the traditional *public utilities*—the local telephone service and the local distribution of electricity, water, and gas—where competition is probably inefficient. There are no readily available rules for identifying such "natural monopolies," and their definition changes over time, as technology changes. It is becoming increasingly clear in the West, for example, that large segments of these industries previously treated as naturally monopolistic—the generation (as distinguished from the transmission and local distribution) of electricity, the purchase and long-distance transport of natural gas, many telecommunications services, and railroad transportation—are probably capable of being effectively competitive; they have therefore been progressively deregulated. Most Western economists, recognizing that all markets in the real world are imperfect, are inclined to define the "naturally monopolistic" sector as narrowly as possible, preferring to let the "naturalness" of monopoly be tested and demonstrated—or disproved—by the competitive market itself, rather than by some prior governmental determination that precludes competition from the outset.

We recognize nevertheless that there is some core group of such utilities, providing essential services, for which neither competition nor unregulated monopoly is acceptable. We can make no better suggestion than that the Soviet Union begin its identification of them on the basis of Western experience.

At the same time, there may well be differences between the two situations that justify drawing the boundary of regulated utilities somewhat more broadly in the Soviet Union than in the West. The most important example that occurs to us is the railroads: the well-developed highway systems in the West make their transportation industries generally highly competitive in serving the needs of most shippers; conceivably in the Soviet Union, with its long distances and less well developed motor transport industries, the monopoly power enjoyed by railroads may be much more substantial and ubiquitous, and therefore require much more comprehensive regulation. The 1980 statute that substantially deregulated the American railroads provided for the continued protection of price ceilings for "captive" shippers—customers lacking any feasible competitive alternatives.

Although recognizing the probable need for regulation to prevent monopoly exploitation of customers of these industries, we strongly emphasize the opposite danger that regulation may be excessively tight. It is a familiar phenomenon worldwide that the prices of basic telephone service or electricity are often held so low as to discourage investment; as a result, the exploitation of consumers takes the form not of high prices but of very poor and primitive service, or an inability to get service at all. This danger is particularly serious in infrastructure industries such as these, upon which so much of the rest of the economy and the prospects for its growth, development, and competitiveness depend.

Even, therefore, if an industry like the railroads must be closely regulated in the Soviet Union to prevent its earning excessive profits in the aggregate, it is also clearly desirable that the companies be given a great deal of flexibility in their pricing of individual services—in particular, the ability to vary markups above variable costs depending on the elasticities of demand. This kind of price discrimination can contribute powerfully to economic efficiency, while also being essential to put the railroads in a financial condition to make major investments in rehabilitation and modernization of their trackage and equipment.

Although *residential construction* is likely at an early point to be effectively competitive, we have already recognized how extremely difficult it would be simply to deregulate residential rents, in view of the very high degree to which they are now subsidized, and have recognized that this is one of the few sectors of the economy in which conversion to a market system is going to have to be gradual. At the same time, the potential benefits of competitive private enterprise in the provision of new housing and of price deregulation, with their promise of increasing supply, improving quality, and eradicating the present fifteen-year waiting period for apartments, and the superior incentives for maintenance and upkeep provided by private ownership are just as important in this industry as in all others.

For these reasons, the local governments, now in charge of housing, should seriously consider transferring an increasing share of the present stock to private owners, while at the same time clarifying the ownership rights in units that have already been sold—for example, by conferring unlimited rights of resale.

Another sector of the economy whose total conversion to an exclusive market basis for organization can only be gradual would be the entire military-industrial complex. If recent changes in the international situation do indeed realize their promise of permitting conversion of a large proportion of these resources to civilian production—which would be a great potential boon for the people of the Soviet Union—that conversion cannot be accomplished immediately. The estimates are that some 7 to 9 million people in the Soviet Union are at present employed in military production and the armed forces. Market forces alone may not be able to effect the transfer of these resources and people at tolerable social costs: continued government subsidization would almost certainly be required.

At the same time, here as elsewhere, the greater danger in our view is that governmental authorities in the Soviet Union will exaggerate the costs and difficulties of the transition and the consequent necessity for continued government planning, and underestimate the efficiency of the market in achieving the necessary conversions—and by so doing deny the economy generally its huge potential benefits. Near the end of World War II there was a widespread belief in the United States that the sudden cessation of hostilities and curtailment of military procurement would result in massive unemployment in the absence of government intervention. In fact, the transition, essentially unplanned and unregulated, was accomplished with startling rapidity, as both military personnel and industrial capacity previously employed in producing armaments responded rapidly to the pent-up demands of the civilian economy. Similarly, in the Soviet Union, every opportunity should be given to the industries now engaged in military production to convert to badly needed civilian products, in whose production they are already heavily engaged: in 1980, enterprises under the jurisdiction of the military ministries produced 60 percent of the tramcars in the USSR, 27 percent of the railroad freight cars, 10 percent of the passenger cars, one-third of the vacuum cleaners, and almost all of the motor scooters, television sets, radios, videocassette recorders, and cameras.[33]

33. Hewett, *Reforming the Soviet Economy*, 174. For a more detailed discussion of the conversion problem, see *Shatalin Report*, 107–13.

Finally, as we have already pointed out, there are major services that the Soviet Union now provides free of charge to its citizens that we expect it would and should continue to do. In the West, education and health care are supplied by a mixture of market and nonmarket institutions, in proportions varying widely among the various countries. Although we see genuine benefits for the Soviet Union from the introduction of competition and market forces into some of these sectors of the economy, we see little likelihood of such changes being either feasible or desirable in the immediate future. There is simply too much else that urgently needs doing.

Chapter Four

Stabilizing the Soviet Economy

William D. Nordhaus

Unfortunately for a considerable period of time in the USSR there has been some kind of "taboo" on the very use of the term *inflation* which was considered incompatible with the nature of socialism.
—A. Khandruev

Courses in Marxist-Leninist ideology . . . have been abolished. . . . The number of required courses has been reduced and new professors, some back from years in exile, are teaching new courses like macroeconomics.
—*New York Times*

The proposals presented in chapter 2—a restrictive monetary policy and a fiscal policy that eliminates the government deficit—are shaped by our view that the Soviet Union today faces a mounting economic crisis. As we emphasized in our discussion in the policy memorandum (chapter 2), problems include issues of inefficient economic structures, distorted prices, large macroeconomic imbalances, divided government, and lack of popular support for steps

Note: Although this chapter is based in part on the discussions of the Study Group that met in Sopron, Hungary, in August 1990 and on discussions at the Study Group Chairmen's Meeting held in New Haven, Connecticut, in November 1990, the views expressed here are the author's responsibility.

A. Khandruev, "In Search of a Reasonable Compromise: Inflation and the Problems of Soviet Economic Stabilization" (Paper presented at the IIASA Conference on Economic Reform and Integration, Sopron, Hungary, July–August 1990); "New Courses and Even Votes at Czechoslovak Universities," *New York Times*, March 1990.

83

to stabilize and restructure the economy. The government budget deficit is unsustainably large, incomes are rising much more rapidly than output, open and repressed inflation is worsening, and there is a flight from currency. For the first time in recent history, national output is actually falling.

As difficult as these familiar economic ailments appear, they pale beside the awesome task of making a transition from a centrally managed to a decentralized market economy and society. In late 1989 and early 1990, the leadership of the Soviet Union had apparently decided to scrap the administrative model of economic organization and to adopt, as soon as is feasible, a market economy.[1] But, in the face of the momentous implications of such a choice, the central leadership faltered and chose instead to reimpose central political and administrative controls, relegating the market economy to a vague and distant vision. Nonetheless, many economists, members of the intelligentsia, and leaders of the republics believe that adopting the market model quickly is vital for the economic health of the Soviet people. The question is not whether, but when and how.

The search for the road to a market economy raises fundamental, indeed unprecedented, economic questions for the leaders of the Soviet Union and its republics. Should reform begin with budget reform or monetary reform to prevent a price-wage-price spiral on decontrol? Or should price inflation and wage controls be used to reduce real aggregate demand? Should there be a first step to get prices close to the market before letting prices go? Or is it hopeless at this late date to try to guess the "right" market price? Should prices be decontrolled now, so that incentives to production are enhanced?

1. An early and moderate plan proposed a staged transition from the administrative system to the market in a process guided by central authorities. (See *Radical Economic Reform: Top Priority and Long Term Measures* (Report presented by L. Abalkin, Deputy Prime Minister, to the Organizing Committee of the All-Union Conference and Workshop on the Problem of Radical Economic Reform, Moscow, USSR, 1989). See also E. Yasin, "Modern Market Institutions and Problems of Economic Reform" (Paper presented at the IIASA Conference on Economic Reform and Integration, Laxenburg, Austria, March 1990). After the Abalkin Plan had run aground, a more radical approach was outlined in the *Shatalin Plan*. This was initially endorsed by both Gorbachev and Yeltsin, but the former retracted his support and instead tightened the administrative screws in late 1990. See *Transition to the Market: A Report of a Working Group Formed by M. S. Gorbachev and B. N. Yeltsin*, Part 1: *The Concept and Program* (Moscow: Cultural Initiative Foundation, 1990). Henceforth cited as the *Shatalin Report* after Academician Stanislas Shatalin, head of the task force.

Or should the monopolies be broken up first to prevent the exercise of monopoly power? This list could be multiplied indefinitely but will give the flavor of the unpleasant dilemmas facing Soviet reformers.

These dilemmas recur in all aspects of the reform process, but they are particularly relevant to issues of stabilization and underlie the macroeconomic measures proposed in the policy memorandum (chapter 2) and elaborated on in this chapter. More than in the other chapters, we must distinguish between measures immediately preceding economic reform and those necessary once reforms have been adopted. As the other chapters stress, the proposals here require the simultaneous implementation of all the major measures listed in the policy memorandum presented in chapter 2. As we said there, "The measures must be taken simultaneously and in view of the crisis as soon as possible. . . . Each of the measures reinforces the others. If adopted together, the five measures can be successful; if adopted singly or over time, they are doomed to failure."

EXISTING ECONOMIC CONDITIONS

Historical Developments

On the whole, the financial and budgetary situation in the Soviet Union was relatively healthy until the mid-1980s.[2] Beginning in 1985, and accelerating up until today, there has been an increasing overall disequilibrium arising from a combination of policy and external factors. The major developments over the last decade were the worsening budget deficit, the acceleration in the growth of incomes, a continued deterioration in the growth of output, and, most recently, a flight from currency and acute shortages.[3]

2. The analysis in this section relies in part on the contributions of the Soviet members of the Sopron study group and on the papers by Gaidar and Kagalovskii and Khandruev (E. Gaidar, "Financial Crisis and Political Problems of Economic Stabilization in the USSR," and K. Kagalovskii and A. Khandruev "Economic Stabilization: Monetary and Fiscal Policy" [Papers presented at the IIASA Conference on Economic Reform and Integration, Sopron, Hungary, July–August 1990]).

3. The literature on the macroeconomics of administrative economies is small but is doubling every year. A thoughtful essay, filled with interesting data and observations, is contained in Gur Ofer, "Macroeconomic Issues of Soviet Economic Reforms," in

1. *Income growth.* A new development during this period was the acceleration in incomes, primarily due to the rapid rise in wage payments by enterprises. The growth of wages (measured by the average monthly pay of workers and employees) rose around 3 percent per year in the period up to 1987; wage rates rose 8 percent in 1988, 9 percent in 1989, and 10 percent in 1990. During the period 1980 to 1990, the average wage in the state sector rose from 168 to 265 rubles per month. The reasons for the acceleration in wages are complex but are essentially grounded in the sharp growth of the bank balances of enterprises and in the liberalization of controls on enterprise wage funds.[4]

2. *Budget.* On the budgetary front, a number of decisions and events led to an increase in the budget deficit since 1985. The anti-alcohol campaign decreased revenues sharply, the fall in oil prices decreased oil export revenues by almost 50 percent in 1986, and the rise in wages led to increasing subsidies to enterprises. In addition, because wages per unit output, and therefore unit costs, were rising for enterprises while prices were frozen, government subsidies to enterprises rose sharply in recent years (primarily to food-processing enterprises). Budget subsidies for food and nonfood retail goods in 1990 totalled around 24 percent of sales. On food alone, government subsidies are more than three-quarters of the value of food sales.

3. *Declining output growth.* The rapid rise in the budget deficit and in incomes led to a sharp increase in aggregate demand. During this period, there was, in addition, a continued deterioration in the growth of real output. The exact growth rates of Soviet output are controversial, and table 4.1 shows a recent comparison of growth estimates from different sources. According to official and unofficial data, there has been a further slowdown in growth in the last five

---

Olivier Blanchard and Stanley Fischer, eds., *NBER Macroeconomic Annual, 1990* (Cambridge, Mass.: MIT Press, 1990).
4. Most studies omit consideration of income earned from private sources, either domestic or foreign. Gregory Grossman ("Roots of Gorbachev's Problems: Private Income and Outlays in the Late 1970s," in U.S. Congress, Joint Economic Committee, *Soviet Economy in the 1980s: Problems and Prospects* [Washington, D.C.: Government Printing Office, 1987]) reports on surveys suggesting that private incomes were perhaps one-third of reported incomes, and moreover that private incomes grew rapidly during the 1980s.

Table 4.1
Growth in National Output in the Soviet Union

A. Historical Data (Average Annual Rates of Growth)

	National Income				Gross National Product	
Period	Soviet Official	CIA	Selyunin-Khanin	Aganbegyan	Soviet Official	CIA
1961–65	6.5	4.8	4.4	—	—	4.8
1966–70	7.8	5.0	4.1	5.6	—	5.0
1971–75	5.7	3.1	3.2	4.0	—	3.1
1976–80	4.3	2.2	1.0	2.1	—	2.2
1981–85	3.6	1.8	0.6	0.4	3.9	1.9

Source: P. R. Gregory and R. C. Stuart, *Soviet Economic Structure and Performance*, 4th ed. (New York and London: Harper and Row, 1990), 389.

B. Recent Data (Average Percentage per Year)

	Growth in Net Material Product
1976–80	4.3
1981–85	3.2
1986	2.3
1987	1.6
1988	4.4
1989	2.5
1990	−4.0

Source: *The Economy of the USSR, Summary and Recommendations: A Study Undertaken in Response to a Request by the Houston Summit* (Washington, D.C.: International Monetary Fund, the International Bank for Reconstruction and Development, the Organization for Economic Cooperation and Development, and the European Bank for Reconstruction and Development, 1990), 4.

years, and the government has projected a 4 percent decline in Gross Material Product in 1990.[5]

Why did growth slow so dramatically in recent years? Numerous causes are given for the slowdown in the period up to 1985: a decrease in the growth of inputs (depletion of low-cost resources such as oil, aging of the capital stock, and deterioration of labor disci-

5. A recent survey of economic conditions with recommendations for reforms is contained in *The Economy of the USSR: Summary and Recommendations*, a study undertaken in response to a request by the Houston Summit (Washington, D.C.: International Monetary Fund, International Bank for Reconstruction and Development, Organization for Economic Cooperation and Development, and European Bank for Reconstruction and Development, 1990), 4.

pline); lowered technological change and efficiency (because of bias against innovation in the planning system, concentration of investment in agriculture, and diversion of research and development activities to the military); exogenous shocks (poor weather and declining prices of oil and other raw materials); and greater complexity of economic activity (with a greater number of products and greater technical complexity).[6]

The actual decline of output in the last year probably has a different origin than the longer-term decline in growth. It is likely to be the result of bottlenecks, reduced labor and administrative discipline, and shortages of materials in key industries.

4. *Shortages.* The conjunction of rapidly growing demand, fixed retail prices, and stagnant potential output has led in the last year or so to severe repressed inflation and increasing shortages. As incomes rise with fixed prices, aggregate demand in constant prices outpaces potential output. In a free market, the result would be a rise in prices—inflation—sufficient to ration out the increased demand. Since most Soviet prices are fixed, there is, of course, minimal official inflation. But as incomes increase more rapidly, the excess demand compounds the shortages. The shelves get barer and barer, lines get longer and longer, and the few goods left in the state stores are rusty tins and rotten cabbage. The free-market or black-market prices rise sharply, the street price of hard currency diverges even more from the official rate, and the free prices in farmers' stalls rise sharply.

Once shortages appear, the dynamics of speculative hoarding gear up as people begin to worry about the value of their rubles and begin to use goods as a store of value. In this framework, it is not surprising that the Soviet economy is experiencing worsening shortages and the disappearance of goods from the stores, and is driven to ration basic goods like soap, meat, cigarettes, and sugar. By an extension of Gresham's Law, overvalued things (rubles) are driving out undervalued things (goods). In other words, the ruble is less and less convertible *internally* by Soviet residents into Soviet goods and services.

6. See Herbert Levine, "Possible Causes of the Deterioration of Soviet Productivity Growth in the Period 1976–1980," in U.S. Congress, Joint Economic Committee, *Soviet Economy in the 1980s: Problems and Prospects* (Washington, D.C.: Government Printing Office, 1982).

The breakdown of both retail and inter-enterprise markets with growing excess demand is described in chapter 3. At the retail level it takes the form of multiple types of rationing, great waste in queuing, and even barter. A recent survey found that the average Soviet adult spends 1.4 hours a day waiting in line (which, if accurate, would equal about one-third of total working time). Under the pressure of shortages, alternative distribution channels are sprouting up. A recent study found that only 40 percent of food is currently distributed in state stores, with the balance distributed in enterprise stores, farmers' markets, special stores serving veterans, invalids, and pensioners, and so forth. At the wholesale level, a complicated set of barter markets for wholesale goods had developed by late 1990, in which trades between enterprises were conducted in free-market barter terms of trade. Such a breakdown of the official distribution channels is a clear sign of repressed inflation.

5. *Effects of partial liberalization.* Tentative and partial liberalizations have served to *destabilize* the economy rather than to contribute to an effective market economy.[7] Virtually every attempt to liberalize has encountered the law of unintended consequences, whereby solving one problem has created two more.

An example of a partial liberalization that proved particularly pernicious was the freeing up of enterprise wages funds, which created a major increase in the incomes of the population (see table 4.2). The impact of this increase on incomes and the budget deficit was described above. The government recognized the peril from the growth in wage income and instituted the "tax on the wages fund," which is an increasing tax based on the rate of increase of total wage payments. This tax (which was imported from Hungary) was in part an attempt to substitute marketlike mechanisms for administrative controls in a philosophy reminiscent of recommendations for tax-based incomes policies in the West.

The wages tax immediately created problems of its own. Its design was flawed because it taxed the wages fund (total wages) rather than average wage rates, thus introducing penalties for enterprises that were expanding output and thus employment, as further described in chapter 6. The wages-fund tax was largely ineffective in

7. A useful early account of the economic philosophy underlying perestroika is contained in A. Aganbegyan, *The Challenge: Economics of Perestroika* (London: Second World, Hutchison, 1988).

Table 4.2
USSR: Incomes and Prices (Annual Percentage Increase)

	1986	1987	1988	1989	1990 (estimates)
Retail price index	2.0	1.3	0.6	2.0	4.8
Average monthly wage	2.9	3.7	8.3	9.4	10.0
Household money incomes	3.6	3.9	9.2	13.1	14.5
Household purchases of goods and services	2.8	3.1	7.2	9.5	13.7
Saving rate (percent of disposable income)	6.9	7.6	9.2	12.0	12.9

Source: *Economy of the USSR,* 49.

reducing wage growth because of successful pressure by enterprises to be exempted and from the enterprises' ability to absorb the tax through higher subsidies.

Economic Perspectives with regard to Changes in Output

This narrative leads to the following diagnosis of the macroeconomic problems that face the Soviet Union as it attempts to make the transition to a market economy. Overall, the current situation is best described as one of *severe repressed inflation.* Analytically, three separate issues must be addressed in stabilizing the economy.

1. *Stock problem.* The "stock problem" denotes the fact that, because of past budget deficits and accumulations of liquid assets by households, household assets today exceed the amount, relative to incomes and prices, that households would desire to hold if goods were freely available. This is often called the "ruble overhang."[8] To eliminate the ruble overhang would require either a reduction of household and enterprise liquid assets or a rise in the aggregate price level. (See table 4.3 for data on the volume of money and credit.)

8. It is technically incorrect to say that there is a monetary overhang in the sense of involuntary holdings of money and other liquid assets. There are goods available at high prices in farmers' markets and in the black market, so consumers can in fact convert their money into *some* goods. It would be accurate to say that monetary assets are in excess of what would be needed to buy today's output at official prices. Put differently, the velocity of money may seem high when calculated at official incomes (in fact, by this technique, velocity has fallen by about 35 percent through 1989). If, on the other hand, we calculate velocity by using black-market prices, velocity may actually have risen over the last decade.

Table 4.3
USSR: Money and Credit (Average Annual Percentage Increase)

	1981–85	1986	1987	1988	1989	1990 (estimate)
Currency	6.0	6.1	7.8	13.6	19.5	21.5
M1	6.8	7.6	15.7	15.4	14.3	13.4
M2	7.5	8.5	14.7	14.1	14.8	15.3
of which:						
Households	7.2	9.4	9.8	11.3	15.0	13.5
Enterprises	8.7	5.5	32.6	22.5	14.5	20.0
M2 (percent of GDP)	—	51.2	56.9	61.2	65.5	72.5
Total credit	8.7	4.2	6.6	11.3	11.2	10.9
of which:						
to firms	8.7	−13.3	−5.0	−6.8	−3.8	−1.3
to government	8.7	18.8	40.3	46.0	30.0	17.2

Source: *Economy of the USSR*, 49.

In a free-market economy, prices would tend to explode upward under the pressure of large monetary assets. The equilibrium price level with liberalized prices would be considerably higher than today's level. There are a number of different ways to estimate the extent of the disequilibrium. An illustrative calculation is the following: The ratio of household liquid assets to income in 1989 was around 0.95, whereas the same ratio was 0.70 in the 1976–82 period (which we might consider a "normal" period). Assuming no budgetary impact of a price liberalization, this would suggest that a rise of prices and incomes of 35 percent would be necessary to bring liquid assets down to "normal levels." Other estimates, which include indexation and wage response, suggest a rise of up to 150 percent as a result of price decontrol. A third set of estimates of the price disequilibrium comes from black-market prices, which are often two to three times official prices. Although no definitive answer to the extent of overhang is possible, there is little doubt that a price explosion of serious proportions will occur when prices are freed.

2. *Flow problem.* In addition to the stock problem, the Soviet economy currently has a serious "flow disequilibrium," which is seen in a large budget deficit that is effectively automatically monetized. Semiofficial data indicate that the on-budget deficit (expenditures less receipts) is approximately 10 percent of gross national product (GNP).

In addition, current pressures for expanded social programs

seem likely to increase the deficit. Estimates are that the cost of enacted or proposed social legislation (pensions, new pay scales, social security, and indexation, for example) would total approximately another 10 percent of GNP. In addition, there are significant "off-budget" expenditures (such as unrepaid credit advances to the farm sector) which add substantially to the budget deficit. Because of the structure of the Soviet banking system, these deficits are monetized immediately in the sense that all net payments to households are turned into cash or savings accounts.

At first glance, a budget deficit of around 10 percent of GNP would not appear extraordinarily large. The danger lies not only in the size of the deficit but in the fact that there are no significant nonmonetary assets (that is, financial assets aside from M2) in which the rapidly accumulating government debt can be marketed. In effect, the ruble overhang is accumulating at a rate of about 10 percent of GNP per year.

3. *Speculation and shortages.* Recently, there has been a significant outbreak of speculative hoarding and flight from the ruble. Following the government's ill-designed announcement of future price increases in May 1990, the shelves in state stores were cleaned out of goods. The unofficial exchange rate for the ruble appears to have fallen in 1990 (from 10 or 15 rubles to US$1 in early 1990 to 20 to 30 rubles to US$1 in summer 1990), another indication of price disequilibrium and speculative panic.

According to Soviet experts reporting in mid-1990, relatively little dollarization has occurred, with unofficial estimates of the dollar balances held by the Soviet population being around US$0.4 billion (as compared with estimates of US$10 billion for Poland in recent times). On the other hand, estimates in the *Shatalin Report* indicated that US$2 billion in hard currency is in circulation.[9]

James Noren presents other evidence of shortages that indicates that shortages have worsened considerably in the late 1980s through the mechanism described above.[10] Noren shows that the increasing problems that occurred in Soviet consumer markets through the middle of 1990 were due to increased demand and not decreased

9. *Shatalin Report*, 61.

10. James H. Noren, "The Soviet Economic Crisis: Another Perspective," *Soviet Economy* 5, no. 1 (January–March): 3–55.

production. In fact, production of consumer goods rose steadily through the middle of 1990.

Other data confirm the worsening shortages in consumer markets. One index is compiled from a survey of emigrants from the USSR during the period 1981–89 concerning the extent to which twenty-two goods were available in state stores and collective farm markets. The percentage of respondents reporting regular availability of the twenty-two foods declined from around 50 percent in 1983–84 to 27 percent in 1989. Availability declined in all regions covered by the survey. Another index of shortage was the extent of rationing. A survey indicated that during the period 1987–89 the extent of sugar rationing rose from 5 percent to 95 percent of respondents, while the percentage of respondents reporting rationing of butter increased from 40 to 60 percent. A third indicator of excess demand is the black-market price of the ruble, which also rose sharply in the period from 1985 to late 1990. In all these cases, it is likely that the shortages were a combination of excess flow demand and some speculative hoarding in anticipation of either price changes or asset confiscations.[11]

Conclusions

These conditions lead to the following two tentative conclusions: First, the time is short. A sense of urgency pervades our policy memorandum (chapter 2) and all the chapters in this volume. There is a significant risk that the Soviet economy is on the verge of a breakdown or of hyperinflation. There is no time for half-measures or for carefully planned stages, sequences, and steps. Decisive actions must be taken quickly or the distribution system may become paralyzed.

Second, given the complete irrationality of the current pricing structure and given the opportunities for arbitrage, the best course may be not to try to reform prices, introduce new plans, unify exchange rates, or undertake some partial move toward the market in the short run. Rather, the only effective approach is to have a *complete and simultaneous systemic change* to the market. That is why we stress the interdependence of the reforms we propose. They must be taken simultaneously and quickly.

11. The figures cited in this paragraph are largely from Noren, "Soviet Economic Crisis."

GENERAL POLICY CONSIDERATIONS

In designing our recommendations for economic stabilization, we had the following considerations in mind. The goal is to replace the centrally managed, administrative system with a decentralized market in a way that minimizes the social cost, pain, and disruption. This means that unemployment should be kept to relatively low levels (those normally found in market economies); that prices should be free to adjust to supply and demand; that the growth of the economy and particularly living standards should be enhanced; and that prices should be stabilized.

The major threat to economic stability will be the threat of a severe inflation when prices are liberalized. In addition, there is likely to be a period, hopefully short but perhaps extended, of irreducible frictional unemployment as people are redeployed from their current jobs to ones that are consistent with an efficient market economy.

The program presented here has been designed to reduce the chances of hyperinflation while insisting upon the primary goals of promoting markets and enhancing long-run economic growth.[12] Any program to stabilize the economy will be extremely difficult; indeed, at many points our Soviet colleagues tell us that the program is impossible (*nevozmozhno*). But the lessons of stabilization policies around the world are that, when governments have had their backs to the walls, when hyperinflation or economic ruin has threatened governments, then everything we recommend has been possible by the test that some countries have actually taken the recommended steps.[13]

A final point is that the program must be simple. It must be easily

12. For a recent study of the dynamics of hyperinflation, with many lessons for the Soviet Union and other socialist countries, see Rudiger Dornbusch, Federico Sturzenegger, and Helger Wolf, "Extreme Inflation: Dynamics and Stabilization," *Brookings Papers on Economic Activity*, no. 2 (Washington, D.C.: Brookings Institution, 1990), 1–64.

13. Many of the lessons of earlier stabilization programs apply to administrative economies on the road to a liberalized system. An exhaustive review of the history of liberalization and stabilization programs is contained in Demetries Papageorgiou, Armeane M. Chokai, and Michael Micacly, "Liberalizing Foreign Trade in Developing Countries: The Lessons of Forty Years Experience" (World Bank, Washington, D.C., 1990, mimeographed).

understood by policymakers and easily communicated to the population through the media. It must not involve complicated multi-stage strategies like the chess game of a Grandmaster or intricate rationales understood only by economists. It must be robust enough to withstand unexpected twists and turns of politics, economics, the weather, and oil prices. (This last sentence was written on the day that Iraq invaded Kuwait and drove oil prices up by over 50 percent, but that fact changed very little in this chapter.)

BACKGROUND ASSUMPTIONS

Any plan to stabilize the economy must begin with some background assumptions about the political situation and about the goals of the effort.

Political Assumptions

The political situation in the Soviet Union changes virtually daily, but before we can begin to describe the economic climate, we need to clarify our assumptions about the political structure in which the economy is operating. The Soviet Union is assumed to consist of a union of republics and to be more or less the same size as it is today. In fact, however, our conclusions would not be affected if the economic unit were to consist of only half or two-thirds of the present population and resources.

We assume there is a common currency in all areas, managed by a single central bank, which is responsible for monetary policy. The country is assumed to consist of a free-trade region, with no internal tariffs or border controls. There would be free migration of goods, labor, capital, and finances within the country. There would be a common external policy, with common tariffs, quantitative restrictions, administration, and regulations. Exchange rate policy would be determined by the central government.

This basic framework allows for considerable variation in the relationships between different levels of government. The structure suggested by the *Shatalin Report* would generally fit into the framework put forth here. There is a great deal of room for alternative structures, such as different tax systems, ownership patterns, government expenditures, and social safety nets among regions. Varia-

tions of these issues will affect other parts of a transition to the market but are incidental to the stabilization issues addressed here.

Economic Assumptions

Our recommendations contain certain presumptions about the evolution of the economy. We believe that it is likely that the economic crisis will continue and may even worsen. Through early 1991 the fundamental factors that are contributing to increasing budget deficits, repressed and open inflation, and shortages are getting worse, not better. The lessons of hyperinflation and economic collapse from other countries suggest that when the population loses confidence in the currency and in economic policy, prices can begin to spin out of control very rapidly. Once the genie of hyperinflation is out of the bottle, particularly in countries with weak political structures, it may take years and a period of great hardship and austerity to get the genie back into the bottle. It is not possible to predict how fast the current economy may deteriorate. Perhaps the system cannot survive for a year; perhaps it can creak along for some time given the inertia and residual goodwill of the population or political repression or both.

In addition, the effectiveness of a stabilization policy will interact with policies in other areas. In order to implement the recommendations on stabilization, we make the following assumptions about policies regarding prices, external policies, and other areas:

• It is assumed that an effort will be made to establish the preconditions for the market in terms of the necessary laws to operate a civilized market economy. These preconditions will be discussed in a later section.

• The most important assumption, recommended vigorously in chapter 3 and strongly supported here, is that virtually all prices should be decontrolled simultaneously and virtually completely. The particular importance of this step for stabilization is discussed below. We have called the day on which prices are de-

14. A word on terminology: We chose the term *D-Day* to represent "Deregulation Day." In the West, D-Day designates the Allied landing in Normandy in June 1944; in the Soviet Union that day is known as "the day of the opening of the Western front." So perhaps the modern D-Day will be known as the day of the opening of the Eastern market.

controlled "D-Day."[14] Complete demonopolization and privatization are clearly highly desirable, but D-Day should definitely not wait for these transitions to be completed.

• With respect to opening the economy, the approach in chapter 5 supports and strengthens our stabilization measures. As explained below, we recommend that the program for opening the economy be implemented exactly on D-Day.

• Once again we stress that it is essential that enterprises must face *hard budget constraints* on D-Day. Unless they face hard-budget constraints, it will be difficult to ensure fiscal discipline and to contain inflation.

POLICY RECOMMENDATIONS: POLICIES BEFORE D-DAY

Our policy recommendations fall logically into two stages. A first set of proposals applies before D-Day, that is, before prices are liberalized and before the economy is opened. A second set of steps apply to the period following D-Day. We discuss each of these two stages in turn.

In the period between now and D-Day, two objectives exist: to create the essential preconditions for D-Day and to keep the ship afloat.

Preconditions for the Market

What preconditions must be established before freeing prices and opening the economy? These topics are discussed in other chapters, but our concern with stabilization makes us view these needs somewhat differently, and we therefore address this issue briefly here.

The absolute preconditions for the market are, in fact, relatively few. It would be a mistake to wait until every law was perfected and every program finely honed. Moreover, it is unrealistic to try to establish a finely tuned commercial code, a full set of stock and futures markets, a carefully crafted social insurance system, and the like. What is needed instead is the most rudimentary framework for the evolution of a market economy. This framework can be achieved relatively quickly.

Among the absolute preconditions are:

• Enterprises must have directors who have the authority to set prices, output, and wages as well as to hire and fire workers and to buy, sell, or borrow financial or tangible capital. It is desirable to have these decisions made by autonomous, financially responsible corporations; these would first be publicly held; privatization would come later. This step would ensure the de jure (and, at least partially, de facto) separation of the enterprises from the state. But whatever the legal structure, somebody (or some body) must have the authority to make decisions.

• The government must enact and enforce laws of property. There must be clear rules regarding who owns what, and how ownership can be transferred, and a system of contract enforcement to encourage longer-term agreements and the development of private capital markets must also be in place. Creditors must have the right to seize quickly the assets of bankrupt debtors.

• There must be banks who perform rudimentary banking functions and refuse to honor drafts, obligations, or checks written by enterprises or people who have no money.

• There must be rules of bankruptcy and liquidation to govern what happens when the claims on an enterprise exceed its liquidation value.

• Above all, there must be hard-budget constraints. This means that there must be a generally accepted system of accounts, a unit of account, and a limit on credit. Enterprises must know that unprofitability ultimately means bankruptcy for the firm and economic ruin for the managers.

These five conditions are what we would call the preconditions for a primitive market economy. In addition, a civilized market would benefit from such measures as unemployment insurance, a social safety net, a stabilized budget system, a full menu of financial assets, and so forth. But markets have operated without these modern features and they are not, in fact, absolute preconditions for the emergence of the market. Moreover, the Soviet Union may not be able to afford either the time or the financial resources to establish these loftier objectives.

Stabilization Policy before D-Day

In the period before D-Day, the major goal of economic policy should be to correct the flow problem, or reduce aggregate demand. The primary tool for accomplishing this involves reducing the budget deficit. In addition there exists a subsidiary role for monetary policy and incomes policies.

1. The first priority during the transition to D-Day is to reduce the budget deficit. Of course, no group would like to see its taxes raised or its subsidies cut. As a result, reducing the deficit faces substantial political obstacles—indeed, the difficulty faced in reducing budget deficits is a problem common to the Soviet and to many Western economies. But one way or another, it is necessary to curb excessive deficits if a stable market economy is to be achieved.

We are not in a position to analyze specific suggestions in detail, and political factors must obviously be taken into account. Yet, certain deficit-reducing measures stand out. One of the early targets should be to reduce or remove subsidies. Subsidies undermine market discipline, distort prices, and lead to wasteful use of resources. We will return later to the point that there are generally more efficient ways of achieving the objectives of the subsidies.

Another target for budget cuts is central spending on investment. Because of the way investment is allocated, the outcome is often highly inefficient. For example, a substantial number of investment projects are simply abandoned. Estimates today are that unfinished construction projects today are equal to almost one year's investment expenditure.[15]

According to most estimates, a substantial amount of spending (and an even larger fraction of effective resources) continues to be channeled into defense, particularly military research and development and defense procurement. Most estimates indicate that defense spending has not decreased at all. Indeed, such reductions might produce a double "peace dividend," for they would strengthen the arguments of those in the United States who wish to reduce defense spending but are blocked by proponents who point to continued high levels of Soviet procurement. Finally, in both the United States and the Soviet Union, the defense establishment siphons off a

15. See *Shatalin Report*, 113–18, for a discussion of the problems of unfinished construction in the Soviet Union.

substantial fraction of the prime scientific and engineering talent, a resource that is increasingly vital to economic health in a technologically sophisticated world. Reducing military research and development and devoting these resources to civilian activities would provide double and triple benefits to both countries.

The allocation of hard currency might be immediately reformed, say by hard-currency auctions; some believe this would reduce the budget deficit by between one-third and two-fifths. Central expenditures in housing and agriculture might be cut sharply (the potential for reduction here being almost one-half of the budget deficit).

2. Credit policy has traditionally been passive in the Soviet Union, based on the historical premise of the "real-bills doctrine," wherein credit is given only on evidence of invoices or warehouse receipts of goods. In principle, credit policies of *Gosbank* could be reoriented in the period before D-Day in order to tighten the screws on enterprise spending. This could be done, for example, by segregating wage and nonwage accounts and freezing wage accounts, or by severely tightening overall enterprise liquidity by freezing a certain fraction of enterprise balances. An alternative approach would be to apply overall credit limitations to the enterprise sector, although this approach would have the difficulty of requiring some kind of nonprice rationing system.

It is not sensible to try to attempt a complete reform of an administrative banking system in the short time before D-Day. Rather, we recommend using the existing system in the most effective way along with promoting the growth of a private banking sector. This recommendation is based first on the view that an attempt to overhaul the banking system to improve the command economy is probably a futile exercise as it is likely to lead to unintended consequences and will waste the time of financial reformers. Moreover, such steps are unlikely to reduce markedly the ruble overhang. A better use of time and energy would be to prepare for a transition to the market by training bankers and preparing to privatize the commercial banking functions.

3. Incomes policies are important in the initial transition period in order to slow the growth of wages and incomes. It is clear that the liberalization of enterprise rules (particularly, the effective abolition of targets for the wages fund) along with passive credit conditions allowed wages to outstrip production by a wide margin since 1985.

In addition, the tax on the wages fund has not yet been effective in slowing wage growth.

The continued hemorrhaging of funds into wages is a serious threat to economic stabilization in the near term. The government should consider tightening controls over wages—either through a sharp tightening of the taxes on the wages fund or tighter credit constraints on enterprises. Unless wages are kept under control during the period of soft budget constraints, the possibility of keeping the ship afloat until D-Day is in peril and the dangers of hyperinflation after D-Day increase.

Another issue during the transition to D-Day concerns the desire for guarantees or indexation during what will inevitably be a period of declining confidence and increasing open and repressed inflation. We recommend avoiding any kind of indexation, compensation, or other real-income guarantees during this period. They serve no economic function, are likely to be abrogated later, and generally will tend to destabilize the economy during the period after D-Day.

4. A major issue of economic reform in the period until D-Day concerns whether there should be attempts to undertake price reforms to bring the system closer to equilibrium. Chapter 3 discussed in some detail why administrative or partial price reform is unworkable. We recommend that policymakers minimize their attempts to reform the administrative system in the period before D-Day. This is not an absolute prohibition, but rather a warning that attempts to rationalize or liberalize are as likely to be counterproductive as they are useful.

The reasons for this recommendation are three: First, there is plenty to do in the near term just to prepare for D-Day. In particular, the program to establish the preconditions for the market essentially attempts to build an entire house in a day. It is better to concentrate all efforts on making the systemic transition than to waste time correcting an imperfect system. Reforming officially controlled prices is like painting a house that is going to be demolished tomorrow. Second, it is clear that there are almost always unintended consequences of reforms and liberalizations (such as the wage boom that followed enterprise liberalization). In a situation that is so full of irrational prices and arbitrage opportunities, changes in the rules are likely to create all kinds of new problems. Third, many of the recommendations will hurt people by raising prices, thereby giving a

bad name to economic reform and (further) damaging the political
prospects for actually making a successful transition to the market.
For example, a 20 percent increase in prices will not put goods on the
shelves; it involves all pain and no gain.

All these recommendations are somewhat complicated, so the
major point to remember is the following: Before D-Day, economic
policy should focus on establishing the infrastructure for the market, stabilizing the budget, and minimizing attempts to improve the
present administrative economic mechanism.

STABILIZATION POLICY ON AND AFTER D-DAY

The next issue concerns the stabilization policy on D-Day. At this
time, it is possible only to lay out the general recommendations.
Given the vast political and economic uncertainties, specific recommendations are not possible. Nonetheless, the general shape of recommendations are clear.

Timing and General Conditions

On or near D-Day, a number of measures will be introduced
simultaneously to liberalize prices, open the economy, and introduce
hard-budget constraints into economic decisions. The following are
the important concomitants of the stabilization package:

1. When should D-Day come? The answer is, soon. Not on January 1, however, for there may be turmoil and confusion, and it would
be better not to have confusion at minus 40 degrees Centigrade.
(Indeed, a grim joke circulating today is that, after four warm winters, the next cold winter will be the last winter of socialism.) Many
believe that D-Day must be implemented quickly if the Soviet Union
is to avoid hyperinflation or a breakdown in the distribution system.

2. The key steps taken on D-Day are the deregulation of prices in
a substantial part of the economy and a hardening of budget constraints everywhere in the economy. The exact strategy for this was
discussed briefly above and is described in chapter 3. The strategic
reason to have complete rather than staged liberalization is that, by
allowing prices to rise sufficiently to clear markets, consumers will
quickly see goods on the shelves. Thus, although D-Day will necessarily be accompanied by certain painful steps, such as inflation and

a fall in real wages, one important benefit will be that at the inflated price level the devalued ruble will be convertible into domestic goods and services.

The proposition that freeing prices will produce goods on the shelves is not merely a theoretical economic proposition. Historical evidence from Germany in 1948 and Poland in 1990 indicates that a rapid liberalization of prices did in fact produce goods in the stores almost instantaneously.[16] By contrast, half measures, such as staged decontrol, run the risk of dispensing pain to consumers in the form of lower real wages without making goods available.

3. Some observers believe that it is at this point that Western economic aid is likely to be most valuable. Given the current short-ages and bottlenecks, along with the decline in production, price deregulation might lead to extremely high prices for certain goods in great shortage (for example, last year cigarettes were selling on the black market for 5 percent of weekly income per pack). To help smooth the transition, some believe that a modest amount of foreign aid might be used to help put goods on the shelves and to ensure that the prices of consumer goods are not exorbitant on D-Day.

Such aid, however, is not essential for our proposals. Indeed some analysts question the wisdom of devoting any foreign economic aid to consumer goods. Such a measure threatens to encourage unre-alistic expectations at a time when the population must be encour-aged to make the psychological transition to a market mentality. Moreover, they argue that whatever economic assistance is available might be better and more productively employed in training pro-grams, technological transfer, and assisting foreign direct invest-ment.

4. Credit for enterprises should be available only on a short-term basis and at positive (and initially probably high) real interest rates. Clearly, it is absolutely essential that any automatic credit link, whereby firms get whatever they need from Gosbank, be severed.

5. We believe that D-Day is the proper time to have an opening of the economy. In an open economy, the exchange rate would float or be determined by the market; the ruble would be freely convertible

16. A full account of the German recovery after World War II, along with details on the German monetary reform, is contained in Henry Wallich, *Mainsprings of the German Revival* (New Haven: Yale University Press, 1955).

for current transactions; and all trade restrictions would be replaced with tariffs at a low and uniform rate.

In addition, stabilization measures will benefit from the undervalued exchange rate recommended in the chapter 5. By undervaluing the exchange rate, business in the Soviet Union will look like a bargain to foreign investors, and Soviet goods will find an eager world market. The world market is *enormous* relative to current Soviet foreign trade. The world market in tradable goods and services is almost 200 times Soviet hard-currency exports. By ensuring that Soviet labor, resources, and goods are a bargain relative to world prices, foreign trade, and therefore integration into the world economy, will be hastened.

6. D-Day would also be the point at which the economy would be open to free entry in all lines of business (except operating missile systems and printing money). The combination of opening the economy to foreign trade and opening the markets to domestic entry and competition would be a major contributor to competition. In addition, the freedom to engage in different activities and start up small firms would provide a shock absorber for unemployment, real wage reductions, or other events that are sure to accompany D-Day.

Stabilization Policies

Given the concomitants of stabilization listed above, we now turn to the measures proposed to stabilize the economy. Before listing the steps, it is important to note that moving to a market does *not* mean abandoning overall economic policy or "leaving everything to the market." It is possible to leave many of the individual decisions about prices, wages, and production to financially responsible firms. But prices and wages are still *indirectly* controlled by aggregative policies that exercise their influence through markets.

Putting this differently, in moving to the market it is necessary to effect a sharp change in the instruments of economic control, to move from microeconomic controls to macroeconomic controls. In an administrative economy, the approach to stabilization involves the *micro* control of individual magnitudes (individual prices, wages, credit lines, and enterprise budgets). In a market economy, these controls must be replaced by policies that *macro* control fiscal, monetary, and other variables. Thus, instead of restricting the credit to particular firms, in a market economy the control is through the aggregate supply of money and credit available to the economy. This shift from micro control to macro control requires simultaneously relaxing controls on the micro variables and imposing strict and disciplined control on the macro variables.

Fiscal Policies

1. The single most important condition for stabilization on D-Day is that government budgets be both tight and under control. The stabilization must be clear, adequate, and complete on D-Day. For simplicity, the target should be a balanced budget.[17] Obviously, the closer the country comes to a balanced budget, the better, for if the deficit is too large, then the deficit itself can lead to excessive growth in incomes and to the unstable dynamics leading to a hyperinflation.

2. We discussed above potential approaches to balancing the budget, and that discussion applies to the period after D-Day as well as before D-Day. A few other remarks apply to the longer-term fiscal structure.

The current structure of taxation is generally economically viable, although it would be useful to make taxation of all enterprises uniform (state, private, and foreign). Moving to a value-added tax such as that used in the European Community would be useful in the medium run, but is certainly not necessary on D-Day.

However, the overall tax rates in the Soviet Union are high relative to levels seen in most market economies. The ratio of total taxes to GNP is approximately one-half, and further amounts are implicitly taxed and transferred through price and allocation policies. It is unlikely that a market economy in the Soviet Union could operate efficiently with as high a level of taxation as today. For example, taxes are about one-quarter of GNP in Japan and about one-third of GNP in the United States. Therefore, in cutting the budget deficit,

17. The concept of the budget differs among different countries. For simplicity, when we speak of the budget, we have in mind the most straightforward system, which is a "cash" concept. In this approach, which provides the basis of the U.S. federal budgetary decisions, the deficit is simply the difference between all outlays (on goods, services, and transfers) less receipts (from taxation and sales of government enterprises). The receipts definitely exclude monetary creation, borrowing from either financial or nonfinancial sectors, and borrowing from the central bank.

preference should be given to expenditure reduction as opposed to tax increases.

3. For expenditure cuts, the discussion under "General Policy Considerations" in this chapter will serve as a useful point of departure for detailed analysis. Again, we emphasize that, in a market economy, subsidies for individual goods and services should be kept to a minimum. Some exceptions to the general rule to abolish subsidies may be desirable, particularly with respect to necessities like food for low-income households; a civilized society should protect the worst-off, such as pensioners, from the ravages of inflation or relative price changes. Measures to protect these groups are discussed in chapter 3 and in chapter 6.

4. In addition to the need to balance the budget, the *structure* of the budget also requires reform. More precisely, the structure of the budget must be such that inflation decreases rather than increases the real budget deficit. This condition, which we call "dynamic deficit stability," is a somewhat technical but critical point and will be elaborated upon here.

Prices liberalization will affect both the real revenues and real expenditures (by "real," we mean those nominal or ruble values divided by an appropriate price index). Expenditure programs that are indexed tend to maintain their real spending levels as prices rise, whereas the real spending on nonindexed programs erodes as prices rise unless they are boosted by discretionary actions. In addition, the real value of taxes tends to erode in periods of rising inflation, both because many taxes are in specific terms (that is, rubles per kilo) and because they are paid with a lag (of say a month, quarter, or year).

The danger of dynamic deficit instability arises if the real value of taxes falls more sharply than the real value of spending when prices rise. This would imply that the real budget deficit would rise, which would tend to produce more spending, more inflation, and increase yet again the real budget deficit. Thus, to avoid spiraling inflation, the structure of the budget must be such that the erosion of real revenues with inflation is less than the decline in real government expenditures.

We did not have the occasion to examine the fiscal structure in detail, but three concrete recommendations will help to ensure dynamic deficit stability. The most important recommendation is to avoid the temptation to use "real" budgeting instead of "nominal" budgets. Real budgeting allows an automatic adjustment of payments when the price level rises. This is commonly used for transfer programs (such as pensions) and is also sometimes used for other government programs. We suggest that budgeting remain in nominal (ruble) terms and that beneficiaries must return for further discretionary increases to compensate for any price increases.

Two other technical recommendations will also help promote dynamic deficit stability. First, all "specific" turnover or other taxes should be replaced with percentage or ad valorem taxes. (A specific tax is one denominated in nominal (ruble) terms per unit, whereas an ad valorem tax is set as a percent of the product price.) This replacement will help prevent the erosion of real taxes when prices rise. Second, we suggest that the tax-payment lag be shortened. Taxes should be paid contemporaneously with wages (say within a week or at most a month), and quickly on other items as well, rather than with the current three-month lag.

5. There is an important interaction between stabilization policy and price deregulation. This arises because administered prices lag behind rising costs, thus leading to greater and greater subsidies. To understand this dilemma today, recall the state of price reforms. The Soviet Union has already freed many prices. As of November 15, 1990, retail prices were in principle freed from central control on many consumer durables and luxury items. On January 1, 1991, all wholesale prices were in principle freed from central control, along with prices at which enterprises sell to one another.

Retail prices, however, remain controlled for items comprising about three-quarters of retail sales, although a retail price reform is planned. With retail prices fixed below market-clearing levels, the government must provide subsidies for the difference between wholesale and retail prices. Such subsidies are estimated to add 200 billion rubles in 1991 to the already swollen government deficit (this being about 20 percent of GNP).

Price deregulation will by itself therefore remove one of the major elements contributing to macroeconomic instability. Only by freeing prices will it be possible to eliminate the need for subsidies for enterprises whose rising costs exceed their revenues based on frozen prices.

Monetary Policies

6. In the longer run, the burden of stabilization policies will necessarily fall on fiscal policies. Monetary policies can, however, play an important role in the short run.

With respect to credit policies, a substantial tightening of credit will be possible and desirable when firms operate with hard-budget constraints. Once individual enterprises are subject to hard-budget constraints, Gosbank should make credit available only to firms that can repay credits; this implies curbing credits to unprofitable enterprises. It is probably unrealistic to completely cut off credits to unprofitable enterprises, but they should be forced to restructure their operations with a view to attaining profitability in a short time.

We emphasized above that stabilization requires replacing controls on individual enterprises with controls on economic aggregates. In monetary policy, this means that the banking system must place overall credit limits on enterprises, much as Western central banks do today. In the beginning, before prices and wages have been stabilized, banks will probably charge high interest rates to enterprises under a regime of tight credit. In the period surrounding liberalization, real interest rates (equal to money interest rates less the rate of inflation) must be positive. Based on the experience in other countries, this implies that money interest rates must be well above today's level, perhaps 20 or 40 percent per year or even higher. After inflation has stabilized and the government budget is safely under control, interest rates can be reduced to levels seen in market economies.

In the transition period, there is likely to be a mixture of enterprises, some operating with hard and soft budget constraints. It will be necessary to cordon off the two sectors so that the lack of discipline in the one sector does not infect the other. For example, it may be useful to allow private firms and deregulated, financially responsible firms to develop an interfirm loan market for funds. But there should definitely be strict limitations on transactions between the financially responsible sector and the less constrained sectors.

Our proposals envision that monetary and credit policies will be administered by the existing banking system. It is not necessary to privatize the banking system in order to have tough credit policies.

Rather, the state banking system must be subject to overall guidelines on credit aggregates, interest rates, and lending guidelines.

In the longer run, it is clearly desirable to develop a private banking system to replace the state-run retail banks. Foreign banks may be able to lend their expertise to this task. But banking is a most complicated industry, and establishment of a private banking system will require careful thought and private banks are unlikely to assume credit allocation in the short run.

7. The steps outlined above will in principle solve the flow problem of the budget deficit. In addition, price deregulation will, at high prices, put goods on the shelves. There remains, however, the difficult issue of the ruble overhang. On D-Day, household assets are likely to exceed the value of assets that households would desire to hold at the current average price level. In order to reduce the real value of household assets—that is, to eliminate the ruble overhang—either prices must rise so that the real value of household liquid assets declines to the desired level, or the assets themselves must be reduced through sterilization or monetary reform.

Some advocate a monetary reform to solve the ruble overhang.[18] An idealized monetary reform proposal might operate as follows: on or around D-Day, the government might convert all existing assets and liabilities into "market rubles" or "convertible rubles"— call them *M-rubles*. The M-rubles would be converted from existing rubles at a rate of, say, one M-ruble to two old, nonconvertible rubles. (The figure of two-to-one is used for illustrative purposes and is unlikely to be exactly the right figure.) Then households would convert *all* cash, savings accounts, and other financial assets into M-rubles at the exchange rate of two to one. The size of household debts appears to be small enough to ignore, but in principle these would also be reduced by 50 percent. Wages rates would not be adjusted; wage rates in old rubles would continue to apply in M-rubles. Other contractual questions, such as those involving enterprise and commodity contracts, will be ignored in this discussion, although these may pose technical issues.

On the basis of the calculations made to date about the extent of repressed inflation (see "Existing Economic Conditions" in this

18. A useful review of the history and theory of monetary reforms is contained in Rudiger Dornbusch "Monetary Reform" (Economics Department, Massachusetts Institute of Technology, Cambridge, Mass., 1990, mimeographed).

chapter), it is plausible that a two-to-one conversion would be sufficient to extinguish much of the monetary overhang. Then, and this
assumption is critically important, taken in conjunction with steps to
reduce the budget deficit and tighten credit, the monetary reform
should prevent a major price explosion on D-Day.

An important part of the deregulation process is that the ruble
will become internationally convertible on D-Day. One major advantage of the monetary reform would be that the new M-ruble would
be immediately able to buy Western goods. This is where the decision about the exchange rate becomes crucial. Estimates of the appropriate exchange rate on D-Day are treacherous, and some research indicates that a rate of 10 rubles to US$1 might be an
appropriate rate if prices were to double, suggesting an exchange-
rate target at current prices of about 5 rubles to the dollar. Accepting
this estimate for purposes of discussion, the new M-ruble would
therefore be completely convertible into dollars for current transactions at a rate of 5 M-rubles to the dollar. For those households
desiring Western goods and exposed to current black-market prices,
which were in the range of 15 to 30 rubles to the dollar during 1990,
the new M-ruble would actually look like a bargain rather than a
confiscation. After the currency reform, the new M-ruble might be
at a floating rate, but that depends on whether a floating or fixed
rate should prevail at the outset of the reforms. This question is
discussed in chapter 5.

Proponents of the monetary reform argue that it is the only practical alternative to inflation; even more important, once a price-level
increase of a factor of 2 or 3 takes place, the chances of triggering
budget expenditures, wage increases, and a runaway inflation are
significant and intolerable. They argue that an across-the-board
ruble conversion would be more equitable than either inflation or
partial conversion or freezing savings accounts. In the ideal monetary reform, all rubles are treated equally, whereas inflation, partial
reforms, or asset freezes will end up mainly hurting the poor, el-
derly, and innumerate who are not sophisticated enough to understand them and are therefore unable to take steps to minimize the
costs of adjustment. Finally, in terms of popular support, experience
from Latin America suggests that although people generally oppose
monetary reform in advance, once a successful reform is behind
them, people are relieved and satisfied that it has been done.

Opponents of monetary reform are skeptical of the ability to produce anything like the ideal neutral ruble conversion analyzed above. There will be pressures to exempt or to attach certain assets; antispeculative sentiment may tend to make the conversion progressive (as occurred, for example, in East Germany); it is likely to be poorly timed; there are many examples of monetary reforms that were introduced as substitutes for, instead of complements to, the necessary fundamental reforms; they tend to undermine confidence in the domestic currency and accelerate dollarization; and they may provoke hostile public reactions. Most important, they can only solve the stock problem (by reducing the monetary overhang) and contribute nothing to solving the flow problem.

In addition, Soviet analysts argued that it would be impossible to keep the plan secret given the necessity of gaining the agreement of the republics, so the task is to devise an effective *anticipated* monetary reform. Opponents point out that an anticipated partial monetary reform (say one converting only large notes or savings accounts, or a temporary freezing of accounts) could be easily defeated by converting assets to exempted assets or goods, or by "leveling" accounts in the case of a progressive reform.[19]

On the whole, it is certainly better to avoid monetary reform if the resulting one-shot price increase would be modest (say 20 or 30 percent), while a neutral monetary reform would be preferable if the price rise was extreme (a factor of 5 or more, which threatens to trigger hyperinflation). In between these extremes, the decision will depend upon the estimates of inflation and the extent to which the actual reform plan resembles the ideal neutral plan sketched above.

But whatever the view about the wisdom of well-designed monetary reforms, it is essential that these be part of a strict stabilization

19. The monetary reform of January 1991 reveals the difficulties of a poorly designed reform. This reform attempted to confiscate unlawfully obtained 50- and 100-ruble notes and aimed to reduce the money supply owned by households (M2) by at most 10 percent. Some newspaper accounts indicate that knowledgeable people had wind of the confiscation and moved into other assets.

The reform is almost certain to be ineffective for large-ruble holders will transfer their holdings to cousins, grandmothers, and people who simply do not have any rubles of their own to convert. The limit on personal conversions is approximately equal to the average monthly wage. Assuming that the average citizen can convert 300 rubles in large notes, this allows for 300 times 280 million in legal conversions, which is 84 billion rubles, as opposed to around 40 billion of notes outstanding.

policy and not be used as a substitute for the necessary measures to reduce the budget deficit and control money and credit.

8. The extent of inflation or the stringency of the monetary reform can be reduced if the ruble overhang can be reduced. With this in mind, two specific steps might be considered to reduce inflationary potential:

The government might attempt to convert some fraction of household liquid assets into equity claims. These claims might be shares of the stocks of privatized corporations or of the housing stock (although the latter appears to suffer from serious technical issues). In addition, liquid assets could be converted into illiquid financial assets. These might include long-term bonds, or special accounts that can only be used for capital transactions (such as purchases of housing or equity claims on corporations).

In undertaking the conversion to illiquid assets, however, care should be taken not to exacerbate the flow problem by incurring large future government interest payments. For example, if the savings accounts were converted into indexed savings accounts or long-term bonds bearing market interest rates, this would sharply increase the government's future interest payments and would therefore threaten to destabilize the economy.

Caution should be exercised in privatizing enterprises so that further government financial obligations are not created. One proposal for privatization would leave enterprises with any positive balances and would reduce any debts to zero. Clearly this would increase the government debt and is to be avoided. From the point of view of stabilization, the best policy is probably to cancel all financial debts and credits of state enterprises and leave them with only their physical assets. A particularly dangerous policy would be to cancel debts, leave credits, and then to transfer shares for free to mutual funds or individuals. This would overnight add another 100 to 200 billion rubles to the ruble overhang because the enterprises have balances of that magnitude.

The point to emphasize is that the enterprises belong to the state. Their assets and liabilities can be auctioned off in a way that is most sensible to the public interest. There is little reason to give windfall gains (or impose windfall losses) on those firms who happen to have positive (or negative) financial balances because of the past whims of the administrative economy.

Other Issues

9. A major set of issues for the period after D-Day concerns how to compensate or index various sectors for the possibility of price increases. In general, we would emphasize the importance of minimizing the amount of automatic indexation of budget claims or of wages or taxes. As we noted in the discussion above, greater indexation leads to a greater threat of dynamic deficit instability.

There is no way to index the entire economy; indexation is best seen as a redistributive measure. The more the system is indexed, the greater is the threat of hyperinflation. Many countries who have indexed their economies have lived to regret it. Moreover, it must be kept in mind that when prices are freed, queues will be reduced, black-market prices will fall, and thus the true cost of living will rise less than will the official retail price index.

With these general considerations in mind, we would allow for one exception in the case of transfer payments to such low-income households as pensioners, for example, who must be protected against the hardships of a severe inflation. For such groups, a high (but not 100 percent) indexation rate would be acceptable. With respect to other groups, the recommendation would be to minimize the amount of indexation. Avoiding indexation will improve the overall stability of the economy.

It is worth noting that the country with the greatest inflation stability, the Federal Republic of Germany, is one in which wage indexation is illegal!

10. A final issue concerns the recommendations on incomes policies. *Incomes policy* is a term used to designate policies that work directly upon the wage and price decisions of individual firms. It could include limits on price or wage increases, penalties or taxes on excessive wages (as in the current "tax on the wages fund"), informal or formal guidelines, and other mechanisms.

Our view is that tight fiscal and credit policies are a necessary and sufficient condition for the ultimate containment of inflation. In ideal circumstances, we would recommend that conventional stabilization policies be augmented by policies to restrain wages.[20] On the whole, however, we recommend avoiding such measures.

20. The case for incomes policies, with suitable cautions, is laid out in Richard Layard, "Income Policies in the Soviet Union" (1990, mimeographed).

The major argument against incomes policies (such as wage guidelines) concerns the danger they pose if policymakers view them as substitutes for the more fundamental requirement of anti-inflation policy—tight aggregate demand and elimination of the ruble overhang. Putting this point differently, the only sure and certain way to ensure that inflation will be contained is the threat of unemployment and bankruptcy that prevents firms from raising prices and wages in an atmosphere of tight budget and credit policies.

Other dangers exist in an economy that is trying to move to the market. Historically, most incomes policies end up with the government putting pressure on individual firms (and sometimes unions) to restrain wages and prices. Such pressure interferes with the principle of free prices and wages. Although the damage may be tolerable in a society with long and deep market traditions, it seems more perilous in a society that is trying to nurture financial responsibility, autonomy, and freedom from central interference with price and wage decisions. Particularly in a mixed system where the government retains some residual powers and can use economic threats to enforce incomes policies, it would seem better to abjure their use.

Given all these limitations, we see at best a limited role for incomes policies. Chapter 6 suggests that incomes policies should be applied only to large enterprises that are likely to be monopolies in their product markets and have strong unions. In contrast, we would forego entirely incomes policies because of the risk that when a government has residual powers and can use economic threats to enforce incomes policies, such policies can weaken enterprise independence and bring back into the political process decisions about relative incomes of different groups.

11. We must be clear on two points about prices. To begin with, the fundamental choice for stabilization policy is between monetary reform (of either the ideal neutral or a messier partial version) and inflation (of uncertain size and duration). To the extent that no monetary reform occurs, the presence of excessive household liquid assets will require a significant price rise to reduce the real value of monetary assets.

At the same time, whether a monetary reform is instituted or not, there is no way of avoiding a major economic upheaval because of the necessary change in relative prices. No stabilization policy can prevent the relative free-market prices of highly subsidized items like food from increasing, although in the process many important consumer goods, such as televisions, automobiles, and jeans, will experience a sharp fall in relative prices.

FINAL THOUGHTS

Many Western observers of the Soviet economy are today pessimistic about the prospects for achieving economic reform. The road is long, political will is meager, and the time is short. The most recent period seems to be a case of "one step forward, two steps backwards." The chasm between the administrative-command economy and the full market economy is wide and deep. Nonetheless, we hope that the chasm will be crossed and that these recommendations will make the crossing less perilous.

Chapter Five

Opening the Soviet Economy

Richard N. Cooper

This chapter addresses the extent and the timing of the opening of the Soviet economy to interaction with the world economy. This involves examining the international convertibility of the ruble, the exchange rate, and commercial policy.

This analysis assumes that the Soviet Union will continue as a free-trade area and as a currency area within roughly its present boundaries. This chapter does not address the pressing political question of the sovereignty of the republics within the Soviet Union, some of which have raised the possibility of instituting separate currencies and establishing restrictions on intraunion trade. Yet if the reforms recommended here and in other chapters are carried out, it would be economically disadvantageous to break up the Soviet Union into diverse regions with separate currencies and border restrictions.

OPEN THE ECONOMY EARLY

The opening of the Soviet economy should be an integral part of the domestic economic reforms from the outset and not delayed until many of the other reforms have become effective. By the opening of the economy, we mean allowing the sale of foreign goods and services within the Soviet Union, promoting Soviet exports to the rest of the world, and encouraging foreign firms and individuals to invest in the Soviet Union, Opening the economy requires establish-

Note: This chapter draws upon the discussion of a study group on the opening of the Soviet economy that met in Sopron, Hungary, in July–August 1990, and was subsequently revised in response to comments made by the participants and by chairmen of other study groups. The chapter is the sole responsibility of the author.

ing early convertibility of the ruble, necessarily at a realistic exchange rate, combined with a trade policy that encourages imports and exports. We return to both these issues below.

There are several reasons for preferring that the opening of the economy occur early rather than late. First, the key to a modern, flexible, and innovative economy is competitive markets, wherein information on new patterns of demand or new technological developments are transmitted to the entire economy through price signals, to which both households and enterprises can respond by adapting their behavior. The Soviet Union has intentionally concentrated production of most manufactured goods in one or relatively few enterprises (see table 3.3). Monopolies do not respond to market signals in the same way that other enterprises do, and their responses are not socially optimal. Some method must be found for introducing competitive pressures on Soviet enterprises at an early stage of restructuring so that enterprises feel these pressures in making their decisions. One way to do this, and for some sectors the only effective way, is to introduce foreign competition, so that Soviet enterprises have a price and a quality standard that they must match in order to sell at home or abroad. This action will strongly reinforce the actions recommended in chapter 3 concerning the establishment of effective competition within the Soviet economy.

A second reason for introducing currency convertibility early is to encourage from the beginning an alignment of Soviet prices with world prices of traded goods and services, subject to such deviations as the economic authorities wish explicitly and consciously to make. If, as we assume, this alignment with world prices is the final objective, then starting the process early would be more advantageous than going through a domestic price deregulation and then having a second major price realignment when the economy is opened. The alternative of administrative price adjustment to approximate world prices is inadvisable, both because it perpetuates the principle of administrative control of prices (as opposed to market-determined prices) and because such control cannot be fully effective in a world with millions of products of diverse qualities.[1]

A third reason for favoring early convertibility of the ruble is to provide goods to Soviet workers whose incentive to work is now

1. The argument against administrative price reform is made in chapter 3.

adversely affected by extensive shortages and to increase the quality and quantity of inputs available to Soviet enterprises. Opening the economy would offer a wide array of new consumer and producer goods, albeit for purchase at high prices. It would not only provide effective goods for households and improved inputs for firms but would also help reduce the ruble overhang, since firms and households would be more willing to hold financial assets, which are not high by Western standards. It would also provide the government with badly needed revenue from taxes levied on imports, as we propose below. Opening the economy early, then, reinforces the proposals made in the previous two chapters.

Fourth, convertibility would provide a strong stimulus to develop export markets. At the exchange rate required to make the ruble convertible, exports would be extremely profitable for newly independent enterprises. Autonomous enterprises would have a strong financial incentive to develop export markets, and that would push them from the beginning to take into account not only the price but also the quality of products that are sold in the world market.

A final reason for current account convertibility is that Council for Mutual Economic Assistance trade is moving to a convertible currency basis and such trade accounts for about 55 percent of both the Soviet Union's imports and exports. To maintain trade in convertible currency when the ruble itself is not freely convertible for current account transactions would require complex administrative controls.

CONVERTIBILITY OF THE RUBLE

For all these reasons, a convertible ruble should be established at an early stage of the reforms. By convertible we mean that all Soviet enterprises and households would have free access to foreign exchange for the purchase of foreign goods or services, but not for the purpose of buying assets abroad or holding foreign currency. Foreign firms operating within the Soviet Union could repatriate their after-tax profits. Obviously a system of monitoring would be required to assure that foreign currency is used for the permitted purposes. In practice, this is likely to require a limit on the amount of foreign exchange that Soviet citizens can acquire for foreign travel.

It also implies a need for Soviet residents to be authorized to open limited foreign currency deposits. It will be necessary, however, to have some procedure for Soviet enterprises to invest abroad in distribution and servicing channels for the sake of promoting exports. In today's world, some foreign investment is often required for effective marketing of national products.

Fixed versus Flexible Exchange Rates

With ready access to foreign exchange, what will prevent an outflow of foreign exchange in excess of what is available? The answer lies in making foreign exchange sufficiently expensive so that, over time, the supply will balance the demand. This condition will require a substantial depreciation of the ruble from the current official exchange rate. We favor devaluing to a specific exchange rate that would then be fixed for at least a year or two in order to provide some stability to the new set of arrangements. Such a strategy, however, has some prerequisites and necessitates careful selection of a specific exchange rate.

With respect to the prerequisites, the most important one is described in chapter 4. There it is argued that the rate of increase in the money supply must be substantially reduced from what it has been in the recent period. No currency can long remain convertible at a fixed exchange rate if the supply of money is growing more rapidly than the domestic demand for it, taking into account both overall economic growth and trends toward a more monetized economy. Reduction in the growth of the money supply requires a sharp reduction of the budget deficit. This will require a sharp turnaround in Soviet fiscal and monetary policy, particularly since events in the last half of 1990 exacerbated rather than ameliorated the budget deficit.

An implication of this overall stabilization of monetary growth is that individual enterprises will cease to have unlimited access to credit when they get into financial difficulty. In other words, enterprises have to operate under hard budget constraints, as discussed in the other chapters. The best way to accomplish this, and to advance the other objectives of economic reform, is to convert most enterprises into joint-stock corporations and to allow the managers considerable freedom in decision making, with the guideline of maximizing financial profits. The experience of Hungary suggests the need for at least some private ownership to assure autonomy from government ministries. If a firm becomes insolvent, such that cumulative operating losses exceed its net value, the management should be replaced and, if the new management cannot improve the firm's financial condition, the firm should be dissolved unless there are special and explicit social reasons for introducing subsidies to preserve it. This system will work well only if enterprises can spend their ruble earnings anywhere in the economy, and if market prices reflect the forces of supply and demand—again with exceptions that are determined explicitly and are maintained by conscious governmental action.

Our preference for a fixed exchange rate depends on the assumption that the macroeconomic balance of the economy has been established. However, a move to convertibility should not be ruled out even if macroeconomic stability has not been established ahead of time. Of course, under these circumstances a new exchange rate could not be fixed, because convertibility could not be maintained indefinitely if it were. But a fixed exchange rate is not required for convertibility, and convertibility could be introduced with a flexible exchange rate (subject to official intervention, but without commitment to a fixed rate), with the expectation that the ruble would continue to depreciate over time. Although this arrangement is not ideal, it would have some pronounced advantages over the current situation of a strongly overvalued ruble accompanied by shortages, rationing, and extensive distortions in resource allocation. The fact of continuing currency depreciation would itself create some pressure for introducing monetary stability. A number of countries around the world that have been moderately successful in their economic growth, such as Brazil and Colombia, have opened their economy to some degree without overall macroeconomic stability and have managed to function even with steadily depreciating currencies. Again, though, we stress that this is very much a second-best solution.

Current account convertibility is achieved by permitting any party that needs foreign currency to import foreign goods or services or to repatriate earnings in the USSR, to buy that currency in the foreign exchange market. Such a market would have to be established (and would quickly be established in London and other international financial centers if not developed in the Soviet Union) and the foreign exchange rate would be determined continuously by supply and demand. Soviet residents who earned foreign exchange abroad would be required to sell that foreign exchange in the market, except insofar as they received permission to retain it for investment abroad. Although the exchange rate would be determined by supply and demand, official intervention in the market (presumably by the central bank) would still be possible for the purpose of reducing sharp fluctuations in the exchange rate. The central bank's source of foreign exchange would be official conversions (for example, from oil royalties) or borrowing abroad.

To repeat, currency convertibility is more difficult if macroeconomic stability has not been established at the same time, but moving to convertibility would be preferable to continuing the current arrangements even if macroeconomic stability cannot be established early during the restructuring period.

Selecting an Initial Exchange Rate

On the other hand, if the political will is found to balance the Soviet budget, a fixed exchange rate would be preferable. A fixed exchange rate helps the government stand by its commitment not to monetize a future budget deficit. Any attempt to cover the fiscal shortfall by printing money will be readily observable by the loss of foreign exchange reserves, followed ultimately by the need for an official devaluation. Thus the monetization has consequences that are very visible. Once the public becomes accustomed to it, the daily market revaluation of the ruble under a floating exchange rate regime would be less dramatic, and hence more conducive to monetizing large budget deficits and maintaining upward pressure on prices in the Soviet Union.

With respect to the choice of an exchange rate, there is no formula to determine the correct rate. The usual modes of analysis involving purchasing power parity comparisons or comparisons based on macroeconomic models that reflect some history of supply and demand responses to price changes are likely to offer little guidance, particularly because the Soviet Union is facing extensive price adjustments. In the end, a decision must simply be made, informed by judgments about how Soviet citizens and enterprises are likely to respond to currency convertibility in the medium run. We believe the choice of exchange rate should allow the Soviet Union to run a slight surplus in the current account of the balance of payments. The objective here is not actually to run a surplus—for we believe the arrangements we propose would in fact encourage a net inflow of foreign capital for some years, thus permitting a current account deficit—but rather to give some encouragement to exports, which would be useful in the early period. If a surplus in fact emerges, consideration can then be given to appreciating the currency at a later time.

On the basis of general considerations, we would guess that the appropriate exchange rate at the outset might lie somewhere in the range of three to six rubles per U.S. dollar for the price level prevailing in the summer of 1990. After allowing for a likely doubling of the price level following price deregulation the rate would be five to ten rubles per U.S. dollar.[2] We emphasize that this choice requires a more informed judgment about the likely functioning of Soviet enterprises under currency convertibility than we are able to give. A number of calculations based on newly deregulated prices and some estimate of production efficiency in some of the key industries should be undertaken as a check on any proposed exchange rate.

In any case, in operational terms the ruble should probably not be fixed against the U.S. dollar alone, but rather against some combina-

2. The rates proposed here reflect the price level that would have prevailed had the price deregulation occurred in the early fall of 1990. Since then, there has been continual inflation and an increase in the money supply, which would make the appropriate rate higher, although we lack current data to pick a precise rate. In November 1990 a commercial rate of about 1.8 rubles per U.S. dollar was introduced, alongside the official rate of 0.6 and a tourist rate of 6 rubles to the U.S. dollar. (The tourist rate has since been devalued to about 27 rubles to the U.S. dollar). The foreign exchange reform of November 1, 1990, was accomplished by a Presidential Decree dated October 26, 1990; it introduced a number of changes in addition to the new commercial exchange rate. They abolished the differentiated foreign exchange coefficient system—effectively a set of multiple exchange rates that varied from commodity to commodity and even from enterprise to enterprise. Further, the decree raised the amounts of foreign currency that enterprises could retain from their export earnings, reduced some import taxes, and imposed export taxes on some raw materials. Although some of these measures are ones we agree with, we doubt they go far enough to enhance significantly the international competitiveness of Soviet industry. See *A Study of the Soviet Economy* (Paris: International Monetary Fund, World Bank, Organization for Economic Cooperation and Development, and European Bank for Reconstruction and Development, 1991), 1:422. (Footnote added by the editors.)

tion of the dollar and the European currency unit (Ecu), or even a basket of currencies that includes the Japanese yen. Most primary product markets in the world operate in dollars, and the Soviet Union will be selling heavily into those markets; on the other hand, most of the USSR's trade in manufactured goods will probably be with Europe, Japan, and the developing countries. One possibility would be to fix the ruble to the SDR, a synthetic unit of account comprising a weighted average of the U.S. dollar, the Japanese yen, the German mark, the British pound, and the French franc. An exchange rate in the range of five to ten rubles to one U.S. dollar translates roughly into an exchange rate of seven to fourteen rubles per SDR.

COMMERCIAL POLICY

An exchange rate aimed at a slight current account surplus cannot be determined without specifying what trade policy will be followed. As part of the move to markets and the restructuring of the Soviet economy—and parallel moves in a number of the Soviet Union's trading partners—the Soviet Union will shift in its trading relations from centralized bilateral bargaining over the exchange of goods to purchase and sale arrangements by enterprises. Under these circumstances, it is necessary to decide whether any preference is to be given to domestic over foreign goods within the Soviet economy.

We can draw upon an extensive analysis of the diverse experiences of economic development in many other countries.[3] The results are not decisive and they lend themselves to diverse interpretations, but an emerging consensus is that, particularly for a country with as developed an industrial structure as the Soviet Union, the best trade policy would involve a uniform tariff duty covering all imports. We recommend replacing all quantitative restrictions on imports with a uniform tariff on all imports in the neighborhood of 10 to 15 percent.[4] Tariffs are more evenhanded than quotas as a way

3. See, e.g., M. Michaely, D. Papageorgiou, and A. M. Choksi, *Liberalizing Foreign Trade in the Developing World* (Oxford: Basil Blackwell, 1991).

4. Note, however, that the *The Economy of the USSR* recommends an average 30 percent rate with a minimal degree of dispersion. *The Economy of the USSR: Summary*

of protecting domestic industry, and they avoid the administrative system that currently dominates and distorts Soviet foreign trade. In addition, tariffs can provide a source of valuable government revenue.

We can envisage the possibility that a few items might bear higher tariffs for the sake of additional revenue, or to discourage consumption, but introducing these exceptionally high tariffs should be strictly limited. In particular, when the aim is to discourage the consumption of luxury goods, excise taxes that apply to all luxury items, whether imported or domestically produced, should be applied rather than tariffs. The excise taxes would penalize both domestic production and importation of the goods whose consumption is to be discouraged and single out goods that can be taxed to raise substantial revenue.

An initial exchange rate of, say, ten rubles per SDR would provide substantial protection to most Soviet enterprises, since at that exchange rate imports would be expensive. We can envision, however, transitional tariffs higher than the uniform rate to avoid a sudden shock of competition to enterprises that are not initially competitive at the chosen exchange rate but have a prospect of becoming competitive in the long run. These transitional tariffs on products should be fixed at 20, 40, and 60 percent, depending on the calculations of initial competitiveness of Soviet enterprises by product and should decline over a period of five to seven years to the long-run uniform tariff mentioned earlier.

This schedule of tariff reduction should be fixed in advance and be nonnegotiable by the enterprises, although the pace of tariff reduction across all sectors might be accelerated or retarded for macroeconomic reasons. It is necessary to resist the inevitable pressures from enterprises to postpone tariff reductions. Of course, many products will not require any transitional tariffs, since the enterprises will be adequately competitive at the new exchange rate. Transitional tariffs should be used sparingly because they tend to perpetuate the principle of administrative control of prices.

and Recommendations, a study undertaken in response to a request by the Houston Summit (Washington, D.C.: International Monetary Fund, International Bank for Reconstruction and Development, Organization for Economic Cooperation and Development, and European Bank for Reconstruction and Development, 1990), 29.

The adoption of this commercial policy, along with the associated other changes we have recommended, would hasten the accession of the USSR to the General Agreement on Tariffs and Trade (GATT). Moreover, the USSR could make the limited purpose and duration of the transitional tariffs more credible to enterprises by committing itself to eliminate them as a condition for full accession to GATT.

Since most international trade takes place in intermediate products, raising the price of imports through tariffs also raises costs to domestic enterprises that purchase them. To avoid blunting the incentive to export at the new exchange rate, a system of import duty drawbacks should be introduced, whereby the tariff is rebated when a product containing an imported input is exported.

A large devaluation combined with transitional tariffs and currency convertibility raises the possible danger of large price increases within the Soviet Union. We believe this danger will be minimal in practice. In the Soviet Union, the problem at present is extensive shortages and a general absence of imported goods, especially consumer goods. The main impact of the introduction of convertibility and devaluation, therefore, will be to widen the purchasing opportunities of both households and enterprises, albeit at high prices. The real wage will actually rise on this account, not fall, as might be the case in an economy that was already extensively open to the world economy.[5]

There are two areas, however, where special attention should be paid to the impact of the currency devaluation on domestic prices. The first concerns oil and gas, the second grain and vegetable oils. The Soviet Union is a large exporter of the former and a large importer of the latter.

With domestic markets linked through trade to foreign markets and domestic prices determined by supply and demand, the domestic price of energy would rise to the world price, converted at the new exchange rate (see table 5.1). No doubt some increase in energy prices is desirable to encourage greater efficiency in the use of energy. The magnitude of the increase implied in our proposal, however, would be a major shock to many energy-consuming enterprises. In order to spread this shock over time, it would be desirable

5. For a simple model where this can happen, see D. Lipton and J. Sachs, "Creating a Market Economy in Eastern Europe: The Case of Poland," *Brookings Papers on Economic Activity*, no. 1 (Washington, D.C.: Brookings Institution, 1990), 90–98.

Table 5.1
USSR: Domestic and World Energy Prices (Wholesale Prices to Industrial
Consumers)

	1990 (ruble 0.58 per US$1)	1991[a] (ruble 1.80 per US$1)
Oil		
in rubles per m.t.	30.0	70.0
in US$1 per m.t.	52.6	38.9
in percent of world market price[b]	26.3	27.7
Coal		
in rubles per m.t.	27.0	50.0
in US$1 per m.t.	46.6	27.8
in percent of world market price[c]	93.1	55.6
Gas		
in rubles per th.cm.	25.0	50.0
in US$ per th.cm.	43.1	27.8
in percent of world market price[d]	33.7	21.4

Source: *The Economy of the USSR: Summary and Recommendations: A Study Undertaken in Response to a Request by the Houston Summit* (Washington, D.C.: International Monetary Fund, the International Bank for Reconstruction and Development, the Organization for Economic Cooperation and Development, and the European Bank for Reconstruction and Development, 1990), 42, and author's calculations.
[a]The ruble prices reflect officially announced new domestic energy prices for oil, coal, and gas, effective January 1, 1991.
[b]World market prices are assumed to be US$200 per metric ton (m.t.) in 1990 and US$140 per m.t. in 1991.
[c]World market prices are assumed to be US$50 per metric ton (m.t.) in 1990 and 1991.
[d]World market prices are assumed to be US$130 per thousand cubic meter (th.cm.) in 1990 and 1991.

to introduce a duty on exports of crude oil, gas, and petroleum products. The level of export duty should allow domestic energy prices to rise more than the general price level, but still shield the Soviet domestic economy somewhat from an immediate energy shock. The duty should be designed to decline over a five- to seven-year period. The export duty would raise revenue for the government, again facilitating stabilization.

Whether the duty should decline to zero, or remain positive over a longer term, would depend on technical judgments concerning the long-run supply of oil and gas in the Soviet Union. If this elasticity of supply is low, a permanent duty would be advisable to capture some of the rents on these extractive products. If by secondary recovery and other technical developments, however, the supply elasticity is high, then the duty should eventually disappear to avoid discouraging production of oil and gas.

It should be noted that this discussion could in principle apply to other mineral products, but oil and gas are clearly the most important and widely used and so the price shock might best be spread over time. This case is not nearly so compelling for other mineral inputs.

The second area of price concern is grain and vegetable oils, both highly visible consumption goods. To avoid a strong political reaction to price increases, it would be desirable to subsidize the import of these products for a transitional period, permitting lower domestic than world prices at the new exchange rate. These subsidies, which should also be phased out over time to encourage domestic production of grain and vegetable oils, would place a claim on the budget and would thus offset a part of the export taxes and the import tariff revenue. Furthermore, with domestic prices for grain and vegetable oils lower than those prevailing in the world market, some mechanism would be necessary to prevent the export of these products at domestic prices, for example, through the imposition of an export tax. Sugar might also be a candidate for this special treatment, but sugar is currently subject to special trading arrangements with Cuba, and we did not consider the future of those arrangements.

A convertible ruble at a realistic exchange rate will open up many new opportunities for profitable and socially productive exports. A key issue affecting the long-run benefits of convertibility for the economy is the response of enterprises to these potentially profitable export opportunities that will be opened up under the proposed arrangements. To what extent, and how soon, will enterprises develop new export markets? We feel that at any realistic exchange rate the current structure of wages paid to the Soviet Union's highly educated work force will make many manufacturing enterprises, for whom wages form the lion's share of costs, quite competitive (see table 5.2).

In some cases, especially with respect to primary products, enterprises will be able to sell into well-organized foreign markets. In

Table 5.2
Hourly Compensation in
Manufacturing (1990 Wage in US$,
index US$ = 100)

Germany	138
United States	100
France	98
Japan	82
Spain	72
Korea	24
Taiwan	24
Portugal	20
Singapore	19
Mexico	12
Poland	6
USSR	3

Source: Olivier Blanchard, Rudiger Dornbusch, Paul Krugman, Richard Layard, and Lawrence Summers, "Reform in Eastern Europe," Report of the WIDER World Economy Group (Cambridge, Mass., 1990, mimeographed), III-14. The figure for the USSR is calculated as follows. The average monthly wage of R257/mo. (See *PlanEcon Report,* vol. 6, no. 46–47, November 23, 1990, p. 8.) yields an average hourly wage of R1.48. At the tourist exchange rate (within the range recommended by this report) of R5.56/US$1 (Ibid., 29), this is 26.69 US¢/hour, and that is 1.76% of the U.S. average of US$15.20. The USSR rate is rounded up to 3 to allow for some wage adjustment after price deregulation. Calculations of the USSR wage rates is by the authors of this report.

The above numbers reflect the hourly compensation paid by enterprises and not the real income of workers. In Poland and the USSR, housing, medical care, and pensions are subsidized by the state, and income taxes are modest compared to many of the other countries in the table. Hence real income in these two countries is closer to the others than the above numbers suggest. For international competitiveness, however, it is the wages paid by enterprises that are significant.

other cases, enterprises will have to develop new marketing channels, which typically requires making expenditures abroad (except insofar as foreigners take the initiative and seek out Soviet products). In many cases, they will have to make domestic investments in quality control and in packaging. In all these cases, the response of potential exporters will be faster if they have access to credit, advanced on the basis of potential export orders. To this end, it is desirable that the new commercial banking system be sufficiently developed to evaluate and make selective credits for the purpose of developing quality export products and export markets. It is also essential, of course, to eliminate the requirement for firms to obtain an export license once price deregulation occurs. (In the absence of price deregulation, some restraint on exporting is necessary to prevent the export of goods that are priced below true costs; but once price deregulation occurs, it is desirable to encourage any firm that believes it can export profitably to make the attempt, except for products such as weapons and nuclear materials, where national security and foreign policy require export controls.)

Another factor that will influence the transition is the response of transportation and telecommunications. In many countries, these services are provided by state enterprises (the United States and Japan are major exceptions), and it is important that adequate services be made available to support the growth of exports.

FOREIGN CAPITAL

The flow of capital from abroad can be very important for the Soviet Union, especially in the form of foreign direct investment. The value of such inflows lies less in the foreign exchange they provide than in the technical, managerial, and marketing skills they can bring to the Soviet Union. The arrangements proposed here, a ruble convertible for current account transactions, including the remittance of profits, combined with a stable and modest import duty schedule, will be conducive to direct foreign investment. On the whole, foreign investment within this framework should be treated neither better nor worse than investment by domestic enterprises. Until such time as this convertibility is established, however, it is highly desirable to allow joint ventures to engage in ruble transactions that have recently been permitted in the Soviet Union. Preventing the regular use of rubles represents a strong impediment to the exercise of business judgment and business flexibility and thus inhibits foreign joint ventures in the Soviet Union.

Other forms of capital inflow are suppliers' credits, bank loans, and official loans of various kinds. The Soviet Union damaged its international reputation in early 1990 by allowing delays in meeting payments due on its obligations. It will take some time to reestablish its earlier reputation as a financially sound and reliable country. On the other hand, foreign sellers will have to learn to evaluate the credit standing of individual Soviet enterprises when they engage in transactions with them. Enterprise transactions will no longer be

Table 5.3
USSR: External Debt and Reserves (In Billions of U.S. Dollars)

	1985	1986	1987	1988	1989	1990 (estimates)
External debt[a]	28.9	31.4	39.2	43.0	54.0	52.2[b]
Short-term external debt	6.9	7.4	8.6	11.2	17.7	10.0[b]
External debt service[c]	—	7.8	8.8	8.2	9.4	13.4
(As a percentage of goods and services)[d]	(—)	(27.7)	(26.5)	(23.1)	(24.2)	(33.0)
Foreign exchange reserves[e]	12.9	14.7	14.1	15.3	14.7	5.1

Source: *Economy of the USSR*, 50.
[a]External debt contracted or guaranteed by the Vneshekonombank.
[b]As of June 1990.
[c]Total debt service on debt contracted or guaranteed by the Vneshekonombank, excluding repayments of short-term debt.
[d]In convertible currencies.
[e]Bank of International Settlements data excluding end-1990, which are staff projections.

supported by the credit standing of the government, either in their corporatized or ultimately in their privatized forms.

By objective standards, however, the existing external debt of the Soviet Union, amounting to around 50 billion dollars, or 40 billion dollars net of reserves other than gold, is not high given the size and potential of the Soviet economy (see table 5.3). With the right re-structuring measures, the Soviet Union has substantial capacity to borrow abroad on commercial terms. At present, the external hard currency debt modestly exceeds hard currency exports, a burden that is not high by international standards, and one that will be lowered by an expansion of exports.

In addition, the USSR will have access to officially guaranteed export credits from other countries. (In January 1991, the Bush administration was working to remove a statutory obstacle to such export credits from the United States.) It may also have access to long-term lending from the World Bank after it is able to join that institution (this is conditional on membership in the International Monetary Fund). Whether the Soviet Union actually has access to World Bank loans will depend on a calculation of per capita income in the Soviet Union after the price and exchange rate adjustments have taken place. (World Bank lending is permitted only to countries with a per capita income on World Bank calculations below around US$4100, a standard the USSR is likely to meet.)

Concessional financial aid to the Soviet Union is unlikely, except possibly from Germany, because there are many low-income countries around the world that have claims to the limited amount of such aid that is available. But, of course, concessional aid is influenced by political factors within each donor country.

In a setting that involves the proposals we make here, however, it is possible that the Soviet Union could raise a stabilization loan in support of the move to convertibility, to lend confidence that the early days of convertibility can be sustained. This loan could come from the International Monetary Fund if the Soviet Union were a member, or it could come from the central banks or governments of the major industrial countries. It is the nature of such a loan that it will not be used if all goes well.

CONCLUSION

The proposals outlined here, while bold, make the most sense for the USSR in the context of the goal of a major restructuring of the economy to bring it closer to world standards. A number of proposals for more limited action have been made. We have not examined all of them, but we find two classes of limited action markedly inferior to our recommendations. The first is a move toward dollarization of the Soviet economy. This involves enlarging the scope for Soviet citizens to engage in transactions in dollars or other hard currency within the Soviet Union and having access to special shops with imported goods. Such an action will hasten internal flight from the ruble, and it is costly to the nation to have to earn through exports the hard currency used in domestic transactions. Introduction of general convertibility for the ruble, at a depreciated exchange rate, would be superior on both counts.

The second class of proposals concerns creation of a parallel ruble, a so-called hard ruble, convertible into foreign currency or gold, that would circulate alongside the existing ruble. If such a development were successful, it would partially avoid the need to earn foreign currency for use in circulation within the Soviet Union. But it, too, would hasten the collapse of the usefulness of the ordinary ruble. Its introduction would also create political resentment toward those relatively few who had access to the hard ruble. Again, a bold movement to convertibility of the ordinary ruble would be preferable.

Much of the economic reform plan outlined in this book and summarized in the policy memorandum (chapter 2) will be painful and politically difficult. Opening the economy is no exception. Indeed, even in market economies more developed than the USSR, trade liberalization demands great political will, as the current round of GATT negotiations and the debates over trade liberalization in some of the newly industrialized countries demonstrate.

Still, we feel that postponing this part of the reform to a later, more tranquil period would be a mistake. It is better for the Soviet economy to undergo a painful adjustment to a new set of relative prices only once. Furthermore, domestic monopolies will be subjected to foreign competition, limiting their ability to raise prices, and, more importantly, setting a standard they will eventually have to meet to stay in business. Finally, Soviet workers will at last be able to buy quantities of high-quality foreign goods that are not administratively limited, albeit at high prices. This should yield, we suggest, an incentive effect that could be a significant stimulus to their productivity.

Chapter Six

Moderating the Social Costs of Unemployment

Wil Albeda

Our policy memorandum (chapter 2) proposes that the social costs of unemployment that will accompany the transition to a market economy be moderated by unemployment benefits. The first part of this chapter elaborates on the unemployment problem. The second part goes beyond chapter 2 to consider longer-term measures that deal with persistent unemployment. The final section examines the difficult questions of wages and collective bargaining.

UNEMPLOYMENT

The Soviet Labor Force

The labor force of the Soviet Union in 1990 was about 140 million people according to official statistics—about 133 million in the civilian sector and 7 to 9 million in the defense sector.[1] The labor force is defined here in the Western sense as including all those employed and all those seeking work. In 1990, open unemployment was minimal, although there was said to be significant disguised unemployment, that is, workers making at best minor contributions to output.

Note: This chapter is based on discussions of the study group on Labor Markets and Employment and has benefited from the collaboration of Aleksandr Shokhin of the Foreign Ministry of the USSR.

1. Estimates based on information provided by the USSR State Committee for Statistics supplied to the IIASA Conference on Economic Reform and Integration, Sopron, Hungary, July–August 1990.

Table 6.1
Estimates of Unemployment with Varying Transitions to a Market Economy

Transition Condition	Long-Term Unemployment	Short-Term Unemployment	Total	Unemployment Rate
	(in millions of workers)			(in percentages)
Modest measures	0.4	3.3	3.70	2.8
Shatalin plan	6.0	6.0	12.00	9.0
Shock version			35.00	26.3

Sources: The first and third entries come from Soviet government studies, and the data were supplied by our Soviet colleagues at the Sopron meetings. The second row is from *Transition to the Market* (Report of a Working Group formed by a joint decision of M. S. Gorbachev and B. N. Yeltsin, Moscow, Cultural Initiative Foundation, 1990), chart following p. 75.

Estimates vary widely concerning future patterns of unemployment and depend on assumptions about the extent and speed of the transition to the market economy. The range is recorded in table 6.1.

Unemployment in a Transition to a Market Economy

The highest estimate of unemployment in table 6.1 is an unrealistic overestimate. This estimate assumes that most of the disguised unemployment would be converted to open unemployment; that is, it presumes that workers making a contribution to production less than their wage would be immediately fired when enterprises receive the right to do so and are under market pressures and hard budget constraints. But this estimate ignores the fact that with price deregulation the revenue of enterprises will rise and hence so will workers' marginal revenue productivity. With higher revenues enterprises will find that it pays to keep some of the presently disguised unemployed on their payrolls. More significantly, this estimate ignores job creation by new enterprises, particularly those in the small business service sector. The importance of this factor is borne out by the fact that cooperatives, which had only a negligible share of non-agricultural employment in May 1987, reached 5.2 million employees in 1990, once the laws restricting their activities were liberalized.[2]

2. *The Economy of the USSR: Summary and Recommendations*, a study undertaken in response to a request by the Houston Summit (Washington, D.C.: International Monetary Fund, International Bank for Reconstruction and Development, Organization for Economic Cooperation and Development, and European Bank for Reconstruction and Development, 1990), 26.

Among the three estimates in table 6.1, we consider that of the *Shatalin Report* to be the best estimate for the reforms proposed in our policy memorandum. We note, however, that the unemployment rate of 9 percent is almost twice the 5 percent unemployment rate experienced in Poland during the first year of the transition to a market economy.[3] A 9 percent unemployment rate is high but not far beyond that experienced by market economies. Even after several years of economic growth, the unemployment rate in much of Europe is about 9 percent. Nevertheless, we warn the reader that there is considerable uncertainty in this estimate. Unemployment could easily be 6 or 12 percent instead of the 9 percent shown in table 6.1.

Frictional and Long-Term Unemployment

Table 6.1 identifies two quite different kinds of unemployment— frictional (or what is called short-term structural unemployment in chapter 4) and long-term unemployment. These two types have quite different social consequences and policy solutions.

Frictional unemployment is a necessary feature of a market economy. Enterprises must be free to fire workers as the demand for their products changes and as productivity gains allow them to produce with fewer workers. At the same time, other enterprises whose demand is increasing will be hiring workers. Frictional unemployment is the necessary bridge between enterprises that are contracting and those that are expanding their employment. (Frictional unemployment also serves as a check on wage demands.) The necessary amount of frictional unemployment will vary with the way in which labor markets are organized. In the United States at present a 4 percent unemployment rate is considered a necessary frictional amount; in Japan, 2 percent seems to suffice. The estimate in table 6.1 from the *Shatalin Report* that half of the unemployment will be frictional seems reasonable.

The social consequences of frictional employment are tolerable and the policy measures required relatively simple. Almost all market economies have a system of unemployment benefits similar to

3. Olivier Blanchard, Rudiger Dornbusch, Paul Krugman, Richard Layard, and Lawrence Summers, "Reform in Eastern Europe," Report of the WIDER World Economy Group (Cambridge, Mass., 1990, mimeographed), III-23.

that proposed in the policy memorandum. The level of benefits should be less than the previous wage, decline with the duration of unemployment, and be paid for a limited period to give recipients an incentive to seek new jobs. In most industrial economies up to 85 percent of job seekers find employment without relying on the public employment service. Information about openings comes from newspaper advertisements, networks of friends, and private employment agencies.

Unemployment Benefits

The *Shatalin Report* proposes a benefit level of 70 percent of the average month's wage during the first three months of unemployment, 60 percent during the next three months, and 50 percent during the last six months.[4] The benefit period is limited to twelve months.

Although such a proposal conforms to the criteria listed in our policy memorandum (chapter 2), it may be that the Soviet Union cannot afford earnings-related benefits in the immediate future. The alternative is a flat-rate benefit that provides a minimum level of support for all unemployed irrespective of their previous earnings. Flat benefits are simpler to administer, an important consideration when the detail and accuracy of records of earnings are low and the number of unemployed may be high.

Limitations on the duration of benefits is important. In the United States, the duration of unemployment compensation is limited to six months. The dangers of unlimited unemployment benefits are illustrated by the Spanish provinces of Andalusia and Estremadura where indefinite part-time unemployment benefits support unemployment rates of over 25 percent.

Market economies often finance unemployment benefits by a special payroll tax on employers with the proceeds segregated in a separate fund from which benefits are paid. Such financing seems desirable, yet as *The Economy of the USSR* observes, high levels of unemployment may require additional financing from general gov-

4. *Transition to the Market: A Report of a Working Group Formed by M. S. Gorbachev and B. N. Yeltsin,* Part 1: *The Concept and Program* (Moscow: Cultural Initiative Foundation, 1990) (*Shatalin Report*), 79.

ernment revenues.[5] Given the geographic diversity of the Soviet Union, unemployment benefits might be best administered by local governments.

We understand that the employment law passed in January 1991 by the Supreme Soviet provides for unemployment benefits, together with retraining and public works employment. It appears to implement the main outlines of our proposal.[6]

LABOR MARKET INSTITUTIONS AND LONG-TERM UNEMPLOYMENT

Definition and Incidence of Long-Term Employment

Long-term unemployment is defined as that which leaves workers jobless for more than a year. Such unemployment is devastating for both the individual and society. Table 6.1 indicates that six million workers might suffer long-term unemployment in the transition to a market economy.

The experience of market economies with long-term unemployment varies considerably. The increase in unemployment in Europe in the eighties was due partly to the duration of unemployment rather than to an increase in the number of workers who lost their jobs. In the United States, 2 percent of workers lose their jobs each month but remain unemployed on average for two to three months. In France and Germany, only 0.3 percent of the workers lose their jobs each month but half of those remain unemployed for over a year. In Italy, Belgium, and Ireland over two-thirds of the unemployed have been out of work for more than a year. Sweden, Canada, and the United States are at the other extreme where only about 7 percent of the unemployed have been so for over twelve months.

The extent of frictional as opposed to long-term unemployment depends in part on macroeconomic policies and in part on the behavior of workers and enterprises. We cannot fully explain why

5. *Economy of the USSR*, 33.

6. See V. Shirokov, "Protection against Unemployment," *Pravda*, January 25, 1991, 1, translated in *FBIS Daily Report: Soviet Union*, January 29, 1991, FBIS-SOV-91-019, 38–39.

some market economies have greater long-term unemployment than others, but there appear to be two contributing factors:

1. The level of unemployment benefits relative to average wages and the duration of such benefits, an issue which has already been discussed.
2. The extent and efficiency of such labor market institutions as employment services, which match up unemployed with employers, and retraining programs, which provide workers with skills that are in demand. The goal should be to have labor market institutions that minimize long-term unemployment at a reasonable cost to governmental budgets.

Employment and Retraining Services

To be efficient, employment services need information about the current conditions in the labor market. (Such information is also valuable for decisions on other aspects of economic policy.)The usual way to measure unemployment is through household surveys that record as unemployed all those seeking work. We think that this is the right way despite the difficulties of measuring the willingness to work.

In the USSR, employment legislation defines the unemployed as those "able-bodied citizens of working age who do not have any earnings for reasons beyond their control, who are actually looking for work, will undergo retraining, and who are registered at an employment agency."[7]

Such a definition may be appropriate for determining eligibility for unemployment benefits, but it is a misleading way to measure unemployment. Individuals who are not entitled to unemployment benefits will not register, and others may forego registration to avoid being entangled in the bureaucracy.

A market economy also needs detailed information from enterprises concerning their past trends of employment by skill and wage levels and their future hiring plans. Since labor markets are localized, data must be collected by cities or regions on a current basis. The sample survey method, this time covering enterprises, seems the best way to collect such information.

7. Quotation supplied by the Soviet experts at the IIASA Conference in Sopron, Hungary, July–August 1990.

Labor market statistics are needed for the efficient operation of the central institution of an active labor market policy—a governmental employment service. Yet, although this employment service needs access to labor market statistics, it need not collect the data itself. A governmental employment service has three functions: (1) administering the unemployment compensation system, (2) matching the unemployed with job openings, and (3) operating retraining programs.

In matching the unemployed with job openings, the employment service will need the cooperation of employers. It should have close links with employers and trade unions and should not focus only on problem workers, otherwise employers shun it as a source of only low-quality workers. As part of the employment function, it should provide counseling to those who register with it.

A public employment service can be supplemented by private employment agencies that match up workers and employers for fees paid by either the worker or the employer. Such private agencies have proved their worth in many market economies. According to the International Labour Organisation Convention employment agencies should be public and free of charge for both employers and workers. This provision, originally designed to eliminate abuses by private agencies at the turn of the century, is now commonly seen as outdated. Several countries have a system of licenses for private agencies that provide an adequate check on abuses.

An employment service can also serve as a major weapon against long-term unemployment by providing retraining. The unemployed in retraining programs would receive allowances, thus providing for their needs after their employment benefits have expired. Although in some cases the service might establish its own schools or contract with existing ones, creating a large system of retraining centers seems inadvisable for several reasons. Such a system is not likely to coordinate well with the demands of enterprises for particular skills or offer the quality of training needed. Vocational education in the USSR already suffers from these difficulties. A system of training centers would be expensive and inflexible. Finally, bringing the unemployed together in centers adds to their feeling of exclusion from society's mainstream.

It seems preferable to emphasize retraining by enterprises that would use classroom and on-the-job training. Such retraining is more responsive to current employer demands for personnel, is cheaper and more flexible, and brings the unemployed into the world of work. Of course, enterprises would need grants to cover the allowances for trainees and the costs of training itself. Experience in the United States shows that such programs must be carefully monitored to prevent enterprises from substituting lower-cost trainees for regular employees in their operations.

Public Employment

Retraining is likely to be inappropriate for some of the long-term unemployed. Thus, consideration might also be given to using employment in local government to support the long-term unemployed. Again safeguards must be developed to prevent such employment from degenerating into disheartening busywork and from undermining the quality of public service activities, destroying the morale of regular employees, or raising significantly the cost of local government services. Thus road building is a poor candidate for using the long-term unemployed for it requires advance planning, a high level of skills, and capital-intensive equipment. Keeping public parks tidy or cleaning streets may be more appropriate work for unemployed unskilled workers. Such employment should be considered a last resort in providing for the long-term unemployed.

Retraining and public employment, however, are preferable to supporting the long-term unemployed by welfare. The experience in Europe is that long-term idleness fosters a culture of permanent unemployment, complete dependence on welfare benefits, and (if benefits are low) poverty. The best policy, of course, is to operate the economy in such a way that only a few become the long-term unemployed.

In contrast to an unemployment benefit system, job matching services, retraining programs, and public employment policies need not be in place when price deregulation and the other reforms occur. Long-term unemployment will take time to develop. Still, planning should begin before the problem of long-term unemployment becomes acute. Such systems might be best operated by local governments since the extent of the problem and the suitable measures will vary by locality. Localities will need financial help from the republics

or the union since some may be particularly hard hit if they specialize in industries with weak demand in a market economy.

A market system also needs to provide for individuals who are
outside of the labor force—the aged, the disabled, and the single
parents with small children. The Soviet Union has in place a comprehensive pension system. With price deregulation, frequent adjustments in pensions and related transfers to those outside the labor
market will be needed to insure the continuation of a minimum
standard of living for these individuals.

Labor Mobility

Labor mobility is important to the equity and efficiency of the
labor market. One of the inherent protections for workers in a market economy is the ability to change jobs if another employer offers
better wages and working conditions. Labor mobility is also important for economic efficiency, for the movement of labor allows enterprises to expand or contract their production. Conditions favoring
mobility also reduce unemployment by making it easier for those
discharged to find new jobs.

Several features of the Soviet economy reduce labor mobility.
First, official permission is still required to live in many cities, although residence regulation has recently become more flexible. Until freedom to move from city to city to seek employment is well
established, there cannot be a Western style labor market.

Second, enterprises compensate their workers partially in kind
through assigning housing and access to special stores, medical
clinics, and vacation travel. Such privileges vary widely among enterprises and are lost by switching jobs, particularly by accepting jobs in
the small business sector. The labor market would function better if
such compensation in kind were gradually converted to cash
payments.

Third, housing is scarce everywhere and often assigned by enterprises or the local government. Waiting lists for apartments are long.
Workers are loathe to move, given the uncertainties of finding housing. We touched briefly on the creation of a housing market in
chapter 3, but we would emphasize that a competitive housing market is important for an efficient labor market.

Finally, enterprises have recently taken upon themselves the task

of distributing food and other consumer goods. The current breakdown in retail distribution has made this function a key one for many
employees. We hope that price deregulation will allow enterprises to
stop serving as retailers to their workers.

WAGES AND COLLECTIVE BARGAINING

Wages with Price Deregulation

Nominally, the USSR still retains a system of wage rates that sets
the monthly salary of each occupation with variations by industry
and region. Yet enterprises have increasingly bypassed this system as
they have been given more freedom to set wages and give bonuses.

Gradually the USSR is attaining a labor market, although a much
distorted and restricted one. Workers are technically free to change
their place of employment, but geographic mobility is restricted by
the need for residence permits and by the frequent unavailability of
housing. Labor shortages in some enterprises and localities have
tended to push wages up, reflecting the limitations on worker
mobility.

Our proposals for price deregulation and corporatization could
increase the current wage inflation. Corporatization is the call for
enterprise independence that would include managerial determination of wages. Free collective bargaining also follows from enterprise
independence. In the current inflationary climate, such freedom
could lead to significant wage increases that would fuel an inflationary fire. Price deregulation will add to the problem, for there is no
avoiding a one-time jump in prices. If wages rise to match price
increases, hyperinflation could result, with prices and wages chasing
one another at an increasing rate. Hyperinflation would convert an
economic crisis into a disaster.

Incomes Policies

During the transition, government control of wages—an incomes
policy—may be necessary. This is particularly so because eliminating
repressed inflation requires a reduction in real wages. That has been
the experience in Poland, for example, where real wages declined
sharply in the first three months after price deregulation. One must

be cautious, however, about overestimating the effect of a decline in real wages. Suppose the price of meat doubles. At the previous low price, it could seldom be found in state shops and was freely available only in the second economy markets at prices two to ten times the official ones. Once the official prices increase, prices in these second economy markets are also likely to fall. The changes in the official price index, which is used to calculate real wages, will then overstate the decline in real wages. This problem of the price index is described in greater detail in chapter 4.

Macroeconomic Reforms

The first line of defense against inflationary wage increases lies in two general economic reform measures. Placing enterprises under hard budget constraints by eliminating subsidies and tightening credit will force enterprises to limit their wage increases to remain financially viable. These constraints should not be weakened by accepting pleas for subsidies and easy credit because wages have increased. Establishing a market system will restrict the ability of individual enterprises to raise wages. Thus the market system has a built-in mechanism to control wages and hence hyperinflation.

Macroeconomic stability is the other essential defense against wage inflation. If the state runs a significant deficit or provides easy credit, it will increase the money supply, adding to demand and permitting enterprises to raise prices and thus wages. The wage increases will raise costs, providing a further need for price increases. The process will continue as long as a significant budget deficit and easy credit continue to add to the money supply. This process is the essence of hyperinflation.

The Dangers of Indexation

We think our proposals, that enterprises be self-financing and that macroeconomic stability be achieved, will reduce the risk of hyperinflation. But these safeguards can be destroyed by a governmental requirement of wage indexation—that is, a mandate that enterprises increase the wages they pay employees by the amount of the increase in the official price index. Full indexation would mean that if the price index doubles with deregulation, enterprises would have to double their wages.

The only way wages can be doubled is if prices are increased sharply. Higher prices, in turn, mean that either the economy plunges into a recession, since at higher prices the goods cannot be sold, or the government adds to demand by running a deficit and providing easy credit. Thus full indexation has a tendency to result in recession or hyperinflation. Gorbachev's Presidential Guidelines recognize the danger of full indexation and call for 50 to 70 percent indexation of wages (with the higher degree of indexation intended for pensions and family allowances tied to the price of a minimum consumer basket).[8] As noted earlier, even such partial indexation could overcompensate for real income changes, because changes in the official price index do not reflect changes in second economy prices or the availability of goods.

Thus, partial mandatory indexation, even if measured correctly, will add to inflation. We strongly recommend against it. In an inflationary situation, the indexed increases become the starting point or floor in determining wage increases, particularly in collective bargaining. The danger of mandatory indexation is apparent from the history of the many countries that have tried it.

We would not change the present tariff system of wages, but we would not index them either.[9] Thus the tariff wages would in effect become a minimum wage system. It does not seem prudent to endure the controversy that altering the tariff system would provoke. With inflation, tariff wages would no longer be very meaningful.

A policy of price increases without mandatory indexation will be politically unpopular; so much so that it could preclude price deregulation. People fear price deregulation; they wonder how they will ever get even enough food at market prices. We are in no position to evaluate the gain in support for price deregulation that partial indexation might provide relative to the problems it poses. From

8. *Economy of the USSR*, 24.

9. The tariff system is a schedule of wage rates set by the State Committee on Labor (*Goskomtrud*) for each occupation, differentiated by branch of industry and by geographic region. It is applied to state employees only (and therefore not to *kolkhoz* workers) and is supplemented by a system of bonus payments. See S. Oxenstierna, *From Labour Shortage to Unemployment? The Soviet Labour Market in the 1980s*, Swedish Institute for Social Research, no. 12 (Stockholm: Swedish Institute for Social Research, 1990), 125–34.

the viewpoint of economic policy, indexation is dangerous. The less of it the better.

Incomes Policy and Large Enterprises

As chapter 3 indicates, the monopoly of a large number of products will be a significant problem with price deregulation and corporatization. Such enterprises will not face hard budget constraints and so will escape one of the constraints against excessive wage increases. Experience in market economies has shown that when a monopoly is combined with powerful and aggressive unions, inflationary wage increases can occur,creating two significant problems. Large wage increases in the monopolized sector can lead to pressures to make comparable increases elsewhere in the economy, thus fueling the inflation. Converting monopoly profits into wages also can slow down the process by which high profits attract entry and thus competition, which we rely upon to eliminate the monopoly.

For large enterprises, then, wage controls may be necessary, particularly if the one plant/one enterprise rule set forth in chapter 3 leaves a substantial number of monopolies. Since identifying monopolies is extremely difficult, wage controls should be applied to all large enterprises—all those with over 10,000 employees, for example. We emphasize, however, that an antimonopoly policy is of crucial importance as a supplement to such wage controls, and it will eventually eliminate the need for them.

What form might these wage controls take? Experience has shown that wage regulation is best formulated as a control on the average rate of increase in wages for the enterprise as a whole. This is preferable to controlling the average rate of increase of total wage payment—the wages fund. Controlling the increase in total wages, a form of control already tried in the Soviet Union, penalizes enterprises whose output is expanding and thus need more workers, while it favors those whose output is contracting and thus are laying off workers.

Controlling the increase in average wages allows the enterprise flexibility in distributing wage increases among workers. Such control is better than regulating increases for each grade of labor, a method that reduces the freedom of the enterprise to adjust wages.

Control by labor grade is more difficult to administer and can easily be evaded by promoting workers to higher grades.[10]

The controls should not constitute an absolute prohibition on above-average wages, but rather should provide for a tax on above-average increases in order to penalize the enterprises that provide inflationary increases. Such a tax would recognize that above-average wage increases impose costs on the economy.

We lack sufficient information even to guess at the correct level of the tax. Similarly, we lack information concerning the proper rate of increase for average wages, but the rate of increase in the unregulated competitive sector should be one guide; another would be the economy-wide average rate of increase in productivity.

We do caution against allowing enterprises with a high rate of growth in labor productivity to give higher wage increases. Productivity growth varies widely among industries, mainly for technological reasons unrelated to the efforts of workers. In market economies there is a weak correlation across industries between the rate of growth of wages and the rate of growth of productivity. This is because competition in the product market forces productivity gains to be passed on to the consumers as lower prices and competition in the labor market forces enterprises to pay similar wages to attract and hold workers.

We are mindful that incomes policies have seldom been successful in the United States and Western Europe. Only when trade unions were willing to cooperate with employers and the government to limit wages and thus inflation did incomes policies enjoy some success. These conditions for cooperation are now lacking in the Soviet Union. As a result, establishing even the limited incomes policies suggested here may use up too much of the government's limited stock of goodwill. That is why we advance the notion of wage regula-

10. The above statements are based on the experience of market economies with income policies. We note, however, that in the context of centrally planned economies, control of average wage increases has not proved to be an effective instrument for wage control. Managers, with the tacit agreement of trade unions, have recruited low-paid employees from such groups as students and pensioners to depress the average wage of their firm and thus permit wage increases for their regular employees above the target amount. Such low-paid fake employees were, in effect, hidden unemployed. This is clearly the experience in Hungary.

tion for large enterprises in a tentative fashion and give incomes policy less emphasis in the policy memorandum (chapter 2).

The other danger of an incomes policy is that it may justify doing less to achieve macroeconomic stability and enforce hard budget constraints for enterprises. It is essential to recognize that an incomes policy is a complement to and not a substitute for enterprise self-financing and tough macroeconomic measures.

Collective Bargaining

Soviet workers have been accustomed to state-controlled trade unions. With the relaxation of controls, it is understandable that workers now prefer unions that are aggressive, independent, and close to them. New unions have developed, often in the form of strike committees.

The difficulty with the rapid rise of collective bargaining is that it takes longer to develop independent employers than independent unions. Our proposals for corporatization are intended to create such employers and a market-oriented system of collective bargaining that is both independent and responsible, with workers and employers both pursuing their conflicting interests.

Strikes are a normal and necessary phenomenon with free collective bargaining. It does happen, however, that a strike can shut down an entire industry that is essential to the functioning of society. No economy can allow itself be held hostage in this way. For such cases it may be necessary to have compulsory arbitration, perhaps through a labor court.

Existing market economies have a wide range of collective bargaining institutions, demonstrating that a market economy is consistent with a variety of forms of union organization. Some collective bargaining is highly centralized (Sweden and Austria); others are not (the United States and the United Kingdom). Furthermore, the extent of unionization varies from 20 percent of the labor force (United States) to 80 percent (Sweden and Austria).

One system of labor relations for the entire Soviet Union seems unlikely and is neither desirable nor necessary. Different republics may pursue different policies and develop different institutions. The European Common Market has shown that a variety of collective bargaining institutions are consistent with a single integrated market economy.

As long as the Soviet Union lacks some form of political pluralism, trade unions will feel tempted to play the role of a surrogate political party. This will compound the difficulties of collective bargaining since union demands will extend to political questions that enterprises cannot resolve. Unions, like enterprises, are likely to look to the government for solutions to problems. As long as the transition to an effective market economy has not been initiated, every economic question will retain its political character. This factor alone makes the development of responsible collective bargaining difficult. We hope the measures proposed here will reduce the politicization of economic decisions, including those affecting wages.

Chapter Seven

Privatization and the Creation of a Commercial Banking System

Kimio Uno

Privatization and the establishment of a commercial banking system are the most difficult phases in the transition to a market economy. In other economies the institutions of private property have evolved over centuries; the problem in the Soviet Union is to condense that history into a few years. To compound the problem, some of the issues have no commonly accepted solutions among Western economists. Furthermore, existing market economies offer a variety of models from which to choose, particularly for the ownership of large, capital-intensive corporations.

Corporatization—making the large, state enterprises managerially independent and self-financing yet allowing the state to continue to own corporate shares—was described in chapter 3 as a relatively quick way of creating firms consistent with a market system. The ultimate goal, however, is privatization. The first part of this chapter examines how privatization of corporations might be accomplished.

The banking system is also to be left in state hands temporarily, but the banks are to begin making loans on a commercial basis and to follow a tight credit policy. The ultimate goal is a privatized banking system with a clear separation between central and commercial banks. The second part of the report examines how this might be done.

Note: This chapter is based on the discussions of the study group on Capital Markets and Privatization that met in Sopron, Hungary, in July–August 1990. It was subsequently revised in response to comments by the participants and by chairmen of the other study groups. The author is grateful for the comments Benjamin M. Friedman, Leonid M. Grigoriev, Robert E. Litan, and Merton J. Peck made on an earlier draft.

In each instance—with the large, state enterprises and the banking system—the use of the state as an owner is designed as an interim
measure, chosen simply because that appears the only way to achieve
quickly the market-oriented institutions that the D-day deregulation
requires. It is not a completely satisfactory solution but preferable to
delaying reforms until the longer process of privatization can be
achieved.

Privatization is necessary, however, because only private owners
can establish an enduring basis for self-financing and managerial
independence. Private owners have a vested interest in the long-run
financial success of the firm. Their vested interest, in turn, makes
private owners guardians of the managerial and financial independence of their firms in a way that the state as an owner cannot match,
as history has demonstrated. Private ownership creates a wall between the enterprise and the state, thereby making the enterprise
responsive to the market.

Of course, in market economies around the world some state
enterprises have functioned well. These are the exceptions and they
occur in largely privatized market economies with strong business
traditions, hardly the situation in the Soviet Union. The more common history of state enterprises is that they become subject to political pressures that divert them from responding to profit incentives,
which is what the market system requires. The 1980s have been
characterized by major actions to convert state enterprises into private corporations. The most notable examples are Margaret
Thatcher's privatization of a large number of nationalized British
enterprises and the very similar process in Japan.

Privatization as a goal of Soviet economic reform was universally
accepted by the economists, from both East and West, who participated in the deliberations leading to this book. Discussions of the
ways to achieve privatization efficiently and equitably generated
more controversy.

PRIVATIZATION OF LARGE STATE ENTERPRISES

We focus on the largest four hundred nonmilitary industrial enterprises that are currently under the jurisdiction of the all-union
ministries. These each have assets of more than 200 million rubles

(see table 7.1).[1] In addition there are two hundred similarly large enterprises engaged in military production. They present special problems because their customers are primarily the state. We set them aside in order to focus on those that are potentially more market oriented.

We focus on these very large enterprises because they present the most difficult questions of privatization. At the other extreme are the small enterprises engaged in light manufacturing, trade, and services. There are thousands of such enterprises. (Table 7.2 presents the size of retail shops; some are very large, but most are small.) These small-scale enterprises can be privatized by public auctions or leased to workers with eventual right of sale, as discussed in chapter 3. That chapter also discusses agriculture and the natural monopolies in such sectors as transportation and communication. Since natural monopolies would be regulated even with privatization, their turn should come late in the privatization process. Agriculture lends itself to privatization in ways similar to small businesses and the service sector.

Of course, there are many medium-sized enterprises, as table 7.1 indicates. Our comments regarding the largest four hundred apply to the largest ones in this middle range, while our comments on the small enterprises apply to the smallest ones in the middle group. Experience will determine where the line should be drawn between the two categories.

Preconditions

Privatization of large enterprises requires several preconditions.

1. *Ownership.* The ownership of each enterprise must be clearly assigned to a level of government—the union, the republic, or the locality. There could be, however, a division of the stock of a particular corporation among levels, but there must be one level of government that controls the privatization process to avoid disputes between levels that will slow down the process. The decision

1. Sergei Aleksashenko and Leonid Grigoriev, "Privatization and Capital Markets" (Paper presented at the IIASA Conference on Economic Reform and Integration, Sopron, Hungary, July–August 1990).

Table 7.1
Size Distribution of Industrial Enterprises in the Soviet Union

Assets of Enterprises (in millions of rubles)	Approximate Number of Enterprises	Total Assets in the Size Class (in billions of rubles)	Level of Governmental Supervision
Over 200	600	360	USSR
50–200	1,600	165	USSR
10–50	6,230	147	Repub./USSR
Less than 10	38,400	95	Repub./Local

Source: Aleksashenko and Grigoriev, "Privatization and Capital Markets."
Note: The net value of fixed capital is used to determine assets.

concerning which level of government should be the initial owner of a particular enterprise is a political one. The important point is that the decision regarding ownership of a corporation be made clearly and permanently in order for privatization to proceed.

2. *Demonopolization.* Many branches of the Soviet economy are highly concentrated, so the problem of monopoly power will be pervasive upon deregulation. Demonopolization should precede privatization, since otherwise shareholders in firms with undue market power will attempt to block procompetitive policies. Moreover, the privatization process itself will be hampered by uncertainty over an anticipated antimonopoly program.

3. *Ownership assurance* and *transferability of assets.* Citizens who hold shares in the newly privatized enterprises must believe that these assets will not be reappropriated or otherwise rendered worthless. They must have free and clear title to any assets they own, and they must have the unrestricted right to resell these assets to anyone who places a higher value on them.

4. *Bankruptcy law.* A bankruptcy law must accompany the privatization process. With the establishment of the principle that enterprises must cover their costs by the revenue from their operations, there is no reason to allow enterprises that are losing money to survive. It is worth pointing out that in the Soviet Union today, not only is there no private equity, but there is no genuine private debt either. What appear to be debts on the books are simply accumulated transfers from one state entity to another. Provisions for enforcing

Table 7.2
Size of State Retail Shops

Floor Space (square meters)	Percentage of Shops
Up to 30	17.4
31–50	20.5
51–100	27.3
101–400	28.1
401–1,000	5.9
1,001–3,500	0.7
Over 3,500	0.1
Total	100.0

Source: Aleksashenko and Grigoriev,
"Privatization and Capital Markets."

contracts and providing damages in the event of nonperformance must also accompany privatization.

5. *Accounting practice.* In view of the fact that the countries of the world are becoming increasingly open and that business is frequently conducted across national boundaries, adjusting accounting practice in the Soviet Union to accord with international standards would allow potential owners, both foreign and domestic, to be informed about the financial condition of particular companies. Such information is required for shareholders to fulfill their ownership role of monitoring the management.

6. *Corporate profit taxation.* Such taxes must be uniform across industries and enterprises and provide an incentive for profit making. A rate of about 50 percent on corporate profits seems appropriate. In the Soviet Union there are now so-called windfall profit taxes with rates as high as 90 percent. Although currently justified by a highly regulated and distorted price system that makes profits a poor indicator of efficiency, the advent of price deregulation will remove this rationale.

Corporatization and the Distribution of Shares

Corporatization sets the stage for privatization by organizing large state enterprises as joint stock companies. It establishes them as managerially independent and self-financing entities. The advantage of a joint stock company is that it makes ownership divisible.

This is the common form of ownership for large corporations in market economies simply because it permits widespread ownership and easy transferability of ownership. Both of these elements are essential if corporations are to be able to raise the large amounts of capital that they will need for restructuring. Moreover, joint stock companies not only allow the ownership of shares to be widespread but permit diverse groups to be easily represented among the owners—management, workers, financial institutions, individuals, and foreign investors—and each may hold varying percentages of the shares.

State property management agencies (PMAs) would be the initial owners of the stock. The PMAs are to distribute the stock of the enterprises once the preconditions enumerated earlier are met. This poses an obvious danger, for the PMAs are to engineer their own demise, something which goes against the natural tendencies of any organization. There seems to be no easy way of creating incentives for the PMAs to push forward on privatization, other than the pressures that come from a state committed to privatization. The drive for privatization of state enterprises in Western industrialized economies came from the political process, not from the state enterprises themselves. One could establish bonuses (perhaps in the form of stock) for PMA managers that would reward them for privatization, but such devices can only supplement the commitment of the political process to privatization.

Another problem is the treatment of the financial assets of enterprises at the time of corporatization. Some firms will have substantial liabilities; others substantial assets, largely in the form of bank deposits. The amounts involved are substantial, enterprise debts were about 370 billion rubles and enterprise bank balances about 235 billion rubles at the end of 1990 (see table 7.3). The current distribution among enterprises of such debts and assets largely reflects the distribution of subsidies and the operation of price controls. Prices have been set by the central planners, basically on the principle of average industry costs. Enterprises with costs above the average have been given subsidies and special credit to continue to operate, whereas those with below average costs have had their profits confiscated. There is little correlation between the present financial health of an enterprise and its viability in a market system. Leaving the

Table 7.3
Consolidated Balance Sheet of the Present Soviet Banking System, December 1990
(In Billions of Rubles)

Assets		Liabilities	
Credit to governments	524.9	Deposits of households	380.2
Credit to enterprises	367.4	Deposits of enterprises	235.8
Credit to households	10.6	Currency in circulation	133.0
		Other Items (Interenterprise and interbank settlement accounts, budgetary transit accounts, and misc.)	153.9
	902.9		902.9

Source: *A Study of the Soviet Economy* (Paris: International Monetary Fund, World Bank, Organization for Economic Cooperation and Development, and European Bank for Reconstruction and Development, 1991), 1:132.

enterprise debts intact would hobble or even threaten bankruptcy for many enterprises. Thus it is necessary to cancel past enterprise debts to allow such enterprises to start with a clean slate.

At the other extreme, some enterprises have substantial bank balances that would in effect allow them to operate with a soft budget constraint by drawing down their balances. As chapter 4 indicates, we propose canceling both the debts and the deposits of enterprises upon corporatization, leaving enterprises with only their physical assets and inventories. (This arrangement still leaves some room for soft budget constraints among enterprises that have accumulated excess inventories which can be sold off. It is infeasible, however, to deal with excess inventories, given the difficulties of distinguishing between excess inventories and those needed for current operations.)

Giving Away versus Selling Stock

One major question is whether the PMAs should privatize the corporations they own by giving shares away to the general public or by selling them. This is a crucial decision central to any privatization program. There is no clear consensus among economists concerning which is preferable. Poland, the Czech and Slovak Federal Republic, and Bulgaria are moving towards the free distribution of shares to the general public, whereas Hungary and the former German Democratic Republic favor selling shares.

Several arguments support free distribution:

1. The objective is not merely to effect privatization, but to build popular allegiance for the reform measures. Citizens who are shareholders have greater allegiance than those who are not. Sale of stocks will make only a small fraction of the population shareholders.

2. There is great concern within the Soviet Union about the current inequality of wealth. Sale of stock would lead to a highly unequal distribution of shares, an outcome that could be especially unpopular in view of the fact that many of those who have accumulated large holdings of wealth are perceived to have done so illegally.

3. A free-distribution scheme sidesteps the need for asset valuation. No one knows what the assets of these enterprises are worth, and any price put upon them would be highly arbitrary. Under a free-distribution scheme, stock prices will emerge as the profitability of a firm becomes apparent under price deregulation.

The mechanics of distributing shares in many enterprises to the public requires the use of financial intermediaries. Privatization via distribution might then involve equity intermediaries in lieu of the PMAs who would be given shares in enterprises, and their shares, in turn, would be distributed to the public. To promote competition, there should be a considerable number of such investment funds—between ten and fifty, for example. The investment funds would derive their income from the dividends on the enterprise shares they own and use such income to pay dividends to the public, who hold shares in the investment funds. The public would be free to shift their assets among investment funds, as these will in time have different rates of return and risk. At some point when capital markets are well established, the funds could sell off their enterprise shares, distributing the proceeds to the holders of their shares.

Many of the participants in the study group on Capital Markets and Privatization at the conference in Sopron supported a free distribution plan; others did not. This reflects the lack of a clear consensus on this point among Western scholars. Despite its attractions, we are dubious of the merits of free distribution on several grounds.

1. Many people, unfamiliar with such investment instruments and nervous about the unstable Soviet business climate, would be likely to sell their shares in the investment funds quickly and at very low prices. Hence the stage where every citizen is a shareholder would be a transitory one, and the stock would end up in the hands of those with the larger ruble balances anyway. The final distribution of shares would thus not be too different from their allocation if they were sold.

2. The Soviet Union is a vast country, with about 300 million people. The sheer logistical aspects of disseminating information and distributing shares are overwhelming, particularly as many villages have no regular means of communication.

3. The stock certificate seems a remote and abstract way of promoting the concept of private property. A piece of paper representing a small ownership share of a large enterprise in a distant city would not be meaningful to many. The concept of private property seems likely to be better promoted by encouraging citizens to invest in small local enterprises and in their own housing, particularly since half the population has less than ten years of schooling and the Soviet Union has no tradition of stock ownership. Further, extremely widespread share ownership may give the managers effective control of the firm as we discuss later.

4. Giving stock away might add to the ruble overhang by increasing the public's financial assets. If they regarded stock as equivalent to cash, they might increase their spending from their ruble deposits, thus adding to the inflationary pressures. To dampen this impact, and to guard against fraud spawned by ignorance at the start, one proposal suggests that the shares given to the public should not be transferable for the first three years. But such a restriction could be easily evaded, and it undermines the idea that the public is being given something of value.

5. Giving the stock away immediately would create future political problems for policymakers. First, it would be much easier to break up monopolies owned by the interim PMAs than by private shareholders. The latter are likely to fight the break up in the political arena, given their strong incentive to maintain monopoly profits for their firms. Second, and for similar reasons, foreign trade liberalization, as discussed in chapter 5, will be easier to achieve while domestic producers are owned by PMAs. Finally,

and again for essentially the same political reasons, any desired environmental regulations would be easier to introduce during a period of interim state ownership under the PMAs.

In selling the stock, the primary device would be the public auction. Stock would go to the highest bidder. Anyone could buy—individuals, foreign investors, other Soviet enterprises, managers and workers in the enterprise, and banks and financial institutions. Auctions must be widely publicized in advance, and the publicity must provide the necessary financial information. Otherwise the shares will be bought by those with inside information, thus casting doubt on the fairness of the process.

The problem with auctioning shares is that corporate assets are likely to be bought at very low prices. The *Shatalin Report* estimates the depreciated value of industrial assets to be 469 billion rubles. The public is unlikely to have more than 50 or 60 billion rubles to invest annually, and these funds are more likely to go for purchases of small enterprises and housing than for corporate shares.[2] Only a small amount of funds will probably be available annually for purchasing shares, even with allowance for foreign and enterprise investment. Thus the vast Soviet industrial establishment could be transferred to relatively few individuals for nominal sums.

We propose that the sale of the stock of large enterprises be spread over several years. It is less of a problem if 10 or 20 percent of the stock is sold at bargain prices than if all the industrial assets are so distributed. As experience accumulates and corporations establish earning records, the auction prices for shares would come closer to reflecting the long-run value of the enterprise. One important source of demand for shares should be other enterprises who would regard shares as good investments for surplus earnings. Suppliers, subcontractors, and large customers of a firm may want to own shares, reflecting their long-term interest in a particular firm. Such ownership is common in some market economies, particularly in Japan.

The difficulty with this way of proceeding is that it spreads the process of privatization over time. But recall that the focus of the

2. *Transition to the Market: A Report of a Working Group Formed by M. S. Gorbachev and B. N. Yeltsin*, Part 1: *The Concept and Program* (Moscow: Cultural Initiative Foundation, 1990) (*Shatalin Report*), 53.

process is on the very largest existing state enterprises; we anticipate that the small business sector could be quickly privatized and in this way create a society familiar with private property.

Worker and management ownership is an alternative to auctions or free distribution. Partial ownership of enterprises by either group can be valuable in promoting an identification with the long-run success of the firm. Workers could be given, or sold at highly favorable terms, perhaps 10 percent of the shares in any enterprise.[3]

Management could be given even more priority in distributing shares in order to give them some of the incentives of owners. This might be done by making shares available to managers only after the enterprise has proved successful, after three years, as an addition to their salaries. The knowledge that these shares will be available could strongly encourage managers to make the economically profitable decisions that shareholders would have made; in other words, the interests of managers and shareholders would be somewhat the same. As a continuing practice, a substantial fraction of management bonuses could be given in shares.

Although there is much to be said for the partial ownership by workers or managers, there is a strong case against either group being the dominant owner. Workers have their greater interest in wages, and thus prefer immediate wage increases over the long-term commitment of funds to capital formation and research and development. Thus worker control has proved largely a failure as the dominant form of ownership in such countries as Yugoslavia. Management likewise has a greater interest in their immediate salaries and bonuses than in the long-term success of the firm.

We stress that the entrepreneurial role is indispensable in carrying out productive activities combining capital and labor and in taking advantage of new technologies and market opportunities. It is a distinctive role not well performed by those with other and conflicting interests in the firm. The entrepreneurial role is essential in making the firm self-financing, independent, and disciplined by the market. In market economies, however, the entrepreneurial role is

3. One argument against the slower form of privatization proposed here is that the workers may simply seize the assets of the firm as their own, given the current confused state of political and legal affairs in the USSR. For reasons discussed below, we view this as inequitable, and we oppose it. As a result, however, the state must be very forceful in asserting its interim ownership claims through the PMAs.

increasingly performed by institutions, such as banks, investment trusts, and other institutional investors rather than individual persons.

Fairness also argues against management and workers becoming the dominant owners. The present capital stock of an enterprise represents the past sacrifices of Soviet society, generally in the form of foregone consumption. To assign property rights over all such past investment to those who happen to be the present managers or workers ignores the investment Soviet citizens as a whole have made in their industry. It would particularly favor those who happened to be employed in the profitable sectors at the time of privatization. A related problem has arisen in Poland and Hungary, where the managers of state firms have contrived to sell their enterprises either to foreigners or to themselves as private owners. This spontaneous privatization has proven to be extremely unpopular and has been referred to as *nomenklatura* capitalism, reflecting the relatively privileged political status of these managers under the old socialist system. To permit this sort of asset transfer would mean effectively assigning initial ownership rights to the old management, and for reasons of equity and efficiency we strongly oppose it.

We favor the sale of shares over other methods of privatization, slow as this method is likely to be. The *Shatalin Report* envisages that 40 percent of assets would still be state owned five years after the start of privatization, and that may be optimistic.[4] This may seem too long, but a hasty and ill-conceived privatization process may be even worse.

We think our proposal is consistent with these words written by Academician Shatalin: "Fundamentally important is that the state cannot and should not give away its property without compensation. Property must be earned, because people do not believe in free property and do not value it sufficiently."[5]

Corporate Governance and the Role of Shareholders

The large corporation has the problem of how the shareholders will monitor and control the managers who run the corporation on a

4. *Shatalin Report,* figure following p. 52.
5. Ibid., iii.

daily basis. The shareholders are numerous, with each share representing only a small fraction of the ownership. No one shareholder has the incentive or the power to supervise or control the corporation's managers. Shareholders do elect the directors who in turn appoint the full-time managers, but with a widely dispersed electorate, managers can easily dominate the election of directors.

Managers can have objectives and interests that conflict with those of the shareholders. The most obvious conflict concerns managerial compensation: managers prefer high compensation whereas shareholders will accept it only to the extent that it improves the corporation's long-run profits. Another common conflict arises when shareholders wish to replace current managers with ones who seem more likely to improve the corporation's performance. A more subtle conflict can arise over corporate growth because managers may prefer growth for the increased power and prestige it provides them as managers, whereas the shareholders are interested in growth only if it increases the firm's long-run value.

This problem of shareholder control over managers is formulated by economists as the principal-agent problem. The shareholders are considered to be the principal employing an agent—the manager—to run the corporation for their benefit. The question then is how the principal—the shareholder—can insure that the agent—the manager—actually does so. This is not purely a private matter of protecting shareholders, for a society based on a market system requires that corporations respond to market signals and be run efficiently in order to serve the social ends of growth and economic efficiency. A central premise of market economies is that corporations are profit-maximizing institutions, and shareholders serve to insure that this occurs. The problem is not merely a hypothetical one dreamed up by economists but has been of central concern to investors and legislators in market economies for many decades.

Western economies have developed several ways of coping with this problem. One of the most common is to relate a portion of managerial compensation to the profit performance of the firm, thus aligning the managers' objectives with those of the shareholders. The use of this arrangement is urged at several places in this volume. A similar solution is to make managers shareholders as well, as just mentioned.

Yet these devices are often thought to be insufficient, particularly when the issue of replacing inefficient managers arises. Dispersed shareholders do not have sufficient power or incentives to organize a campaign to change the directors who will replace the managers. One solution is to have a dominant shareholder who alone holds enough shares to change the board of directors. That need not be a majority of the shares; 20 to 30 percent is often thought to be sufficient to give such power. In Western economies, dominant shareholders are often individuals of great personal wealth (often inherited) who can augment their own holdings by borrowing to buy more shares and thus achieve control of a corporation. Such individuals are unlikely to exist in the Soviet Union for some decades. And it may not be desirable for them to emerge.

Another way to achieve shareholder control is through blockholders, usually defined as those with 5 percent or more of the stock of a corporation. Their holdings are large enough to encourage them to take time to monitor carefully the performance of managers and to take actions to change them if necessary. They differ from the dominant shareholder in that blockholders must organize other shareholders to exercise control.

Again there is the question of where blockholders might arise in the Soviet Union, since to be a blockholder of a major corporation still requires significant capital, although less than would be required to be a dominant shareholder. One possibility is that the state PMAs, formed at various levels of government, could act as competing blockholders. Multiple and competing PMAs as shareholders would provide some check on one another. For example, an All-Union PMA might hold 40 percent of the shares of a firm, a republic PMA could hold 20 percent, a local government PMA could hold 15 percent, and the balance could be held by, or promised to, the workers and management.

Institutional investors (investment funds, banks, other corporations, pension funds, and insurance companies) can also provide some of the control and monitoring functions of blockholders, even when they themselves hold a smaller percentage of the stock. Compared to individuals, institutional investors still have larger share holdings and so have an incentive to develop professional managers to monitor the corporations in which they have invested. Furthermore, their major activity is investing and their own success turns on how well they do it.

Institutional investors are important in most Western economies. In the United States they hold 58 percent of corporate stock and in Japan 73 percent.[6] It will take years to develop a comparable set of institutional investors in the Soviet Union. However, two kinds of institutional investors could develop more quickly in the Soviet Union—banks and investment funds. As discussed subsequently, a banking system already exists in the Soviet Union, and these banks could become institutional investors. We would allow banks to buy stocks through auctions, but consideration might be given to placing two limitations on their purchases: (1) no bank could hold more than 5 percent of the stock of a particular corporation, and (2) no bank could have more than 10 percent of its total assets invested in stock. The rationale for these limitations is that stocks are risky investments, and banks should have diversified assets and not be overcommitted to risky assets. Diversification serves to minimize the risk of bank failure. Some people also feel that banks should not become too powerful in the economy. These limitations have developed in Japan and similar ones are common in many market economies. In Germany, however, banks are major stockholders, and this has not created any particular problems.

The other type of institutional investor that could develop quickly are the investment funds common in market economies. These firms aggressively sell their shares to individuals and institutions and in turn invest the money in a portfolio of corporate stocks. From their stock dividends, the investment funds in turn pay dividends to their individual investors. Such financial intermediaries are attractive to individuals because a small investment can be diversified among many enterprises, and they provide individuals with professional management of their investments. They are useful to society for they yield another group with an incentive to monitor large corporations carefully. As the stocks of large corporations become available for purchase, investment funds could develop without requiring any particular policy action or incentives. It is important,

6. For the United States, F. M. Scherer, "Corporate Ownership and Control," 46 (data for 1979). For Japan, Merton J. Peck, "The Large Japanese Corporation," 23 (data for 1982). Both in John R. Meyer and James M. Gustafson, eds., *The U.S. Business Corporation* (Cambridge, Mass.: Ballinger, 1988).

however, to have regulations in place that would allow investment funds to be created.

Finally, the Soviet Union will need a stock exchange in which both individuals and institutions can buy and sell their stock. Easy transferability and the resulting liquidity are important advantages of share ownership.

The stock market also performs the function of monitoring corporate performance. Those with increasing profits will see the price of their shares rise; those with financial problems will see the price of their shares decline. In market economies, the behavior of stock prices is the most important corporate scorecard, and it creates powerful pressures for managers to run their corporations well.

Despite shareholders' significant influence, it is important not to exaggerate the importance of shareholder control over managers. Most Western economies seem to function well with many large corporations that are management controlled and lack a dominant shareholder. For example, in 1963, 169 of the 200 largest U.S. corporations were controlled by a self-perpetuating management.[7] These included such notable companies as International Business Machines (IBM), General Motors, and American Telephone and Telegraph (AT&T). If a firm encounters competition in its markets, managers are forced to be profit-maximizers simply to insure the firm's long-run survival. Thus it is not surprising that various studies have found either no statistically significant difference or only a modest one between the profitability of management and shareholder controlled firms with otherwise similar characteristics.[8]

Throughout this study we have emphasized the importance of competition. We think that this is of primary importance in economic reform and that the problem of insuring that managers serve their stockholders may be of secondary importance. The crucial objective in privatization is to separate large corporations from the direct control of the state and to make them responsive to competi-

7. Robert J. Larner, "Ownership and Control in the 200 Largest Corporations," *American Economic Review* (September 1966): 777–87. Corporate takeovers and management buyouts in the 1980s have reduced the number of large corporations that are management controlled. There is no recent study of the proportion of large U.S. corporations that are management controlled, but it remains a substantial number.

8. F. M. Scherer, *Industrial Market Structure and Economic Performance* (Chicago: Rand McNally, 1976), 34.

tive markets. If privatization can achieve that, we would regard it as a success.

CREATING A BANKING SYSTEM FOR A MARKET ECONOMY

In a market economy, the banking system is the key institution for providing credit to enterprises and achieving macroeconomic equilibrium. These two roles are assigned to different entities in market economies, creating what is termed a two-tier banking system. We consider it essential that the Soviet economy establish a two-tier organization—one tier being the central bank, and the other the commercial banks. The central bank would set monetary policy through its controls over the commercial banks; the commercial banks would collect deposits from individuals and enterprises and would make loans, primarily to enterprises. Until recently, the Soviet banking system was, in effect, a one-tier organization consisting of one mammoth institution, *Gosbank*.

The content of monetary policy was discussed in chapter 4. Here we discuss the institutional reforms that are necessary to carry out that monetary policy effectively. These are not insignificant or cosmetic reforms, for money and the banking system had an essentially passive role in the traditional Soviet system. Plan construction and implementation were for the most part carried out in physical, as opposed to financial, terms. Prices bore little, if any, relation to scarcity and demand, and therefore financial flows merely served as a means to check plan implementation. There were essentially two circuits of money, *beznalichnye* (enterprise money) and *nalichnye* (household money). These were effectively separated, meaning that a large government budget deficit, expressed in soft credit to enterprises, did not necessarily have adverse macroeconomic consequences. The reforms of 1987 and 1988 broke down the barrier between the two circuits of money, and as a result excessive money and credit creation began to yield longer lines and greater deficits of goods, given largely fixed retail prices.

We take as the starting point the Soviet banking system as it was in the summer of 1990, the time the preliminary report on this topic was written. Taking that starting point serves to identify the key issues. Subsequently we examine the changes introduced by the banking legislation approved in December 1990 and compare them to our own recommendations. In recent years the Soviet system has consisted of Gosbank, the major institution, and a set of specialized banks serving with loans and deposits the specific sectors indicated by their titles. These specialized banks are: the Industrial Construction Bank (*Promstroibank*), the Social Housing Bank (*Zhilsotsbank*), the Agricultural Bank (*Agrobank*), the Bank for Foreign Economic Relations (*Vneshekonombank*), and the Savings Bank (*Sberbank*). Only the Savings Bank collected deposits from individuals, and it was by far the largest.

Creating a Central Bank

Gosbank, the existing State Bank, is the obvious candidate for the role of the central bank. The specialized banks are the best candidates to become commercial banks.

Gosbank, as the central bank, needs safeguards, either by legal stipulation or by custom, to protect its independence from the government. Monetary policy is crucially important in a market economy and so Western economies in varying ways and degrees have made their central banks independent from the government.[9] The management of the central bank must be free to set monetary policy to avoid the twin evils of inflation and recession. It must not, as in the Soviet Union, be a passive instrument to finance whatever deficit the government chooses to create.

One recurring issue in the Soviet Union is whether each of the fifteen republics should have its own central bank. The Federal Reserve System, the central bank for the United States, has twelve separate banks. Monetary policy, however, is set largely by what is called the Open Market Committee whose members are seven Federal Reserve governors in Washington and five members chosen from the heads of the twelve separate banks. The system operates as a single central bank. It is a political decision whether there should be one central bank, as in Japan and most Western countries, or several nominal ones, as in the United States.

9. No Western central bank operates totally without government control, but all have more independence than government departments. The level of independence varies by country; the central banks of the United Kingdom and France, for example, are less independent than those of Germany and the United States.

In either case there can be only one monetary policy with a single currency. Monetary policy can be set centrally or with the participation of the central banks in the republics, but there must be a single policy. If there is easy credit and low interest rates in some republics and not in others, borrowers will flock to the easy credit republics, thus nullifying tight credit elsewhere. Individual countries can have differing monetary policies, but that is possible only because they have different currencies and changes in the exchange rates offset differences in monetary policy.

To maintain a single currency, therefore, the Soviet Union must have a single monetary policy and hence a single, coordinated central banking system. As argued elsewhere in this volume, a single currency and a unified common market for goods and services is one significant economic advantage that the Soviet Union has achieved. A large common market and the advantages in productivity and specialization that a large free trade area affords are said to explain much of the economic success of the United States. The European Economic Community has spent many difficult years trying to create such a market.

Creating Commercial Banks

The best candidates for the role of the commercial banks are the several specialized banks listed previously. We recommend that they pass through a process of corporatization, analogous to that of other corporations. They should be organized as joint stock companies, with the stock initially held by state PMAs. The former specialized banks should also be divided into a number of smaller units to compete with one another, just as many large industrial associations and enterprises should be split up during the corporatization period. They should be managerially independent and self-financing. Their income would come from the interest on the loans they made and they, in turn, would pay interest on their deposits. (As with other corporations, the stock of these commercial banks would eventually be sold to the public at auction.) Even with PMAs as interim owners, the objective of commercial banks would be to maximize their profits.

The new commercial banks will realize their income by making loans to enterprises. In making loans it is essential that commercial banks allocate credit to insure that its use passes the market test of profitability. Past practice in the Soviet Union, where financing was made available to enterprises according to the credit plan, cannot work in a market economy. The allocation of credit, of course, determined the allocation of real resources of labor and capital among enterprises.

Given the minor role of other financial institutions in the Soviet Union for the foreseeable future, commercial banks will be the main source of credit to enterprises, both for such financing of physical investment as the expansion of manufacturing facilities and for working capital to cover the time lag between production and sales. Loans to enterprises must be made at market rates of interest, adjusted for the risk that the loan will not be repaid. There should be no government credit subsidies, for once prices are deregulated these lose their present rationale.

In the medium to long run, the Soviet capital stock will need to be expanded and investments made to raise productivity. Given this great need for investment, some observers favor a system of capital rationing in which some loans are made at less than market rates of interest according to governmental priorities. In the context of the Soviet Union, such a method opens the door to a return to central planning. It is better to rely on the market for the allocation of credit and hence the selection of investment projects. Given the profit objective of the new commercial banks, they will allocate credit according to market criteria.

The other function of commercial banks is to collect deposits from households and enterprises. Bank deposits are the efficient way to carry out financial transactions, and they are the most common way in which current earnings can be saved for subsequent use. Commercial banks attract deposits by the interest they pay depositors. As discussed subsequently, the rate of interest on deposits must be high enough to attract and retain deposits.

Central Bank Control of the Newly Established Commercial Banks

The major characteristic of the old banking system is captured by table 7.3, which consolidates the balance sheet of Gosbank with all the specialized banks. Such a consolidation is appropriate since the

Table 7.4
Balance Sheet of the Central Bank in the Two-Tier Banking System

Assets	Liabilities
Government debt	Currency in circulation
Loans to commercial banks	Deposits from commercial banks to meet reserve requirements
Loans to PMAs for bank equity	Bonds issued to commercial banks

banking system operated as one bank, dominated by Gosbank. The balance sheet makes clear that over half the assets of the banking system were credits to the government, reflecting the past role of the banking system in financing the state deficit. This overhang of government debt creates a problem in the transition to a new banking system. We will suggest a possible solution subsequently.

The system that we recommend is portrayed in table 7.4 for the central bank and table 7.5 for the commercial banks. These show the assets and liabilities of each level of the two-tier system, although with no numerical magnitudes since these will depend on how individuals and enterprises react to the transition to a market economy.

The central bank would hold three types of assets (see table 7.4). The first would be the old debt of the government, which would carry a very low rate of interest to avoid a major increase in interest payments and thus increases in the government deficit. The second would be the loans the central bank would make to the commercial banks. Changing the interest rate on these loans would be one way the central bank could execute monetary policy. Raising the rate would cause the commercial banks to raise the rates on their loans, thus tightening credit. Lowering the central bank loan rate (called the rediscount rate) would ease credit. The third kind of central bank asset would be loans to PMAs to enable them to make equity contributions to the commercial banks.

The central bank would have three kinds of liabilities as well. The first would be currency in circulation. The second would be deposits from the commercial banks to meet their reserve requirements. By changing the reserve requirements, the central bank could also tighten or ease credit. The third asset would be the bonds—backed by government credit—that the central bank would issue to the commercial banks to give them assets and income. By selling or

Table 7.5
Balance Sheet of Commercial Banks in the Two-Tier Banking System

Assets	Liabilities
Deposits in central bank to meet reserve requirements	Old deposits of individuals (insured; former savings banks only)
New credits to enterprises	New deposits of enterprises
Bonds issued by central bank	New deposits of individuals (not insured)
Stock equity	Loans from central bank

buying back these bonds from the commercial banks the central bank could also tighten or ease credit. These are commonly called open market operations. Such bonds would represent only a fraction of the old government debt held by the central bank. Their function would be to give the commercial banks assets and interest income at the outset of corporatization.

Two of the assets of the newly established commercial banks would correspond to the liabilities of the central bank: deposits to meet reserve requirements, and the bonds issued by the central bank (see table 7.5). New credits to enterprises would reflect the fact that enterprises will need to borrow from the banks to obtain working capital and to finance long-term investment. Much of these borrowed funds would be used in turn to create enterprise deposits in the banking system. Both loans and deposits are labeled "new" in table 7.5 to reflect the proposal made above to cancel old enterprise debts and deposits at the time of corporatization.

The stock equity, shown in table 7.5 as an asset, reflects the fact that we recommend that the commercial banks meet the international standard set by the Basel agreement specifying that commercial banks must have an equity cushion of at least 8 percent of their deposits. The initial owners would be PMAs and they, in turn, will need to borrow the funds from the central banks to provide equity. When the commercial banks are privatized through the sale of their stock by the PMAs (to be discussed subsequently), the proceeds from the sales can be used to retire this debt of PMAs to the central bank.

The difficult question concerns the treatment of existing deposits by individuals. As prices are deregulated and goods become available, there would be withdrawals of deposits for purchases of goods and services. Anticipation of inflation would further accelerate the process of bank withdrawals. The new commercial banks would then need to borrow from the central bank to meet their cash needs. The central bank, in turn, would need to print currency to meet the demand from the commercial banks for currency.

This is the monetary side of the one-time jump in prices discussed elsewhere in this volume. Inflationary as it is, we recommend accepting the consequences of this one-time price jump, including the withdrawal of individual deposits.

Nevertheless, it is necessary to minimize the depletion of individual bank deposits. To serve this objective, we propose deregulating interest rates for both loans and deposits for this will result in positive real rates of interest, that is, interest rates that exceed the rate of inflation. Of course, the monetary policy of the central bank would be the major determinant of interest rates through its rediscounting activities, its setting of reserve requirements, and its open market operations.

But how will the commercial banks obtain the income to pay high rates of interest? This is a special problem for Sberbank, by far the largest of the present specialized banks and the one now with individual deposits. In the past the function of the Savings Bank was to collect savings from the population and channel these funds into covering the state deficit. The Sberbank is to be transformed and divided into commercial banks; these will continue to collect deposits, but they will also make loans to enterprises and to local governments at market rates of interest. The resulting interest income will enable them to pay high rates of interest on deposits, but that may not be enough. If it is not, then it will be necessary for the central bank to pay high rates of interest on the government bonds the central bank issues to these former savings banks. These interest payments will need to be repaid by the government to the central bank, thus adding to the state deficit. Recall, however, that chapter 4 stressed the importance of eliminating the state deficit.

The problem then is to seek a way to reduce the withdrawal of individual deposits while minimizing the addition to the deficit. We would propose achieving this objective in the following way.

Deposits in the Savings Bank are now de facto completely guaranteed by the state. The Savings Bank, once divided into several new commercial banks, would distinguish between old and new deposits.

Old deposits of individuals would retain the implicit deposit insurance guarantee they now have and carry a low rate of interest relative to those elsewhere in the economy.

New deposits by individuals and enterprise would carry higher rates of interest in order to compete with the new commercial banks, particularly those formed out of the other specialized banks. These accounts, however, would carry no deposit insurance. The combination of deposit insurance and lower interest rates will appeal to some of the population and thus reduce the flight of individuals out of existing savings accounts at a lower level of interest rates than would otherwise prevail. The lower interest rates would, in turn, reduce the need to pay high interest rates on the government bonds that finance interest rates on the old individual deposits and thus reduce the additions to the government deficit.

Although the proposal for distinguishing between old and new individual deposits has its problems, it is still better than the alternative of freezing individual bank deposits to prevent their withdrawal. We are strongly against freezing individual bank accounts. In a society where markets are only beginning to exist, freezing individual bank accounts is obviously extremely detrimental to creating consumer confidence in the system.[10] Nor are we in favor of indexing bank accounts, given our general concern with indexing as an instrument for hyperinflation.

Privatization

We consider private ownership of the specialized banks (now the newly established and restructured commercial banks) to be the ultimate goal, just as it was for the nonfinancial corporations. And we would achieve this goal by auctioning off the stock of banks, held initially by state PMAs, to the general public. There are, however, some special preconditions for privatization that apply particularly to commercial banks. These preconditions need to be established as quickly as possible during the corporatization stage.

1. *Demonopolization* must be completed. Even when corporatized, the former specialized state banks must be free to compete among one another for both loans and depositors. Banks should be free

10. The partial freeze of deposits in January 1991 has certainly led to a decline in consumer confidence.

Table 7.6
Comparison of the Proposals Made in this Chapter with Those of the New Soviet Banking Legislation
(Proposals made in this chapter come first; corresponding parts of the Soviet legislation follow)

I. Two-Tiered Banking System

A. Make Gosbank an independent Central Bank, safeguarded from political pressure.

Article 1 of the Law on Gosbank (LGB) makes Gosbank the central bank of the USSR. Article 6 makes it accountable to the USSR Supreme Soviet, which sets limits on the amount of credit it can grant to the ministries of finance of the USSR and the republics (Article 21). The Supreme Soviet of the USSR cannot remove members of the Gosbank governing body, its central council, though the law does not prohibit the president from doing so (Article 43).

B. This chapter does not recommend whether the republics should have their own central banks, but notes that, if there is only one currency, then there must be one, unified central banking system (as in the United States).

Article 2 of LBG creates "a unified system of central banks based on a common monetary unit and performing the functions of a reserve system." The central banks of the republics are thus subordinate to Gosbank USSR.

II. Commercial Banks

A. Corporatize the existing specialized banks, after breaking them up into a larger number of competing units. Eventually they are to be privatized. Foreign participation and competition is to be allowed.

New commercial banks are encouraged. The specialized banks are also made into joint stock companies, and foreign participation is allowed. [IMF/BRD/OECD/EBRD, *A Study of the Soviet Economy* (Paris: International Monetary Fund, World Bank, Organization for Economic Cooperation and Development, European Bank for Reconstruction and Development, 1991), 2:370–71].

B. Regulate the commercial banks according to international standards; let them set interest rates to clear the market. (See below on Savings Bank).

Interest rates are generally to be market-determined, though Article 16 of LGB mentions indirect Gosbank USSR regulation, and Article 17 contains provisions for emergency short-term credit controls.

III. The USSR Savings Bank (Sberbank)

Gosbank USSR guarantees old deposits 100 percent, and new ones, like those in ordinary commercial banks, are not state guaranteed. This implies an interest rate differential.

Table 7.6 (*Continued*)

Gosbank USSR guarantees 100 percent of household deposits in the Savings Bank, but not in other banks, which must establish special reserve funds (Article 38 of the Law on Banks and Banking Activity [LBBA]).

IV. Gosbank Control of Credit and Monetary Policy

A. Gosbank USSR is to manage credit and monetary policy through the use of the usual instruments: rediscounting, reserve requirements, and open market operations.

Article 14 of LGB says Gosbank USSR sets the volume and price of credit provided by Gosbank USSR and the central banks of the republics to commercial banks; it establishes reserve requirements; and it buys and sells securities and foreign currency.

B. Gosbank USSR must not provide concessionary credit to the government for purposes of financing budget deficits. The government must borrow at market interest rates, like everyone else, from the public.

Article 21 of LGB governs credit provision of Gosbank USSR and the central banks of the republics to the ministries of finance of the USSR and the republics. The Supreme Soviet of the USSR limits this credit, but the president can, "in exceptional cases," permit excess credit above those limits.

V. Privatization of the Commercial Banks Held by PMAs

Eventually, these banks are to be auctioned off to the highest bidder. Effective preconditions for this are: (1) demonopolization, (2) establishment of a bank supervision system, (3) training of bank managers (probably abroad), and (4) development of a modern physical banking infrastructure.

Although both the LGB and the LBBA say the commercial banks are to be joint stock companies, they say nothing about who will own the stock, much less about preconditions for its transfer.

Source: This table was compiled by the editors from the USSR banking legislation, translated in *FBIS Daily Report: Soviet Union,* December 31, 1990, FBIS-SOV-90-251, 34–47.

USSR is nominally free from political pressure, its ability to maintain this independence seems questionable. Under the new banking legislation, the president has the effective ability to force Gosbank to cover a fiscal deficit (Article 21). Further, in an environment marked by rapidly changing laws and regulations, the formal independence of the central bank might prove only too easy for a future government to reverse.

In market economies, policy credibility is essential to its effectiveness, and this is true most of all for a nation's central bank. If the public believes the central bank will not monetize a fiscal deficit, inflation and a flight from the nation's currency are less likely to occur. If the monetary authority is not credible, however, no amount of on-paper independence will stop such flight. Soviet political leaders should give serious consideration to the importance of establishing—through deeds as much as through laws—such real credibility for Gosbank.[12]

A CONCLUDING COMMENT

The policy memorandum presented in chapter 2 gave less emphasis to privatization and the creation of a commercial banking system.[13] This is not because they are less important measures but because they take time. Privatization is essential to achieve a complete separation of the enterprises from the state, and this constitutes the essence of a market economy. Through its commercial banking system a market economy allocates the resources for investment and channels savings into the real economy. This chapter position at the conclusion of this book does not indicate that the topics it discusses are of any lesser importance in creating a market economy.

Since this is the last chapter, it is useful to summarize the primary thesis of this book. This thesis is a manifesto for economic reform, although it is stated in the sober prose of economists. The sober, straightforward prose does not lessen the urgency of the manifesto's message.

In 1902, Lenin borrowed the title *What Is To Be Done?* from the nineteenth-century novel by Chernyshevskii, and we have elected to borrow it from him.[14] In his book, Lenin emphasized the importance of a vanguard party—his soon to be formed Bolshevik party—in leading the masses to revolution. In some sense, Lenin's *What Is To*

12. See *Study of the Soviet Economy,* 1:373–74, for a further discussion of this point.

13. These last few paragraphs were added by the editors.

14. Nikolai G. Chernyshevskii, *What Is To Be Done? Stories about New People* (Ann Arbor, Mich.: Ardis, 1986; first Russian ed., 1862); Vladimir I. Lenin, *What Is To Be Done: Burning Questions of Our Movement* (New York: International Publishers, 1931; first Russian ed., 1902).

Be Done? provided much of the organizational framework for the events that followed. We claim no similar historical import for the chapters of this small volume. Yet it is true that, without some logical and consistent program, the Soviet transition to the market is impossible. And for that we can see no alternative to some form of the proposals put forward here.

The Soviet economy is suffering from acute shortages and threatening inflation, with both policymakers and the people gravely concerned about the future. It will take time to achieve tangible gains. As a result, short-term policy measures such as price freezes, rationing, forced delivery of goods, and increased government subsidies will be tempting. Some such measures may be needed in order to keep the economy afloat. Yet they must be temporary exceptions rather than long-term policy, and they must be employed as sparingly as possible.

Long-run resolution of the problems of the Soviet economy can only be achieved through increased efficiency, which can only be realized through increased individual responsibility. All the measures discussed throughout this book are directed at creating such responsibility. Furthermore, as the experience of the European Economic Community suggests, a market system may provide a way sovereign nations can live together for their mutual advantage. The Soviet Union needs the market system to permit the sovereignty of its republics while retaining the economic advantages of a large national economy.

Painful as it will be, it is illusory to believe that there exists an alternative to a transition to a market economy. The status quo seems certain to lead to deteriorating efficiency and economic disintegration. A market economy promises, not tomorrow but in decades hence, a prosperity comparable to Western economies. For tomorrow it promises hope.

Economic Policy and the Reforms of Mikhail Gorbachev A Short History

Petr O. Aven

The economic situation of the USSR is catastrophic. In 1990 peacetime output declined for the first time, traditionally stable prices began to rise sharply, and most goods were no longer reliably available in the state stores. Unemployment and strikes, hitherto unknown, exacerbated social tensions.

This appendix is an evaluation of recent Soviet economic policy organized chronologically and with an emphasis on the period between October 1989 and March 1991. A survey of Soviet public opinion in January 1991 indicated that about 40 percent of the population thought that perestroika was a mistake. These results are not surprising. While the intelligentsia gained a free press, travel abroad, and various political freedoms, most "ordinary" people regarded the level of consumption as the main criterion for judging the success of perestroika, and that has declined since 1985.

THE ECONOMIC SITUATION OF THE USSR IN THE MID-1980s

Table A1 shows official Soviet statistics on growth rates together with the more believable "alternative" estimates of Grigorii Khanin.

Note: This appendix reflects many discussions with Soviet colleagues, in particular with those who in the course of 1990 found themselves at the center of events. In particular, I would like to single out E. Gaidar, S. Shatalin, A. Shokhin and E. Yasin. T. Richardson is responsible for the translation from Russian into English. The views expressed here are solely the responsibility of the author.

179

Table A1
Soviet Annual Growth Rates
(Average Annual Percentage)

	1961–65	1966–70	1971–75	1976–80	1981–85
Net material product Official data	6.5	7.4	6.3	4.2	3.5
Alternative estimates[a]	4.4	4.1	3.2	1.0	0.6
Fixed assets	9.6	8.1	8.7	7.4	6.4
Number of employees	4.4	3.2	2.5	1.9	0.9
Domestic fuel production[b]	25–30[c]	25–30[c]	28.6	20.6	9.6

Sources: *Promyshlennost' SSSR* (Industry of the USSR), 1988, p. 6; *Material'no-tekhnicheskoe obespechenie narodnogo khoziaistva SSSR* (Material-technical provisioning of the national economy of the USSR) (Moscow: Finansy i statistika, 1989), 65.
[a]Estimates of G. Khanin, "Ekonomicheskii rost: Al'ternativnaia otsenka" (Economic growth: An alternative estimate) *Kommunist,* 1988, no. 17:85.
[b]Growth during the five-year period (measured in tons of coal equivalent).
[c]Estimates of A. Aganbegyan, "Perestroyka: Recent Developments in Restructuring the Soviet Economy" (Paper delivered at IIASA, Laxenburg, Austria, Dr. Bruno Kreisky Lecture Series, no. 3, 1987), 2.

Even though Khanin's estimates differ markedly from the official ones, both have the same pattern—a significant reduction in rates of economic growth in the second half of the 1970s and the start of the 1980s.[1] Table A1 also illustrates one of the causes of the fall in growth rates—the partial exhaustion of Soviet reserves of fuel, raw material, investment, and labor resources.

Exogenous factors also played a role, especially the acceleration of the arms race and the fall in export prices for Soviet exports of energy. Still, the main reason for the fall in growth rates was that the economic mechanism created by Joseph Stalin was no longer effective after the seventies.

Soviet industrialization policy was designed to maximize the production of goods deemed crucial to rapid development—the output of heavy industry and raw materials. Such output has grown sharply

1. According to official statistics, the best postwar Five-Year Plan (FYP) was the eighth, the first FYP under L. Brezhnev and A. Kosygin. According to Khanin, the best was the seventh, the last FYP under N. Khrushchev. In comparison with the official estimates, the alternative estimates of Khanin show a significantly sharper fall in the rate of economic growth, practically to zero at the start of the 1980s.

since the 1930s, but little attention was paid to their costs. The system was well-suited to achieving simple, stable goals, such as maximizing the growth rate of steel production, but it proved resistant to changes in objectives. Once achieved, the level of production of a given product was seldom reduced, even when the product was no longer needed.[2]

One explanation for the relatively successful economic development of the USSR until the 1970s is that the goals of industrial policy accurately reflected the rational priorities of early industrialization—namely, the expansion of heavy industry and raw materials production. Further, the economic system set up with these goals in mind was effective in achieving them. Over time, however, these priorities became outdated, but the command economy was not capable of redirecting its efforts. In other words, the centrally planned economy was adequate for industrialization but ineffective for post-industrial development. The reason was the growing complexity of the economic system as economic growth continued and the resulting need to decentralize decision making.

Complexity here refers to the difficulty of coordinating production given the dramatic increase in the number of products and services as well as the number of technologies that can produce them. This complexity also stems from an increase in the rate of technical change in products and processes. Even in the 1950s and 1960s complexity was reducing the effectiveness of the "command" system. The idea of command presupposes the observability of the commanded," which became increasingly difficult in a complex economy. In dealing with this massive coordination problem, the Center—meaning economic planners in Moscow—was forced, first, to limit its "field of view" by concentrating on important branches. Key branches for industrialization not only were supplied with inputs and labor resources on a priority basis, but were also strictly controlled. It is no accident that the fall of discipline and the rise in thievery and corruption were particularly noticeable outside these key sectors (as in agriculture and services).

2. Tractors are one of the best examples. Their production continues to increase, although less than 80 percent of the tractor parks have sufficient tractor drivers and many brands cannot be sold for any price. In 1985 the USSR produced five times as many tractors as the United States. *SSSR i zarubezhnie strany v 1987* (Moscow: Finansy i statistika, 1988), 137.

Second, the Center, unable to manage the ever-growing volume of information, became more and more inclined to make simple decisions. For example, older technologies were preferred by planners over modern ones, simply to facilitate coordination of economic activity.

Third, the inability to use all the relevant information led to the use of a small number of indicators for evaluating the performance of the firm. However, orientation "to the indicator" significantly changed the incentives for managers, provoking price increases, falsification of reports, and so forth.

Indeed, for a command economy to work, even in theory, certain assumptions need to hold:[3]

• The Center must have a relatively accurate assessment of the capabilities of its subordinates (both ministries and enterprises).
• The Center must formulate its commands or targets on the basis of these accurate assessments.
• Subordinates must be held strictly responsible for carrying out these commands.

Until the 1960s, the actual economic mechanism corresponded roughly to this theoretical model. With the increase in complexity of the economy, however, the assumption that the Center had "objective knowledge" about the capabilities of subordinates no longer applied. Moreover, the Center's ability to collect and analyze large masses of information did not keep pace with its information requirements. To an ever-increasing extent, the economic planners became dependent on information provided to them from below.

Informational dependence of the Center on enterprises led to a weakening of the commandability of the system and eventually to the replacement of a command economy by a "bargaining" economy, in which relations between higher and lower organizations were characterized more by exchange than by subordination. The higher units had, as chips in this bargaining process, material—technical resources, money, and various ways of rewarding managers—while the subordinates had as chips the fulfillment of

3. Note that these assumptions mirror those in much of the Western literature on economic planning, namely those of honesty (no adverse selection) and obedience (no moral hazard)—the Editors.

production targets (or promises of their fulfillment).[4] The impossibility of objectively evaluating the actual situation of an enterprise (which always had a thousand reasons for not fulfilling the plan and justifications for increased resources) led, therefore, to the collapse of the discipline a command economy requires.

The informational dependence of the Center and the development of bargaining facilitated the development of branch lobbies. Beginning in the 1930s, Mafia-like interest groups or lobbies developed in many branches of industry to press the Center to allocate resources to their branches. Cadres for all-union functional departments, such as Gosplan or Gossnab, were recruited from these branch lobbies, further enhancing their influence at the top. The most important branch lobbies were the military industry and the energy complexes.

The emergence of these branch interest groups was partly a cause and partly the result of the growing uncommandability of the system. They complicated the planning process by forcing the Center to consider their interests, particularly since not all economic coordination could be done explicitly at the top. Yet this very complexity meant that bargaining and local interest groups were inevitable.

The multiplicity of issues subject to bargaining and the complexity of achieving an agreement in any individual case also strengthened the importance of informal ties.[5] The local Party organization became an important institution for informal coordination, serving not only as a directive force but also as a middleman or arbitrator in the many horizontal bargains that took place.[6]

Economic legislation itself became an object of bargaining as well. Exceptions to the rules became the rule. Corruption was promoted by the nonenforcement of the laws, while bribes and personal services became part of the resources used in bargaining. This process led to a further softening of the budget constraints on enterprises. Excess demand for investment resources was not effectively controlled by the Center, and this led to a real waste (*razpylenie*) of

4. See P. Aven and V. Shironin, "The Reform of the Economic Mechanism: The Realism of the Projected Transformations," *Problems of Economics* (June 1988): 33–48.

5. See L. Csaba, "Some Lessons from Two Decades of Economic Reform in Hungary," *Communist Economies* 1, no. 1 (1989): 17–30.

6. This was particularly true in agriculture, where the local Party organs put forward the interests of the kolkhozy in relations with machine building or repair enterprises.

resources. By the time Mikhail Gorbachev came to power, more than 350,000 construction projects were being carried out, with an average duration approaching ten years.

In general, the importance of decisions taken at the top steadily fell, and the role of the Center gradually devolved simply to covering up the losses incurred by inefficient management at the bottom. Underfulfillment of plans, the share of which increased from year to year, became the norm.

Until 1985, the soft budget constraints for enterprises created by a bargaining economy did not lead to a sharp growth of wages. The claims of workers were held in check by administrative controls, combined with a prohibition on strikes. As opposed to the industrial branch lobbies, which united managers and the Party apparatus, the workers were not effectively organized and were without a way to exert pressure. As a consequence, inflation was channeled less into the growth of personal incomes and more into unneeded production and construction projects.

Despite effective wage controls, the slowdown in economic growth began to affect the consumer market. The food supply became a major source of social tension, with, for example, the growth of per capita consumption of meat stagnant in the 1970s and 1980s. Attempts to ration consumption and to distribute goods at workplaces only increased inequality. Higher income groups had access to the restricted systems of supply, permitting them to purchase goods at subsidized prices. Because of such access, in 1984 a family with a monthly income per person of 150 rubles paid an average of 2.96 rubles for a kilogram of meat, while a family with an income of less that 50 rubles paid 3.93 rubles.[7] In this system, most of the subsidies went to the well-off groups.

The weakening of observance of the law and the growth of corruption, both of which started in the economic sphere, gradually spread to all of society. The last years of the Brezhnev leadership were the apotheosis of irresponsibility, lawlessness, bribery, and protection rackets, and they led to growing protests. Thus the Soviet leadership that took power in 1985 was faced with a declining rate of economic growth and increasing social tensions. Changes were in order, but those that were introduced made the economic situation

7. Estimates of the USSR State Committee on Statistics.

worse. These included an ill-conceived program of industrial re-structuring known as "acceleration" (1985–1987), timid and poorly thought-out institutional reforms (1987–1989), and the government's responses to "populist" pressures (1988–1989).

THE ACCELERATION PROGRAM (1985–1987)

The need for a major restructuring of the economy was clear by the late 1970s. It was to be achieved by increased capital investment in the priority sectors of industry, with particular attempts to modernize the military industry and machine building. In this sense, Gorbachev did nothing new; he only continued, with great fanfare, what had begun under his predecessors.

As in the short period of Andropov, there was an emphasis on strengthening discipline and action against corruption and protection rackets. Overall, no attempt was made radically to reform the economy, but rather the focus was on using the old methods better. The growth of household consumption was once again "temporarily" put off.

According to the ideologists of acceleration, the key to success was the development of machine building.[8] If from 1981 to 1985 capital investment in this sphere grew by 24 percent, then the growth from 1986 to 1990 would have to be 80 percent to meet the objectives. At the start these objectives were achieved; capital investment grew by 17 percent in 1986. However, already by 1987 the share of investment in machine building had returned to its 1985 level, and then it continued to decline.[9]

Renovation and the renewal of capital stocks were the other key recipients of capital investment. Depreciation and underinvestment had combined to yield a highly skewed age structure for the capital

8. The machine-building sector is essentially the set of branches producing "all forms of machinery and equipment, cable products, electronic products, machine tools, precision instruments, transportation vehicles and equipment, agricultural and construction equipment." See D. Bond and H. Levine, "The Soviet Machinery Balance and Military Durables in SOVMOD," in U.S. Congress, Joint Economic Committee, *Soviet Economy in the 1980s*, vol. 1 (Washington, D.C.: Government Printing Office, 1982), 300n.

9. A. Aganbegian, *The Challenge: Economics of Perestroika* (London: Hutchinson, 1988), 5; *Narodnoe khoziaistvo (Narkhoz) SSSR v 1989* (Moscow: Finansy i statistika, 1990), 534.

stock. Thus, by 1986, 68 percent of the machinery and equipment in industry and construction was at least six years old, and almost 15 percent was over twenty years old.[10]

Between 1986 and 1990, according to the plans, 45 percent of operating equipment was to be replaced. Achievement fell well short of the plan. The renewal rate did accelerate briefly from 3.1 percent of the value of all investment in 1985 to 4 percent in 1986 for civilian machine building. Abel Aganbegyan, at that time close to Gorbachev, was not satisfied and promised that in 1987, 7.5 percent of the stocks in civilian machine building would be renewed, and in 1990 the rate of renewal was to reach 13 percent.[11] These plans were never fulfilled and the renewal rate remained at its 1985 level.

One source of the failure was poor interindustry coordination. The accelerated development of machine building needed at least some minimal investment in infrastructure, as well as investment in the metallurgy and the energy sectors. The Center was not powerful enough to secure the necessary interbranch (interindustry) coordination.

Another reason for the failure was that the consumers of machine-building products were not prepared to use the new modern technology made available to them. Rather, the increase in the output of the machine-building industry contributed to the further growth of uninstalled equipment (see table A2).

Many economists doubted whether the choice of machine building as the key recipient for increased investment was the right one. Although between 1960 and 1985 the capital-labor ratio almost doubled, there was virtually no increase in labor productivity.[12] Using capital equipment more effectively would have been a better goal in this view. More investment in metallurgy, rail transport, light industry, and the oil industry, and less in machine building, might have made a greater contribution to economic growth.

The inflationary consequences of increased investment in machine building reflected the failure to make offsetting reductions in investments in nonpriority branches. The pressure of branch inter-

10. *Nauchno-tekhnicheskii progress v SSSR* (Moscow: Finansy i statistika, 1988), 60.

11. Aganbegyan, *Challenge,* 5.

12. G. Khanin, "Ekonomicheskii rost: Al'ternativnaia otsenka" (Economic growth: an alternative estimate) *Kommunist* 17 (1988): 89.

Table A2
Excess Equipment in Inventories at Beginning of Year (Current Prices in Millions
of Rubles)

	1981	1986	1988
Metal-cut lathes	98.3	163.6	173.9
Foundry equipment	12.7	15.7	22.0
Electronic equipment	52.4	99.7	107.7
Agricultural machinery	15.7	23.2	34.6

Source: *Material'no-tekhnicheskoe obespechenie,* 197.

est groups hindered any such redistribution of investment. Simply
put, to give more to one branch was easy, but to take it from another
was usually impossible. Thus, officials in agriculture not only prevented any reduction in their investment levels but were even able to
achieve increases.[13] In this way, the redistribution of capital investments turned into their uncontrolled growth with inflationary
consequences.

By 1987 the failure of acceleration had become obvious, and the
growth of investment was sharply curtailed. Yet the measures to
reform the economy that were taken in response to the failure of
acceleration themselves increased the inflationary forces and made
any return to the past impossible.

INSTITUTIONAL REFORMS (1987–1989)

The word *reform* first appeared in the lexicon of the political
leadership somewhere in the middle of 1987, when it became clear
that the acceleration campaign had failed. Prior to this, the leadership only spoke about the "perfection" of the economic mechanism.
That year saw passage of the Law on State Enterprise, which introduced the state order (*goszakaz*) system. Such state orders were eventually to be accepted "voluntarily" by the firm and were to cover only
a portion of the enterprise's output; they were to sell the rest at free
prices. In other words, the diktat of the Center was to be replaced by

13. Capital stocks in agriculture grew by 15 percent from 1985 to 1989, although the
volume of production was 8 percent less. *Narkhoz,* 418, 481.

decentralized planning. In practice, the goszakazy simply represented a new name for the old obligatory plan targets.

The enterprises were to be given considerable freedom in the use of their financial resources. The 1987 legislation also emphasized careful definition of the mutual obligations of the state and the enterprise. Many of the concepts had been tested in an earlier "large-scale experiment" that applied to a limited number of enterprises.

The incentive mechanism embedded in the Law on State Enterprise is often called a system of "indicative" or indirect planning. The government remained responsible for the production of a specific list of goods and for the formation of central plans. Control over enterprises was to be accomplished by means of economic levers such as tax rates, price controls, economic "normatives" (governing the use of retained earnings), and interest rates on credit, as well as some direct limits on the use of various types of resources. Soviet proponents of "the new course" asserted that this indirect regulation would be more effective than the old planning directives.[14] In fact, actual practice did not confirm their assertions.

The normatives, which also regulated payments to the state budget, were to remain stable for the duration of a Five Year Plan. This was to provide greater incentive to enterprises, who could thus earn higher profits without fear that these would be confiscated in the future. The problem was that the promise of stability of normatives strengthened the enterprise in its bargaining with the state. It became significantly more complicated to extract financial resources from a disobedient or wealthy enterprise, because such extraction now directly violated the official policy. At the same time it was very difficult to avoid softening constraints for firms experiencing financial difficulties. If the firm adopted a plan sent down from above, then the state had to take responsibility for its financial status. As a

14. See, for instance, N. Petrakov and E. Yasin, "Ekonomicheskie metody tsentralizo-vannogo planogo rukovodstva narodnym khoziaistvom" (Paper presented at the all-union conference Problems of the Scientific Management of the Economy, Moscow, November 1986). The economic mechanism that was introduced in the USSR began more and more to look like the 1968 Hungarian system on paper. In fact, the proponents of the reform admitted they borrowed liberally from the Hungarian experience. Most of all this dealt with the regulation of incomes. Unfortunately, they paid no attention to the negative experience of Hungary with this sort of mechanism.

Table A3
Distribution of Profits of State Enterprises (In Percentages)

	1980	1985	1986	1987	1988	1989	1990
Total profit	100	100	100	100	100	100	100
Transferred to the state budget or branch ministry	59	56	51	50	48	46	45
Left at the disposal of enterprises	38	40	46	47	50	52	51
Used on other goals	3	4	3	3	2	2	4

Source: *Narkhoz*, 620; *Statistical Press-Bulletin*, no. 22 (1990): 10. For 1990, estimates are from the USSR State Committee on Statistics.

result of this asymmetric situation, payments to the state budget out of enterprise profits fell (see table A3). Exceptions were frequently granted that reduced the financial obligations of the firm. Thus, in 1989, only 28 percent of state enterprises paid into the state budget the 3 percent of the value of their capital stock required by regulations. The rest paid little or nothing.

Other factors strengthened the bargaining power of enterprises. Thus, the Law on State Enterprise for the first time permitted enterprises to sell and exchange capital stock as well as products that were produced above state orders. The importance of the control of materials supplied by Gossnab (which had traditionally played a major role in the management of enterprises) fell significantly. The Center had practically only financial incentives to control enterprises.

Table A4 demonstrates the decentralization of capital investment after 1986. This, however, did not lead to the better use of investment spending. In the absence of a capital market, the intersectoral mobility of capital investment was limited, and firms made investments mostly in "known" production processes.

Corresponding to the political campaign for democratization, the Law on State Enterprise transferred many powers from enterprise management to labor collectives, which in 1988 began electing the enterprise directors.[15] This change also weakened further the position of the Center in bargaining, as the managers found in the workers a powerful source of support for extracting resources from

15. In 1990 this practice was abolished.

Table A4
Decentralization of Capital Investment in the State Sector (In Billions of Rubles)

	1986	1987	1988	1989
Total capital investment (constant prices)	172.0	189.6	192.9	200.8
Capital investment from enterprises' production development funds (constant prices)	5.3	33.2	77.2	102.4
Ratio between 2 and 1 (%)	3.1	18.2	40.0	51.0

Source: *Narkhoz*, 529.

the government. The new possibility of strikes became another bargaining tool of the enterprises. The transfer of enterprises to leaseholding—a system in which management and workers lease plant and equipment from the state and thus become financially independent—further strengthened their position vis-à-vis the ministries. Though it had become difficult to extract resources from a purely state enterprise, it was now practically impossible to do so with a leaseholding enterprise.

To sum up, a number of changes led to reduced power of the Center relative to that of the enterprises. Much in the way of resources, which had been pumped into the economy as a result of the incompetent investment policy, simply sat in the accounts of producers. The growth of these funds was greater than had been thought. The aggregate size of the production development fund of enterprises from 1985 to 1988 grew almost eightfold; in 1989 the growth comprised 28 percent. The material incentive fund grew fourfold from 1986 to 1989, and in 1989 it grew by 36 percent.[16] From 1987 to 1989, payments out of enterprise profits to the state fell by 11 percent, and this was one factor in the growth of the budget deficit.

The multiplicity of types of money had served as an important control instrument for many years, enabling the government to support a relative balance between the real and the monetary sides of the economy, even under conditions of budgetary expansion and fixed prices. Resources from the production development fund, for

16. *Statistical Press-Bulletin*, 1990, no. 22:11.

example, could not be used for wages. The wall between the monetary and the real economies markedly eased the problem of monitoring and control. However, decentralization under the Law on State Enterprise significantly weakened the partition between the two spheres. The growth of financial assets that could be used as the enterprise saw fit increased the inflationary pressure on prices.

The influence of the new incentive mechanism on the growth of prices was observable as early as 1986. Consumers, however, were protected against a rise in most prices, since the increased costs of the enterprises were financed by increased state subsidies. From 1985 to 1989 enterprise subsidies grew from 66.4 to 97.6 billion rubles and by 1989 were 20 percent of state budgetary expenditures.[17]

Thanks to the subsidies, the increases in wholesale prices were not considered a problem for the producer until 1990. The main thing was a worsening of shortages. Barter was the natural response.[18] As for the consumer goods market, the state was able to control retail prices more effectively than wholesale prices so that open inflation at the household level was minimal; from 1985 to 1989 retail prices increased only 13 percent.[19] Yet goods became increasingly unavailable and rationing became much more common than before.[20]

Until 1988, the control of personal incomes was the main instrument for maintaining a relative equilibrium on the consumer goods market. Indeed, next to fulfilling its planned output target, the most important indicator of success for an enterprise was staying within its planned wage fund. The situation completely changed in 1987 with the passage of the Law on State Enterprise. From then on, the wage fund was a predetermined proportion of enterprise revenue (or, more precisely, the remainder after all the necessary payments to the budget and deductions into the various funds had been made). In the overall context of decentralization, the rules for redistributing monies out of the wage fund were significantly weak-

17. Ibid., 6.

18. According to A. Vavilov and O. V'iugin, "Reforms in 1991: Money, Prices, and Finance" (Institute of Economics and Forecasting of Scientific and Technological Progress, Moscow, 1991, mimeographed), barter today comprises more than 15 percent of interenterprise trade.

19. *Statistical Press-Bulletin*, 1990, no. 22:18.

20. By late 1989, potatoes were rationed in 33 oblasts, butter in 20, and tea in 16.

Table A5
Growth of Wages and Personal Incomes (Percentage Rates of Growth)

	1986	1987	1988	1989	1990 plan	1990 actual
Average wages of workers and employees	3.2	3.6	8.2	13.1	n.a.	10.9 (32.0)[a]
Personal incomes (nominal)	3.6	3.9	9.2	12.9	7.1	16.8

Sources: *Statistical Press-Bulletin*, 1990, no. 22:19; for 1990, A. Vavilov and O. V'iugin, "Reforms in 1991," 4.
[a]10.9, growth of wages in the state sector alone; 32.0, growth in cooperatives.

ened. The growing right of the enterprises to spend their resources as they wished served to destroy the wall between the household (*nalichnye*) and enterprise (*beznalichnye*) circuits of money.

As table A5 indicates, personal income grew sharply. Various attempts to limit the growth of personal income by—for instance, a tax on wages—were unsuccessful.[21] The Center was not strong enough to counter the pressure from below, and the gradual growth of incomes became a rule of the game.

In part this new rule was determined by the development of individual and cooperative forms of management, legalized in 1986 and 1988, respectively. Even though restricted by various limitations on their activities, by mid-1990 more than five million people worked in more than 200,000 cooperatives.[22] Cooperatives added to inflationary pressures because they changed social conceptions about a normal income. Higher incomes in the cooperative sector put a great deal of pressure on state enterprises to pay higher wages.

The relaxation of controls on economic activity in the USSR exceeded the rate of change during this period in the other countries of Eastern Europe. Unfortunately, this decentralization, which was not accompanied by a hardening of budget constraints, led only to intensifying inflationary processes, the seeds of which were sewn during the program of acceleration.

21. See P. Aven and S. Aleksashenko, "The Soviet Tax Reform at the Beginning of 1991," in P. Aven and T. Richardson, eds., *Essays in the Soviet Transition to the Market* (Laxenburg, Austria: IIASA, forthcoming).

22. *Statistical Press-Bulletin*, 1990, no. 20:42. For a detailed analysis of the development of the cooperative sector and privatization, see S. Aleksashenko and L. Grigoriev, "Privatization and Capital Markets" (Paper presented at the IIASA Conference on Economic Reform and Integration, Sopron, Hungary, July–August 1990).

POPULISM AND OTHER MISTAKES OF
THE GOVERNMENT (1988–1989)

As the system created by the Law on State Enterprise demonstrated its flaws, populism began to displace the public's belief in communist ideology. The new group of peoples' deputies who were elected in 1989, many of whom made it to the Kremlin by calling for "justice," gave populism a new push. At times, it seemed that they were competing with each other and with the government to promise the people more. New pension legislation was adopted, expenditures on health care were increased, and the minimal period of paid state leave was lengthened—all of which added to the state budget deficit. It was not acceptable to ask how these expenditures were to be financed; there were no overt opponents of such increased expenditures. Neither the Ministry of Finance nor Gosbank became counterweights to the populism.

By the start of 1990 the financial system of the USSR was at the edge of catastrophe. The main factors in reducing government receipts were falling tax and other payments by enterprises (as a result of the 1987 reforms) and the decrease in income from foreign trade.[23] Bad investment policy, the growth of subsidies, and the populist increases in state spending led to the sharp growth of budgetary expenditures, and thus the deficit. As a result, the level of inflationary pressure in the Soviet economy reached previously unheard-of levels.

Under pressure from the population (or, more accurately, individual social groups) the government adopted various mistaken policies. The anti-alcohol campaign was one of the most widely known of Gorbachev's early initiatives. Unfortunately, it was as useless (from the standpoint of the struggle with drunkenness) as it was inflationary (from the standpoint of losses to the budget). Its quiet death in 1989–1990 demonstrated the weakness of the government.

Further, at the start of 1989 a somewhat unexpected campaign began against the cooperatives. Even at their outset the cooperatives met with opposition. Public opinion surveys showed that the share of

23. From 1985 to 1989, income from the export of oil fell from 28.2 to 18.6 billion rubles. Overall income from foreign trade was reduced from 66 to 38.2 billion rubles. See E. Arefieva, "Opening the Soviet Economy" (Paper presented at the IIASA Conference on Economic Reform and Integration, Sopron, Hungary, July–August 1990).

the population in favor of closing the cooperatives was never below 40 percent.[24] By 1989 pressure on the government and the parliament led to a sharp limitation on the sphere of activity of cooperatives and an increase in their tax burdens. Middleman-type cooperatives (the most necessary in establishing a market infrastructure) were totally forbidden. The consequences for supplies to the market were felt immediately.

At the end of 1989, people began for the first time seriously to consider the prospect of a collapse of perestroika (if not the economy itself). The struggle over the course of the reforms now became more intense.

IN SEARCH OF A WAY OUT (LATE 1989–EARLY 1991)

The All-Union Conference on the Problems of Economic Reform, in October 1989, marked a new stage in the search for a policy to deal with the crisis. The conference discussed a paper entitled "Radical Economic Reform: Top-Priority and Long-Term Measures," prepared by the Commission on Economic Reform of the Council of Ministers of the USSR.[25] This commission had been created earlier in 1989 with the goal of working out a comprehensive program of reform. Academician Leonid Abalkin, an economist with a reputation as a "market socialist," headed the commission.

The plan proposed that the process of economic perestroika be radicalized and divided into three parts. The first, in 1990, was to be a preparatory stage. In the course of this year the requisite market legislation would be prepared. These new laws were to include measures on property, legalizing various forms of entrepreneurship, a new tax system, and a new banking system. The plan also proposed extraordinary measures to reduce the state budget deficit, limit the growth of personal incomes, and restrict credit. All loss-making en-

24. *Obshchestvennoe mnenie v tsifrakh*, All-Union Center for Public Opinion Studies, Moscow, 1989–1990, various months.

25. "Radikal'naia ekonomicheskaia reforma: pervoocherednye i dolgovremennye mery (material dlia obsuzhdeniia)," *Ekonomicheskaia gazeta* 43 (October 1989): 4–7, henceforth cited as the Abalkin plan.

terprises were to be transferred to leaseholding. Indexation of incomes, considered by the plan's authors to be a necessary precondition for even a gradual liberalization of prices, was foreseen.

The second stage, from 1991 to 1992, was to see the new market mechanism introduced. The share of free trade, that is, products produced above the state orders and sold at unregulated prices, was to increase sharply. Wage determination was to be completely decentralized. All of the loss-making collective and state farms were to be closed.

The new system was to be fully implemented during the third stage, from 1993 to 1995. This stage was to include an antimonopoly program and the introduction of a two-tiered banking system. By the end of 1993, 25–30 percent of state enterprises were to be transferred to leaseholding, and by the end of 1995 as much as 30–40 percent of state property was to be transformed into joint stock companies. By this time macroeconomic stability was to be have been achieved.

The program had obvious weaknesses. Incantations of the nation's "socialist choice" or the "Leninist ideas of NEP" were substituted for concrete actions. Some sections of the program were very vague, particularly on financial stabilization. Considering the seriousness of the situation at the end of 1989, whole sections were notoriously conservative (for example, the section on property). In general, the program was more an ideological manifesto of the need for change than a precise plan of reform.

Still, one should not underestimate its importance. For the first time in the thirty-year history of Soviet reforms, a scheme of sequential changes was proposed. Had it adopted this plan, the government could not have counted on success, but it could have used the program as a basis for more radical and detailed proposals.

The government of Prime Minister Nikolai Ryzhkov rejected even this moderate Abalkin plan, and presented its own program to the Congress of Peoples' Deputies in December 1989.[26] The government program looked formally much like the Abalkin plan. Yet it differed in several key ways. In the Abalkin plan enterprises were to be accorded the immediate right freely to sell 5–10 percent of out-

26. N. I. Ryzhkov, "Effektivnost', konsolidatsiia, reforma—put' k zdorovoi ekonomike," *Ekonomicheskaia gazeta* 51 (December 1989): 8–13.

put, and by 1995 this share was to rise to 80–90 percent.[27] There was to be a gradually widening sphere of free trade (where free trade meant in terms of pricing, production and the decision to export), with the growth of the share of commodities produced above goszakazy. In the government program, the emphasis was on the need to strengthen plan discipline, and the notorious goszakazy were still to play an important role. For most industrial products, these state orders were to be reduced only from 100 percent to 90 percent of planned production. In addition, the Ryzhkov program advocated new sanctions for unfulfillment of goszakazy, and also rejected the principle of voluntary acceptance by the enterprises of the state orders.

The government program included a two-stage plan for administrative price reform. In 1991 wholesale prices were to be increased, followed in 1992 by retail prices.[28] At the same time, the Ryzhkov government promised not to raise retail prices without consulting with the public, a commitment that would complicate matters a few months hence. The government program was, moreover, silent on property relations. Although the Abalkin plan was cautious in dealing with property, it did propose that all loss-making industrial enterprises be shifted to leaseholding in 1990, and those in agriculture in 1991. The government plan was adopted by the Congress of Peoples' Deputies, and even Abalkin expressed his support for the Ryzhkov plan.

A powerful wave of strikes shook the country in January and February 1990. Work time lost for those two months alone was almost nine million person days, compared with seven million for all of 1989. Industrial output for the first quarter fell by 0.7 percent in comparison with the corresponding period of 1989, largely owing to strike activity. At the same time, the incomes of the population grew by 13.4 percent in the first quarter of 1990, and the production

27. Over the course of the first four to five years of the Abalkin plan, wholesale prices for raw materials were to approach in a coordinated way the world prices; the prices on goods in the processing branches were thus to be freed as the share of products produced above state orders grew.

28. This, it would later turn out, was the macroeconomic analog of the oldest joke concerning sequential reform of a socialist economy. It goes as follows: The British decide to change to the continental system of driving on the right instead of the left. But to soften the impact on the population, trucks are to begin driving on the right as of January 1, and cars are to follow suit six months later.

development funds of enterprises grew by an annual rate of 12 percent.[29] The availability of consumer goods continued to decline. The worsening situation radicalized the participants in reform, particularly the group of specialists who had, in October, prepared the Abalkin plan and who continued to work in the hope that their new and more radical proposals would be requested sooner or later. This hope was tied directly to the president, who had in March been granted executive power by the Supreme Soviet. Nikolai Petrakov, well known for his promarket views, was made Gorbachev's personal economic adviser. His participation with a group from the Commission on Economic Reform influenced the program that was prepared in the spring of 1990 under the president. Rumors of the introduction of this radical "presidential" plan spread rapidly.

The presidential program reflected the necessity to deregulate prices in order to achieve a meaningful enterprise reform as well as macroeconomic stabilization. Subsidies could at one stroke be eliminated by price liberalization, whereas prices regulated by the government would not permit a hardening of enterprise budget constraints. An "unjust" price was a sufficient basis for a firm to request discretionary reductions in taxes, favorable credit terms, or direct subsidies.

The question of price deregulation, then, was central to the new program. In contrast to the October variant, this deregulation was not tied to a reduction in goszakazy, but rather the goszakazy were to be carried out at free market prices.

In April the proposed program was discussed twice by joint sessions of the Presidential Council and the Parliamentary Federation Council. Neither the president nor these bodies decided to support its Polish-style shock therapy. Rather, on May 24, 1990, the prime minister presented a new variant of the government plan to the Supreme Soviet that was similar to Abalkin's plan of October.[30] Even though by past standards the government had been radicalized, it was still not keeping up with the pace of events.[31]

29. *Statistical Press-Bulletin*, 1990, no. 12:3.

30. "Ob ekonomicheskom polozhenii strany i kontseptsii perekhoda k reguliruemoi rynochnoi ekonomike" (Report of N. I. Ryzhkov to the third session of the Supreme Soviet of the USSR, *Pravda*, May 25, 1990).

31. The sequential appearance of various reform programs gives the impression of a struggle between radicals and conservatives. In some sense, this impression is correct,

The core of the May government program (and its difference from the October plan) was its proposal of widespread and simultaneous future administrative price increases. The government realized the seriousness of the inflationary situation, as well as the impossibility of increasing only wholesale prices (because the latter would cause subsidies to increase). On January 1, 1991, procurement prices in agriculture were to increase by 55 percent and industrial wholesale prices were to rise by 46 percent. Consumer prices were to increase by 43 percent on average, but food products were to double in price. The government was, however, willing to limit the price increases, since the share of goods with unregulated wholesale prices was to be not more than 40 percent, and at retail no more than 50 percent.

The announcement of a future price increase was part of the government promise to consult with the population, and its impact was dramatic. Nikolai Ryzhkov had barely finished his speech before goods began to disappear from the shelves and lines in front the shops doubled. Under intense political pressure, the government suffered a major setback in the Supreme Soviet, for the price increases were not acceptable to the deputies and the program was not adopted. It was sent back to the government with an admonition to return in September with a new program.

In May and June deposits of individuals in savings accounts shrank. An unheard of 9 billion ruble reduction in retail inventories occurred. The rate of growth of sales of light industrial products increased from 2 percent in 1989 to 20 percent in 1990. By October 1990, of the 115 consumer goods that the State Committee on Statistics (Goskomstat) follows, not one was still freely available. By June 1990, prices on the black and collective farm markets had increased by 18 percent over their level of a year before, and in November by 44 percent.[32]

The course of events, and the evident inability of the central government to take the country out of the crisis, led the republics to work on their own reform programs. Still, all of the institutional

---

but frequently the same people participated in the preparation of various, often mutually contradictory, programs. The preparation of these documents was usually accompanied by many compromises made by the economists involved.

32. See E. Gaidar, "V nachale novoi fazy," *Kommunist* 2 (1991): 14–15.

levers and material resources remained in the hands of the Center, and confrontation between the republics and the Center did not seem useful to the leaders of the republics. They chose instead to put pressure on the Center to develop a better program, with all hopes again resting on the president. The union government continued to elaborate its May plan, although it became apparent that there was little hope of change in its views.

Inspired by their economic advisers, a short peace between the Russian leader Boris Yeltsin and President Gorbachev gave birth to the well-known Five-Hundred-Day Plan. This program was produced in August by a group of economists headed by Academician Stanislav Shatalin, a member of the Presidential Council, and Grigorii Yavlinskii, Head of the Economic Reform Commission of the Russian republic.[33]

The Shatalin-Yavlinskii plan repeated much of the spring presidential program. Nevertheless, the Five-Hundred-Day Plan took a further turn toward radicalism. Some of the sections, though not all, were written more precisely, and the question of mutual relations between the Center and the republics was posed in an entirely new way.

The core of the program was the idea of a two-stage reform; macroeconomic stabilization was to come first, starting on October 1, 1990. The second stage, price liberalization, was to begin no later than July 1991. In the first stage, state expenditures were to be sharply reduced. Given the importance of these reductions in spending, this part of the Five-Hundred-Day Plan was written in an exceptionally precise way. The expenditures of the Ministry of Defense were to be cut by 10 percent, and those of the KGB were to be cut by 20 percent. Foreign aid was to be cut by 70–80 percent and subsidies to loss-making enterprises were to be cut by 30–40 percent. Capital investments were to be reduced by 20–30 percent. All long-term (three-to-five-year) investment programs were to be canceled, and not one budget item costing more than 100 billion rubles would be permitted. These actions were to eliminate the budget deficit by March 1991.

33. See *Transition to the Market: A Report of a Working Group Formed by M. S. Gorbachev and B. N. Yeltsin*, Part 1: *The Concept and Program* (Moscow: Cultural Initiative Foundation, 1990). This report is also known as the *Five-Hundred-Day Plan* or the *Shatalin Report* after the Chairman of the Task Force, Academician Stanislav Shatalin.

A critical part of the stabilization process was to be the privatization of state property. The sale of land, housing, and the small- scale of enterprises was to reduce household monetary assets. Thus, by the end of 1991, almost 70 percent of food stores and as much as 80 percent of the cafes and restaurants were to be in private hands. At least half of this ownership transfer was to be accomplished by the spring of 1991.

Restricting credit by administrative measures and high interest rates was assigned an important role in achieving macroeconomic stability. The most obvious antimonopoly measures were to be implemented in the first stage by eliminating production associations and splitting up enterprises that produce similar goods.

The stabilization program was intended to prevent a sharp jump in prices once they were deregulated in the second stage. There was to be an immediate corporatization of state enterprises to transform them into fully independent and self-financing, if state-owned, organizations.

Of course, the program was not free of internal inconsistencies and confusing points. Thus, no detailed prescription for corporatization was included. Indeed, in the first stage, with regulated prices, such corporatization would not have been possible. Too many potentially viable enterprises would have been in financial difficulties because of government price controls. It was planned to reduce enterprise subsidies by 30–40 percent at the start of stage one in October 1990; in other words, their budget constraints were to be hardened. It remained unclear how effectively this burden of additional stringency would be distributed across the economy and the consequences of a complete prohibition on subsidies in the second stage were not understood, but it was recognized that many enterprises would need temporary assistance. The Five-Hundred-Day Plan proposed the formation of extrabudgetary stabilization funds to distribute monies to enterprises. The Polish experience showed, however, that such funds would remain in the control of the government and could be allocated according to criteria that have little to do with competitive effectiveness.

Such a danger seemed more real because the Shatalin-Yavlinskii plan retained the concept of state orders (*goszakazy*). Henceforth, of course, these were to be distributed on a voluntary basis but enterprises would receive tax preferences and cheap credit as inducements. Bargaining over the size of the goszakazy would have been institutionalized, especially since the bargaining power of enterprises would have increased still further. It was not clear why one of the bargaining chips of the Center could not have been disbursements from the stabilization funds.

Also unclear was the idea to freeze all economic ties between enterprises (as long as the purchaser confirmed them) until June 1991. This measure was also aimed at stabilizing the current situation, but it was naive to expect that enterprises, knowing about their approaching freedom, would temporarily follow the command not to change the structure of their production. The emphasis (in the first stage of the reform) on repressive methods to maintain plan discipline contradicted the general logic of the reform and would not have been effective. In general, the program failed to overcome the main shortcoming of all the models of market socialism—the continued responsibility of the government for market performance.

Serious internal contradictions were also embedded in the proposed mechanism of mutual relations between the republics and the Center. The Shatalin-Yavlinskii plan recognized the sovereignty of the republics over the national wealth located on their territory. The land and its capital were to be considered the property of the republic in which they were located, with a few exceptions. The republics were to conclude an economic union, and together with the central government were to regulate the economy.

The resolution of the specifics of economic policy would have required an interrepublican consensus, and this was hardly possible. In particular, this was true of the management of the central banking. It was to be a reserve system composed of republic central banks with representatives of these republican banks and the president of the reserve system as its managing council. This body was to take all the important decisions in the area of credit and monetary policy; the republican banks were to implement these policies. It was unclear how this collective organ would work in practice, as the interests of the various republics seemed too different.[34]

34. Defending their plan, the authors of the program cited the U.S. Federal Reserve system, which, of course, is effectively run by a single Board of Governors in Washington, and not by representatives of the fifty states. There are about a dozen regional

A consensus on the price issue also seemed doubtful. The plan proposed that most regulated prices (mostly on raw materials) be set on the basis of an interrepublican agreement. Given the contradictions among the various interests, a practical agreement among the fifteen different points of view seemed unlikely.

Implementation of the Five-Hundred-Day Plan would have met with some very serious difficulties. In particular, the breakdown of the five hundred days into stages of one hundred to two hundred days had a demagogic flavor. However, its adoption would have been a singular demonstration of the determination to introduce a market economy. It would have initiated real action toward macroeconomic stabilization and corporatization. With all the republics signing the program, it would have provided breathing room to prevent a collapse of the unitary Soviet market.

The reasons why Mikhail Gorbachev decided at the last minute not to support the Shatalin-Yavlinskii program are known to him alone. The resistance of economic managers at various levels must have been important. Indeed, in a Soviet-type economy a union of the Communist Party, the government, and the directors of enterprises must certainly play an enormous role, since informal coordination and personal ties have always smoothed out the failures of economic plans. After 1985, this mechanism of informal coordination was dealt a serious blow. Local party organs, traditionally one of the key institutions for maintaining coordination, were largely removed from economic life. The apparat lost its orientation as the generally accepted rules of the game ceased to function.

Yet the mechanism of informal coordination still existed. Government officials and most of the enterprise directors remained loyal to Mikhail Gorbachev. Had he supported the Five-Hundred-Day Plan, the president would have risked being without their support. The prime minister announced that his apparat would not carry out this program, and the president had no other apparat.

The president also gave no support to the latest government variant, put forward by the prime minister and the Council of Ministers at that time, though their plan became more market-oriented. The Five-Hundred-Day Plan, and threats by people's deputies to support

---

Federal Reserve banks, but these follow the unitary monetary policy set by the Board of Governors.

it, had forced the government to radicalize its own proposals, although not on the questions of price deregulation and the rate of corporatization and the role of the republics.

Gorbachev's action resulted in still another compromise variant, drafted by a commission headed by Abel Aganbegyan, who emerged from political obscurity. This plan, however, was too close to the Five-Hundred-Day Plan for the government's taste. (Shatalin himself said they were 99.5 percent the same.) In September the Supreme Soviet rejected both the Shatalin-Yavlinskii plan and the Aganbegyan compromise.

The public, tired of the arguments and the obstruction of the various plans, was becoming apathetic and anxious for some kind of resolution. Thus, on October 19, the Supreme Soviet adopted the "Basic Directions for Stabilizing the Economy and for the Transition to a Market Economy."[35] Its major authors were Abel Aganbegyan, Stanislav Shatalin, and Evgenii Yasin, one of the chief architects of the Five-Hundred-Day Plan and the preceding presidential program. This new document was vague—it would have permitted any interpretation by whomever had the power to implement it—and Gorbachev placed its fate in the hands of the current government.

During this time, expectations of administratively higher prices prompted the enterprises to delay concluding contracts at the old prices and drove collective and state farms to cut back on deliveries to the state system. By the start of October, only 25 percent of 1991 output had been covered by contracts, compared with 65 percent the year before.

By the end of September, the fear of going without meat had forced the government of Russia to increase its procurement prices then, instead of waiting until the start of 1991, when the union government planned to increase them. Almost no one noticed that this decision stood in direct contradiction to the logic of the Five-Hundred-Day Plan, which the Russian parliament had almost unanimously adopted. The Russian decision forced the union government to speed up the introduction of the new procurement prices across the entire country.

Under parliamentary pressure, Gorbachev legislated by decree a

35. "Osnovnye napravleniia po stabilizatsii narodnogo khoziaistva i perekhodu k rynochnoi ekonomike," *Pravda*, October 18, 1990.

new set of prices, effective January 1, 1991. As in the May plan of Ryzhkov, 40 percent of wholesale prices were to be deregulated; for these goods the new price lists were to provide only a lower bound.

Simultaneously, Gorbachev decreed all economic ties to be inviolable for the entire year of 1991. The actions of the government left no doubt about the future interpretation of the "Basic Directions." Although during the course of 1990 a series of market laws was worked out, including new tax legislation[36] and rules for the formation of corporations, the Center did not really speed up the pace of reform. Of the two directions of reform in 1988—decentralization and clarifying the mutual obligations of the Center and the enterprises—only the second was pursued. On the other hand, movement backward was possible, as was reflected in the freezing of economic ties.

Having frozen contracts and raised prices, the government had to absorb the losses of those enterprises in financial difficulties, leading to a further growth of subsidies. A reform of retail prices was also unavoidable, as the gap between them and wholesale prices had grown sharply, and covering these losses with subsidies was becoming unfeasible. Thus, while the growth of retail prices before 1990 took place primarily outside the state trade network, after that the prices in state stores started to take off. There was no doubt that given Gorbachev's rejection of a price deregulation, this process of periodic administrative price increases would continue.[37]

The key differences between the government of Valentin Pavlov, formed in early 1991, and that of his predecessor, Ryzhkov, were its understanding of the problem of excess liquidity and its readiness to take decisive and unpopular actions. Its measures were shaped by the old administrative system, and as a result, all its attempts to reduce inflation so far have met with failure. In early 1991, 50 percent of the resources in enterprises' production development

36. See Aven and Aleksashenko, "Soviet Tax Reform."

37. One thing the government did was to encourage the "creeping" increases in prices. However, the government later decided to implement a one-time reform. In part this was owing to stubbornness (the new price lists were already prepared), in part to pressure from below (neither the republics nor the trade network wanted to have to answer for the inevitable price increases), and in part to budgetary considerations (dragging out the reduction in subsidies would have been senseless).

Table A6
Growth Rates of Selected Indicators, Official Data (Percentage Rate of Change)

	1990	First Quarter of 1991 (compared to the same period of 1990)
Gross national product	−2.0	−8.0
Net material product	−4.0	−10.0
Industrial production	−1.2	−5.0
Oil production	−6.0	−9.0
Ferrous metals production	−3.0	−7.0
Construction	−13.0a	−10.0
Food production	+1.4a	−2.0
Meat production	−3.0	−14.0
Exportsb	−6.0	−18.4
Importsb	−2.1	−45.1
Personal incomes	+16.8	+24.1

Sources: *Ekonomika i zhizn'*, no. 4 (1990); *Izvestiia*, April 10, 1991; *Statistical Press-Bulletin*, 1991, no. 3:53 and 1991, no. 4:51; USSR State Committee on Statistics, press releases, various numbers in 1991.
aFor nine months of 1990 (January–September).
bIn current prices.

and material incentive funds were confiscated by the state, but this had little effect.[38] Valueless money continued to be pumped into the economy.

A January 1991 monetary reform was no help. Fifty- and hundred-ruble notes were made invalid and they could be exchanged freely for smaller notes only up to an amount equal to the average monthly wage. To convert the rest, one had to reveal the source of the money. Household savings deposits were also frozen, though citizens had the right to withdraw up to five hundred rubles per month. The government hoped that this measure would significantly reduce demand while reducing the impact of low income groups who had little savings.

No serious reduction of demand was achieved. Unjustified savings were minimal, and there were many ways of getting around the limits on exchanging the large notes. Under popular pressure, savings accounts were unfrozen as early as February. The inflationary

38. It was "recommended" to enterprises to use these resources for the floating of shares of the labor collective. In other words, the resources were taken in return for the share of the collective in future earnings.

expectations created by the measure were more significant than the reduction in the ruble overhang.[39]

A new factor further contributed to Soviet inflation—the non-fulfillment by the republics of their obligations to make payments to the central budget. At the start of 1991, the Center made expenditures as if the revenues promised by the republics would be forthcoming. In the first quarter of the year the union, however, received less than 40 percent of these planned receipts.[40] On April 2, 1991, retail prices were administratively increased, meaning that most of the arrangements between the Center and the republics ceased to function. By April, the cumulative annual deficit had reached the level planned for the entire year.

Production has declined sharply because of the financial disorder, the overall feeling of indecision, the breakdown of the informal coordination mechanism, and an increasing numbers of strikes (see table A6). The increase of retail prices, implemented in April 1991, indicates the start of a new, previously unknown stage of open inflation. It turned out that the Five-Hundred-Day Plan had underestimated the inflationary pressures in the economy. New prescriptions were necessary, ones that would be more radical and more painful than before.

39. It is true that the goal of the monetary reform was not only stabilization of the consumer goods market but also the imposition of Central control on the banks, including the republican banks. This goal of the government was achieved.

40. *Pravda,* April 23, 1990.

Participants in the Economic Reform and Integration Conference at Sopron, Hungary, July–August 1990

CONFERENCE STAFF

Friedrich Schmidt-Bleek
  Leader, Technology, Economy, and Society (TES) Program,
  International Institute for Applied Systems Analysis (IIASA),
  Austria.
Merton J. Peck
  Leader, Economic Reform and Integration (ERI) Project,
  IIASA, Yale University, USA.
Petr O. Aven
  ERI Project Coordinator, Research Scholar, IIASA.
Evgenii Yasin
  Senior Soviet Adviser, USSR State Commission on Economic
  Reform.
Sergei Aleksashenko
  Soviet Conference Coordinator, USSR State Commission on
  Economic Reform.
Thomas J. Richardson
  Conference Rapporteur, Yale University, USA.
Christoph Schneider
  Research Assistant and Conference Rapporteur, ERI Project,
  IIASA.
Shari Jandl
  Administrative Assistant and Conference Organizer, TES
  Program, IIASA.
Gabrielle Schibich
  Secretary, ERI Project, IIASA.

STUDY GROUPS

Prices and Competition

Alfred E. Kahn, Chairman
    Cornell University, USA.
Vladimir Capelik
    Central Institute of Mathematical Economics, USSR Academy
    of Sciences, USSR.
Carl Kaysen
    Massachusetts Institute of Technology, USA.
Klaus-Peter Möller
    Institute for Applied Systems Research and Prognosis (ISP),
    Germany.
Viacheslav Shironin
    All-Union Institute of System Studies, USSR Academy of
    Sciences, USSR.
Marton Tardos
    Institute of Economics, Hungarian Academy of Sciences,
    Hungary.
Sidney Winter
    General Accounting Office, USA.

Labor Market and Employment

Wil Albeda, Chairman
    Universities of Utrecht and Limburg, Netherlands.
Barry Bosworth
    Brookings Institution, USA.
Alan Gladstone
    International Labor Office, Switzerland.
János Köllö
    Institute of Economics, Hungarian Academy of Sciences,
    Hungary.
Vladimir Kosmarskii
    Soviet Center for Public Opinion and Market Research, USSR.
Richard Layard
    Centre for Economic Performance, London School of
    Economics and Political Science, United Kingdom.

Alice Rivlin
  Brookings Institution, USA.
Aleksander Shokhin
  Foreign Ministry, USSR.
Sóren Wibe
  Swedish University of Agricultural Sciences, Sweden.

Economic Stabilization

William D. Nordhaus, Chairman
  Yale University, USA.
Joshua Charap
  Ministry for Economic Policy and Development of the Czech
  Republic, Czech and Slovak Federal Republic.
Rudiger Dornbusch
  Massachusetts Institute of Technology, USA.
Egor Gaidar
  Editor of the Department of Economic Policy, *Pravda*, USSR.
Konstantin Kagalovskii
  Moscow Institute of Construction Engineering, USSR.
Aleksander Khandruev
  Scientific and Research Institute for Money and Banking,
  USSR.
Assar Lindbeck
  Institute for International Economic Studies, University of
  Stockholm, Sweden.
Karol Lutkowski
  Ministry of Finance, Poland.
Kalman Mizsei
  Institute for World Economics, Hungary.
J. Michael Montias
  Yale University, USA.
D. Mario Nuti
  European University Institute, Italy.
Jacek Rostowski
  Ministry of Finance, Poland.

Opening of the Economy

Richard N. Cooper, Chairman
  Harvard University, USA.
Elena Arefieva
  Institute of World Economy and International Relations, USSR
  Academy of Sciences, USSR.
János Gács
  Institute for Economy, Market Research and Informatics,
  Hungary.
Urpo Kivikari
  Institute for East-West Trade, Turku School of Economics and
  Business Administration, Finland.
Robert Lawrence
  Brookings Institution, USA.
Paul Gerd Loeser
  Central Advisory Group of the President of the Commission of
  the European Communities (CEC), Belgium.
Vladimir Musatov
  Institute of USA and Canada Studies, USSR Academy of
  Sciences, USSR.
Richard Portes
  Centre for Economic Policy Research, United Kingdom.
Todor Walchev
  Institute of Economics, Bulgarian Academy of Sciences,
  Bulgaria.
John Williamson
  Institute of International Economics, USA.
Salvatore Zecchini
  Special Counsellor to the Secretary General, Organization for
  Economic Cooperation and Development, France.

Capital Markets and Privatization

Kimio Uno, Chairman
  Faculty of Policy Management, Keio University at Shonan
  Fujisawa, Japan.
Iulia Babicheva
  State Bank of the USSR, USSR.

Gerhard Fink
  International Business Research, Austria.
Benjamin Friedman
  Harvard University, USA.
Leonid Grigoriev
  Institute of World Economy and International Relations, USSR
  Academy of Sciences, USSR.
Manuel Hinds
  Trade and Financial Division, World Bank, USA.
Robert Litan
  Brookings Institution, USA.
Vitalii Naishul
  Institute of Economics and Forecasting of Scientific and
  Technological Progress, USSR Academy of Sciences, USSR.
Dušan Triška
  Ministry of Finance, Czech and Slovak Federal Republic.

Index

Abalkin plan, 194–96, 197
Accounting practices, 153
Aganbegyan, Abel, 203
Agriculture, 28, 77–78, 100, 181, 183 n
6, 187, 196, 198. *See also* Food
Alcohol, 45, 86, 193
Antitrust laws, 27, 62, 72–73, 74–75,
145. *See also* Monopolies
Assets, of enterprises, 112, 154–55,
158
Auctions, hard currency, 31, 100
Austria, 147
Automobiles, 2, 51, 69–70, 73–74

Bank accounts: freezing of, 3, 14, 172,
172 n 10, 205; of enterprises, 86,
154–55; interest on, 168; treatment
of existing, 170–72, 175–76; guaranteed, 171–72, 173, 174
Bank, central, 121, 165, 166–67, 169–
70, 171, 173, 175, 201. *See also Gosbank*; Macroeconomics
Banking system, Soviet: finances government debt, 6–7, 165, 166, 169–
70, 171, 176–77; provides easy
credit, 20, 31, 100, 165, 168; must
regulate credit to enterprises, 25, 26,
31, 59–60, 98, 108–09, 167–68, 170;
privatization, 31, 100, 108, 109, 149,
170, 172–73, 176, 177; restricts capital, 77; should be two-tier, 149, 165–
66, 168–69; balance sheet, 155, 168–
69; specialized banks, 166, 167, 171,
172–73, 174; reform of, 172–77, 206
n 39; private banks, 173–74. *See also*
Bank, central; Banks, commercial;
Credit; *Gosbank*; Interest rates
Bankruptcy: necessary for market efficiency, 25, 60, 120; need for laws, 26,
59, 98. *See also* Budget constraints,
hard
Banks, commercial, 76, 128, 163, 165,
167–74, 175–76, 177
Barter, 2–3, 24, 40, 43, 54, 55–56, 89,
191. *See also* Distribution
Belgium, 137

Black market: prices, will lower after
D-day, 22–23, 35, 42–43, 110; exchange rate, 29, 36, 88; inflation in,
29, 88, 91, 198; popularity during
the crisis, 40, 89. *See also* Distribution
Bread, 46 n 8. *See also* Food
Brezhnev, Leonid Ilyich, 8, 184
Budget constraints: hard, 25, 32, 41,
60, 97, 98, 102, 108, 143, 145, 146;
soft, 101, 108, 155, 183, 184, 192,
197. *See also* Credit
Bulgaria, 155

Canada, 137
Capital: -intensive industries, 71; diffi-
culties obtaining, 77; rationing, 168;
equipment, 185–87, 189–90. *See also*
Banking system; Credit
Cement industry, 66, 73
Central bank. *See* Bank, central;
Gosbank
Chemical industry, 69
Collective bargaining, 144, 147–48. *See
also* Unions
Commercial banks. *See* Banks,
commercial
Communications, 28, 129
Communist Party, 6, 177
Competition: efficient, 5, 52 n 13; requires price deregulation, 24, 70, 97,
104; limits monopolies, 27, 35, 68–
69, 70–71, 117, 173; enterprises
must be free to choose markets, 27,
68–70, 74, 76, 77, 104; in small business sector, 28, 77; international,
stimulates Soviet enterprises, 34–35,
74, 117, 132; improves quality, 69;
promoted by antitrust agencies, 75;
eased by transitional tariffs, 124; goal
of privatization, 164–65; in banking
system, 167, 172–73. *See also* Market
economies; Monopolies
Computers, 173
Construction, 99, 184
Consumer goods, 2, 4, 35, 117–18. *See
also* Distribution; Food

213